MORE LETTERS FROM THE EDGE

MORE LETTERS FROM THE EDGE

MARGARET RANDALL

New Village Press • New York

Published in the United States by New Village Press
bookorders@newvillagepress.net
www.newvillagepress.org
New Village Press is a public-benefit, nonprofit publisher
Distributed by NYU Press

Paperback ISBN 978-1-61332-275-8
Hardcover ISBN 978-1-61332-276-5
eBook Trade ISBN 978-1-61332-277-2
eBook Institutional ISBN 978-1-61332-282-6

Library of Congress Control Number 2025936974

This book is printed on acid-free paper, and its binding materials are chosen for strength and durability. We strive to use environmentally responsible suppliers and materials to the greatest extent possible in publishing our books.

The manufacturer's authorized representative in the EU for product safety is Mare Nostrum Group B.V., Mauritskade 21D, 1091 GC Amsterdam, The Netherlands.
Email: gpsr@mare-nostrum.co.uk.

Manufactured in the United States of America
10 9 8 7 6 5 4 3 2 1

This book is for our fast-disappearing world, in which justice was the goal, solidarity the means, art the reward. And with the fervent hope we can bring it back.

Don't read anything
except what destroys
the insulation between yourself and your experience.

—Louise Erdrich,
(Anishinaabe poet, Turtle Mountain Band)

I will have spent my life trying to understand the function of remembering, which is not the opposite of forgetting, but rather its lining. We do not remember. We rewrite memory much as history is rewritten. How can one remember thirst?

—Chris Marker

Eyes without memory see nothing.

—Carmen Castillo

CONTENTS

INTRODUCTION

AS I WORKED ON the book just before this one, *Letters from the Edge: Outrider Conversations,* I felt a deep communion with its protagonists, friends who have inhabited important places in my life. Those long gone came alive through their letters; I could see, hear, feel, almost touch, them. Those who are still alive seemed to be speaking from the full range of our knowing one another; the passage of years collapsing beneath the renewed delight their ideas and our shared memories bring. What convinced me that our correspondence transcends personal relationships and would be meaningful to readers was my sense that I'd unpacked a new historical medium, one that reveals—through the immediacy of actual conversations lifted out of time—a layer of intimacy and truth too often lost to memory.

Context, yes, but also skin and bone, an expression or gesture, a paintbrush moving effortlessly in a hand, a poem read in the voice of the poet who wrote it. And a hands-on reality that is largely absent in this digital age: the physicality of type made from hot lead becoming words on a page and a flatbed press printing those words onto paper to produce a book you hold in your hands. The experiences of creative women, forever threatened by patriarchal fear and control. Women and men unafraid to stand against war, genocide, destruction of our habitat, silencing, and censorship. Heartache and discovery, the joy of face-to-face contact. What happens right in front of you, not in some nebulous cyberspace or saved to an invisible cloud. The here and now of making and doing.

Who does the making and doing is important. And I began to understand that those who make the history that counts share a common quality. They are outriders, people who for various reasons face obstacles that force them to make courageous choices, choices that defy society's stultifying penchant for putting us all in safe boxes, frighteningly alike. Risk is vital to progress, and those who are willing to risk give us valuable gifts, push us all forward.

In *Letters from the Edge: Outrider Conversations,* I defined the term *outrider*:

> Outriders[1]: those who live and work outside the norm. Who represent a rupture with tired values and a ferocious resistance to their imposition. Who have the integrity to reject society's seductive efforts to mold them into its cowering attitude of

1. The word *outrider* did not originate with me. I first heard it spoken by the U.S. poet Anne Waldman, who, in her book *Outrider* (Albuquerque: La Alameda Press, 2006), writes, "Outrider is a line of demarcation. It's words—obsession for the honor, dignity of a mind ill at ease, restless, jumping from desk to orally standing-at-attention, examining itself. A maker of poetry. Parallel to a maker of many things." Thank you, Anne, for this brilliant word, for curating Naropa University's Jack Kerouac School of Disembodied Poetics for five decades, and for so much else. *Outrider,* the 2024 documentary about Waldman, directed by Alystyre Julian, explores the term further. I use it here to define someone who has faced social stigma and pushed through that to create.

> predictable acquiescence, thus making it more difficult for political and corporate powers to co-opt them to their advantage. Who reject the idea that there are only two choices, a "good" and a "bad," and demonstrate with their lives and in their work that we can all create other choices that enhance our journey.
>
> Outriders are often artists and others who are bridges—between cultures, between languages, between ideas. They can bring people together and strengthen communities. Sometimes they are forced into exile by political excess or violence and construct such bridges by their own example. They must resist the very real possibility that cruel displacement may destroy their will. Those who do resist emerge at pivotal moments in history with a collective force, sometimes following periods of social oppression, censorship, and defeat. When they do, the communal explosion may be termed countercultural.

My earlier book introduced five such people. A Communist poet with an imagination that led him to reject a narrow party line as well as fight and survive the rude assault of the state. A woman who dared question anthropology's male establishment and deciphered the meaning of an ancient culture by meeting it face-to- face. A publisher who spoke truth to power. A poet who embodied an identity and allegiances considered mutually exclusive at a time when she most needed understanding and encouragement, and who continues unwaveringly today. A painter who works with materials and a sensibility invisible to the mainstream and resists the rules of an art world sadly caught up in commodity culture.

More Letters from the Edge, the book you have here, is a continuation of this approach. Four more outriders speak through letters, interviews, and other fragments of memory, illustrating the fact that when we take risks, we tear down the walls and open the doors our debilitating social constructs impose. We are fond of applying whatever set of tools is currently in vogue to analyze previous eras, their cultures and ideas. Why not go to the source, read the words the protagonists wrote at the time, accompany them on their journeys, absorb the attitudes and efforts of those who were there?

In this book you will meet Jane Norling, a woman who defied her class and education to seek out those of her generation who were applying their talents to their passion for social change. Formally trained in art at a prestigious college, she left a promising job with a New York publisher to journey across the country and take her place among those who were contributing their creativity to the causes of the day. They rejected war, rose above racism, and confronted gender inequality. With others, she painted some of the great community murals of the 1980s, and explored the possibilities of public art that spoke to people's needs and aspirations.

No journey is straightforward, and Jane struggled for years with the issues creative women have faced for millennia: Can we be mothers and artists at the same time? How do we avoid the gender subservience always ready to trap us in its web? And what about our art itself? Must it always carry a political message? Can't art have its own presence, independent of point of view or with no point of view at all? Through a correspondence that spans decades, we accompany this woman in her struggles. In so doing, we touch many of the visceral questions of our time.

You will meet Robert Schweitzer, a man whose outrider parents knew how to give him the freedom to be his authentic self, the self-confidence he needed to make creative choices long before they became part of our popular discourse. Many of us, whether our parents were supportive or not, had to arrive at our identities by pushing back against parental influence. Robert found his by taking his parents' lessons further than they had been able to.

As a young boy, he asked for a dollhouse for Christmas. His mother and father didn't argue that dollhouses were for girls—wouldn't he prefer a gun or a truck? The joy he experienced in rearranging the furnishings in that "girl's toy" was reflected years later in his brilliance as an innovative curator of art. Early involvement in day-care centers taught him that education is the door to lifelong curiosity and creativity, and the educational ideas he introduced in his museum work as well as in college classrooms enabled generations of his students and others to engage in learning that would change their lives. And when he turned his attention to the injustices that plague us, he invariably stood up to authority, patiently but firmly explaining how it was misdirected, abusive, just plain wrong—and what a better option might be.

The Cuban Revolution was a defining event for those, like me, fortunate enough to have participated in its "David facing Goliath" reality. Here was a tiny island nation standing up to its powerful imperialist neighbor and demanding the right to self-determination. The first such experience on this continent, and the longest-lasting. Its goals of universal health care, education for everyone, and equality in ownership and work are desirable by any measure that prioritizes human well-being.

But from the revolutionary victory in 1959, the United States used every weapon in its arsenal to discredit a country that had dared stray from its sphere of influence. A succession of anti-Communist U.S. administrations accused Cuba of poisoning this hesphere with dangerous ideas. Year after year, we lied about the revolution in our media, blockaded and invaded Cuba's shores, boycotted its trade and forced other nations to do the same, introduced crop-killing plagues, and repeatedly attempted to murder its leaders. This constant death-dealing pressure couldn't defeat the revolution, but it has had a long-term effect; in addition to Cuba's own internal errors and occasional corruption, covert and overt U.S. intervention eroded the revolution's possibility for success. Supporters and attackers alike often distort the Cuban reality. Books from both camps tend to be one-sided, if not complete fictions.

I lived in Cuba from 1969 to 1980. I have often referred to that time as the revolution's glory years. A privileged bourgeoisie had fled the island, but those who remained were being educated, their health-care needs were being met, and there was virtually no unemployment. Creativity was encouraged and supported. When problems arose, we were confident they would be addressed and resolved. New ideas and initiatives were fresh, and enthusiasm was high.

Today, Cuba is a pale memory of what it was back then. Dramatic changes in the global balance of power, especially the collapse of the Socialist Bloc in 1989–1990, have made it increasingly difficult for the country to confront unrelenting pressure from the United States. The economy is in shambles and, like many other countries that still call themselves socialist, an authoritarian state capitalism rules. Still, each time I visit I come away with a deep appreciation for those elements that remain, however diminished. There is a pride and solidarity I haven't found anywhere else.

Those who remained in Cuba despite successive waves of emigration embody those qualities most solidly. Not the clones of Marxist-Leninist rhetoric, who simply go along with the program, questioning nothing, but those true revolutionaries who courageously maintain a critical lens, contesting what doesn't work and supporting the change that is still possible.

Arturo Arango is such a person. I have known him since he was a university student, already a brilliant thinker and writer, one of the young poets who hung out at my apartment during the 1970s, singing, reading to one another, sharing ideas. Now a successful novelist and professor of film scripts, Arturo travels the world to attend conferences and teach. But he has never wanted to leave his homeland. His relationship to the revolution has always been from the inside. Through our correspondence, readers will be able to go beneath the surface of facile rhetoric and explore a reality that exemplifies resistance and might have produced a society of true justice had imperialism desisted in its destructive campaign to destroy it.

The final voice in this book tells a story as painful as it is moving and meaningful. Kathy Boudin, a member of the Weather Underground in the 1970s and 1980s, wanted to be part of our generation's struggle for justice. She chose a radical route to that end, involving armed actions repugnant to the mainstream sensibility.[2] After years underground, she began to question the organization's strategy and tactics. She had begun to think about surfacing and continuing to organize for change while at the same time examining personal inherited and psychological factors that she was beginning to realize might have influenced her decisions.

It was during this confusing time that Kathy agreed to participate in "one final action." She and her partner dropped their fourteen-month-old son off at a babysitter and joined others in

2. The Weather Underground, or Weather Underground Organization (WUO), was a far-left Marxist militant organization founded in 1969 on the University of Michigan's Ann Arbor campus. The group emerged as a faction of Students for a Democratic Society (SDS).

attempting to rob an armored vehicle to secure funds for the revolution. The action went bad. Two law-enforcement officers were killed, as well as a security guard. Kathy and her comrades were caught, and she was sentenced to twenty years to life at a New York state correctional facility. A symbol of "domestic terrorism" in the eyes of the public, this thoughtful, introspective, and deeply compassionate woman began the long road to self-understanding, healing, and eventual freedom.

Kathy and I met when she had been in prison for more than five years. We became immediate friends. I visited her regularly during my teaching stints on the East Coast, and we wrote to each other and talked by phone when I was in New Mexico. Her letters, more than any I've had the privilege to receive, document a journey few have been forced to undertake. At first, she put her energies into prison projects of undeniable benefit to the inmate population, helping to create programs for incarcerated mothers and their children, literacy classes, and aid to victims of HIV/ AIDS. She obtained a master's degree. And she wrote—articles and books that have been useful to other prisoners and a general readership. But, although she herself wasn't armed and didn't pull a trigger, she continued to be plagued by the knowledge that she had been involved in an action that resulted in the deaths of three human beings. She spent decades trying to inhabit the feelings of the victims' families.

After twenty years in prison, Kathy went before the parole board for the first time. It denied her request for release. And the event sparked the renewed indignation and stigmatization of that sector of the population still enraged by her actions decades before. Two years later, her second appearance before the board ended differently. Considering her valuable contributions while in prison and what they saw as her true expressions of regret, the authorities gave her back her freedom after almost twenty-three years. On the outside, Kathy obtained a doctorate, established a center for prison reform at Columbia University, and continued to advocate for change in our egregious penal system. She enjoyed a deeply appreciated freedom before dying of cancer in 2022.

Now I invite you to enter these lives and their outrider sensibilities through their own words.

1

JANE NORLING: PAINTING THE BEAUTY OF STRUGGLE

JANE NORLING IS A painter, muralist, and graphic designer. She has used the latter skill to finance her more serious art but also to support progressive political efforts. Her creativity can be seen in much public art from the 1970s on: posters, murals, and large panels in public buildings, all of which tell a real people's history, encourage natural solutions to social problems—such as her *Leche Materna* poster supporting breast-feeding and the images she created to make people aware of the wrongness of the war in Vietnam, the excessive imprisonment of people of color in the United States, and the destruction of our Earth, pollution of our air, overprocessing of our food.

For more than fifty years, Jane created community murals in and around the San Francisco Bay Area—sometimes alone, more often with others. In one of the following letters, she describes the grateful reaction of passersby as she and two friends worked on the enormous *Our History is No Mystery* mural in Haight-Ashbury. She designed promotional materials for social and human rights movements and progressive political campaigns, from women's rights to local and international liberation struggles. She worked for many years at People's Press in San Francisco, a community-based print shop that produced books, pamphlets, posters, and other materials that addressed the issues of those times. In 1972, that organization selected her to go to Havana, Cuba, where she spent several months studying new silk-screen printing methods at the design department of the Organization of Solidarity with the Peoples of Africa, Asia, and Latin America (OSPAAAL).

That's where we met. I had arrived a couple of years earlier, having fled repression in Mexico following my participation in that country's 1968 student movement. As was the case with so many visitors from the United States, Jane got in touch. I was immediately moved by her receptivity to the issues that were important to us both, and by the way she channeled her passion into the quick sketches she made wherever she happened to be. We soon became close friends. It is a friendship that continues to this day.

Jane was born into an upper-middle-class family in Virginia. Art called out to her from an early age. As she told Aaron Hughes:

> I was always an artist, holding pencil to paper, drawing to interpret my world, dreaming of the shapes out the window, gazing at clouds. In grade school complying with kids' requests to draw pictures of them because I was good at representation. In high school I had jobs as a furniture decorator, holiday window painter, sign painter, and tile setter for business owners in the small town where I lived. I'm fortunate to have had solid encouragement from my parents and grandmother.
>
> I loved book design and learning a skill but was also hearing the voices of people demanding justice, an end to the war

> [in Vietnam], and for a society truly based on civil rights. In 1970, I quit my plans to marry a man I was with at the time and headed to San Francisco, where I joined like-minded people determined to make political change. My one year at Random House had given me the basics of book design that became a foundation for my fifty years of work in graphic design.[3]

Jane always understood that she could do her best political work through her art, but, as for so many others, class conditioning and unresolved emotional issues often got in the way, holding her back. For years, she was also troubled by a perceived contradiction between political and "fine" art, feeling guilty when her heart and hand produced the latter, believing—erroneously, I think—that all art must have a social message.

Throughout her adult life, she struggled to come to terms with all that kept her from her creativity. Our friendship, expressed in the many letters we wrote to each other from the mid-1970s on, was often a place where she questioned herself, feeling free to express her vulnerabilities. I encouraged her, and eventually she was able to overcome these obstacles. She also encouraged me, throwing herself into support work when I came back to the United States in 1984 and was ordered deported because of the content of some of my books.[4] Despite being a

3. "Jane Norling on Women's Rights, Human Rights, & Fifty Years of Art and Activism," an interview in *Justseeds* by Aaron Hughes, March 17, 2018.

4. In 1967, living in Mexico and married to a Mexican, I took Mexican citizenship. When I returned to the United States in 1984, this facilitated the government's case against me. Invoking the ideological exclusion clause of the 1952 McCarran-Walter Act, it claimed my work went "against the happiness and good order of the United States." The Center for Constitutional Rights (CCR) defended me through multiple trials over the following five years. I won the case in 1989. For more details about my case, see *Coming Home: Peace Without Complacency* (Albuquerque: West End Press, 1990).

struggling single mother at the time, she didn't hesitate to launch and head my Bay Area defense committee and worked tirelessly for the next five years to help me win my case.

Jane's path wasn't easy or straightforward. Along the way, she had to deal with a biased education typical of her class and time, the damaging family secrets that have plagued so many of us, self-doubt and indecision, a draining five-year relationship with the addict who fathered her child, single motherhood, a battle with breast cancer, and more. But her commitment was solid, and she faced all those challenges with conviction. Her art was a constant.

I had problems of my own to work through and overcome. Writing was my mode of expression. From our respective struggles and achievements, we saw and heard each other.

I lived in Cuba and Nicaragua before returning to the United States. Jane lived in Northern California. These were years of multiple struggles, and in our letters we exchanged news of what was happening in our respective communities. We also got together whenever possible. In the following fragments of our decades-long correspondence, readers will be able to trace our parallel, often intertwined, paths. You will get an idea of how we saw the world back then and glimpse our various involvements in the efforts to change it for the better.

La Habana, Cuba September 6, 1973
"Year of the XX Anniversary"

Dear Jane:

I haven't written in a while. Heavy times here. It seems like each day has so much that hits hard, that somehow must be absorbed and worked with—and then there's never enough time to do the absorbing or working-with.

I have completely rewritten the woman book. It's now 170 pages and works in chapters. There are ten chapters following a very long (38-page) introduction. I love the introduction. It's a pretty thorough study of women in Latin America, including working and peasant women, prostitutes, ideological penetration from the North, population control. And the chapters are complete entities as well. Each is built around that original material we got together, and you get a real sense of what the country is like, the context that produced a particular document or testimony or poem or account.

The kids are back, and it's been intense/beautiful being with them, hearing what they have to say, what they feel about their experiences. It was important for them to have gone on that trip. I am constantly amazed by their maturity, their astuteness, and their inner lives. All the kids are back at school now: Gregory at the Lenin, Sarah and Ximena where they were last year. And little Annie went from *círculo* to pre-school which has made her very proud because it means having a real teacher, real classes, a uniform, etc.

I'm deep into the FMC [Federation of Cuban Women] work which I love, and also deep into preparing for Peru.[5] Ever since I signed the contract two weeks ago now, I've been wondering how I'm going to do all the work. In three months they want me to write two books and give a series of lectures. They are going to pay me a fortune: $1,379 a month plus $28 a day for expenses, plus my travel both ways. All this is payable when I turn in the work to the satisfaction of "the

5. At the end of 1973 and the beginning of 1974, I was contracted by the United Nations International Labor Office (ILO) to spend three months in Peru researching women's lives and suggesting policies to improve them. A Socialist military officer, Juan Velasco Alvarado, had staged a coup against the repressive government of Fernando Belaúnde Terry. Velasco undertook radical land reform, recognized the cultural identities of the country's large Indigenous population, and made sweeping changes in education and other areas. His death, in 1977, cut these efforts short.

Secretario General," whatever that means or is. So, you can imagine how I feel. All kinds of insecurities creeping in as well as excitement and a desire to produce something that really will help Peruvian women in some small way.

I want/need news of you, the press, etc. Please write.

Love, much much love, M.

During the 1970s and 1980s, I had the great good fortune of witnessing social change in several volatile parts of the world: Cuba, Peru, Vietnam, Venezuela, Chile, Nicaragua. Before I got my Mexican passport back, the Cubans facilitated travel papers; afterward, I was able to travel with my Mexican document again.[6] The contacts I made during my years in Cuba gave me access to key players and opportunities for participation and on-the-ground learning. But as was true for all women with children, especially back then, I also struggled to combine motherhood with these opportunities. This was a theme in many of Jane's and my letters.

Paris—August 29th, 1974

My dear, dear, sister Jane:

Met Arlene's plane yesterday afternoon and she gave me the envelope right off.[7] It was several hours later before I could devour its contents: your life, the struggles you've been going through, the pain and also the strength.

6. I lost my Mexican passport in 1969 when two paramilitary agents came to our house and took it at gunpoint. I wasn't able to get another until I took my case to the Mexican ambassador to Cuba in 1980. He was progressive, listened to my story, and issued me a replacement the following day.

7. Arlene Eisen Bergman had written a book about Vietnamese women. The North Vietnamese Women's Union invited the two of us to travel together.

One day about a week before I was due to leave Habana, I suddenly got a very sharp pain in my lower abdomen. Almost passed out from it. And a slight fever. In something like two hours it was gone, though the "echo" lasted several days. A doctor friend said: "maybe gall bladder." Since it went away, and since I was pretty frantic with things to do before leaving, I put it out of my mind. Two days before I left, I was stricken again, this time with more fever, more pain, vomiting, dizziness, couldn't get off my back for those two days. As the trip time got closer, the doctor began plying me with an emergency plan he devised based on his assumption that it's my gall bladder (by this time there was no time for tests, of course). I somehow made it to the airport, walked across the field to the waiting plane, made the trip with the help of continued medication, waited out my layover in the Madrid airport, and arrived in Paris.

I was met there by my old dear friend/brother who is one of the closest comrades I have. Brazilian, out of Chile. He and his wife have a three-month-old baby girl who is amazingly calm and strong despite their history of struggle, torture, hardship, months in an embassy, and the fact that she and he have been given asylum in different European countries. Just being with the three of them gave me strength. I had sent him a telegram about my arrival but expected he'd be in a difficult living situation and that I probably wouldn't be able to stay with them. Wrong. I'd forgotten what solidarity is. The solidarity committee here got him an apartment rent-free for a year and I'm welcome to a tiny corner of it.

So, those were my first two days. Slowly beginning to eat again. Learning the city, the metro system, looking, listening, learning. Loving the experience of being in Paris and finding that the terrible culture-shock and depression that grabbed me during my first weeks in Peru weren't present even during my first minutes here. The reason for this may be that the class struggle, the contradictions, the misery, are so naked, so bare, so right out there in our poor devastated countries that coming from Socialism to them is physically and emotionally painful. Coming from Socialism to developed colonialist France is only intellectually painful.

You know the French workers and peasants have serious problems, you know there's poverty and misery, you even see a certain amount of it on some Paris streets, but it's a distant cousin to that misery we know in Peru, Bolivia, Nicaragua (what must it be like in Bangladesh, Indonesia, throughout Africa or Asia?). Everything here is so efficient, so streamlined and automatic—and of course that hits me constantly, and I think: if we only had this kind of transportation system, this kind of service, this kind of computerized facility for dispensing with the necessary means to an end in Peru, in Bolivia, even in Cuba. Yet I know that in Cuba, even in our transition, we have resolved the basic and most important human problems: health, education, housing, food.

Love, Margaret.

[flip side of postcard with photo of two new shoots of a plant emerging from barren ground]

Paris—September 6th, 1974

Dearest Jane: How I miss you! So far, the experience isn't easy. The other day Arlene and I visited with women from the Vietnamese Women's Union here in Paris, a beautiful experience. They gave me this photograph which symbolizes new life growing even from the most devastating death and destruction—a bomb crater. I wanted to share it with you, energy for you now. Arlene leaves Paris tomorrow via charters and I fly out next Thursday direct—we'll actually be on the same plane for the last hour or so from Vientiane to Hanoi. I can hardly believe it's so soon. Love, strength, Margaret.

Paris, October 17th, 1974

Dearest Jane:

Back in Paris, typing up my notes from the Vietnam experience, writing a few initial articles, poems, etc. Sometimes walking or going to a movie. Paris is a good place for this because somehow it seems like the people have maintained a semblance of dignity. Not like so many capitalist countries where the cracks are already deeper. Emotionally, though, this trip has been too long already, and I want to be home. I feel a deep need for the children and for Cuba.

The more I think of the experience with Arlene, the more I realize how hard it was. I am sure she also felt the need of another kind of sister. Now that I have some space to analyze the problems, I can see that they are essentially ideological. Two revolutionaries can have ideological differences that affect how they relate to one another. Even though Arlene identifies as a Marxist, for her sisterhood comes first. Although I am a woman—oppressed as a woman, struggling to liberate myself as a woman and deeply connected to my sisters everywhere who are engaged in the same struggle—for me class comes first. And this was reflected in the way we interacted.[8] All my love, M.

---

8. In the 1970s, social activists too often prioritized one set of social contradictions. In time, we have come to understand that successful struggle lies in understanding the intersection of all contradictions: class, race, gender, and other issues of identity, cultural as well as economic. Arlene Eisen Bergman's book, *Women of Viet Nam* (San Francisco: People's Press, 1974), remains an important look at the heroic women of that nation. Jane Norling designed the beautiful cover. Half a century after traveling to Vietnam with Arlene, I met her oldest son, Tongo Eisen-Martin, when we both performed

La Habana, Cuba—February 24th, 1975

Dearest Jane:

The Latin American women book, so long in the works and finally quite a bit enlarged and necessarily changed, will be published by Casa de las Américas for International Women's Year. I'm very glad about it, spent several weeks just rereading, revising, adding things, etc. I added a whole chapter about Nicaragua, which I think is the best in the book. It's in process now, Spanish translations being done of those parts that needed that. I still very much feel that the beginning of this project, our work together, makes it partly yours. If you still have the photographs that we searched for together at the COR archives, I need them, please send.

I'm enclosing something I thought might interest you and others there: On March 8th the Family Code goes into effect here, and the clauses relevant to men and women sharing housework and childcare will also from now on be read into the civil marriage ceremony. It's really an important step, I think, and so I copied the article in *Granma* and am sending it on.

The project I'm so deeply into now, and that's filling my days, nights, dreams, was sparked by the new chapter I inserted into the women book, the one on Nicaragua. The chapter is based on an interview with a young woman combatant from the Frente Sandinista de Liberación Nacional *[FSLN]*. Contact with that woman gave me the idea of doing a whole book on

---

at the Jack Kerouac School's fiftieth anniversary Summer Writing Program in 2024. Tongo is a brilliant poet deeply involved in today's struggles for social justice. He had his six-month-old daughter, Sankara, with him, and the legacy continues.

her—on Nicaragua, really, but seen through her life experience.[9] I think it will be a monologue, broken now and then by specific visual images from the Nicaraguan reactionary press, the social pages, the regime's description of its own poverty, repressive operations, etc. I'm going through ten years of newspapers from that country and have so far recorded some 200 pages of sessions with this woman. To do the book, every day I am juggling work hours and robbing time from my "real" work. It's very exciting. I can't remember being so in love with a project.

Gregory is taller than I am now, into manhood somehow though still only 14. Sarah, too, beginning to get breasts. Ximena close behind. Little Annie very wise and funny.

Much love, Margaret.

La Habana, Cuba—April 16th, 1975
"Year of the First Congress"

Jane, dearest sister:

I saw people from the Brigade[10] quite a bit this time around. A couple of Sundays ago we spent some time together

---

9. The woman was Doris Tijerino and my book about her came to fruition throughout 1975. It was published in Spanish as *Somos Millones* (Mexico City: Extemporaneos, SA, 1977) and in English as *Inside the Nicaraguan Revolution: The Story of Doris Tijerino* (Vancouver: New Star Books, 1978).

10. The Venceremos Brigade was formed in 1969 by a group of young people in the United States in solidarity with the Cuban Revolution. The people who came together to initiate the project represented a broad cross section of the radical movements of the time: Students for a Democratic Society (SDS), the Student Nonviolent Coordinating Committee (SNCC), the U.S. Communist Party, the Black Panther Party, and the Young Lords, among others. The first brigades had as many as seven hundred participants, who traveled to Cuba, worked cutting sugarcane, met with representatives of liberation struggles around the world, and learned about the revolution. Over the next fifty years, more than ten thousand young people would participate in the experience. During the decade I lived in Cuba, groups from

in groups, then last Sunday, another free day for them, I met with some twenty women in the morning. We talked about women's lives here and they taped. Then, somehow, we all shared lunch. I don't think I've ever before cooked here for 20 guests! I boiled the carcass of a chicken (our meat ration for nine days!). I added some potatoes and other things I had to the broth, and there was bread, and I think everyone was happy. That afternoon many others came over, as well as some of the Chilean comrades.

Did you know that Fernando[11] had a stroke, a light one but his left arm and the left side of his face were slightly affected. Worse, his blood pressure won't stay down without medication, and it is getting in the way of his work. What could be sadder than a Vietnamese freedom fighter who can't work? He will be returning to Vietnam in June. Last night we had a party for him, and for Minh who will be leaving next Wednesday. Remember them? The Vietnamese are rising up all through the south—so beautiful![12] Love, M.

Caracas, May 18th, 1975

Dearest Jane:

Surprisingly, I was invited to this First Congress of Venezuelan Women which will take place from the 21st to the 25th here in Caracas. I came on the 15th through Barbados (itself an interesting one-night experience: a tiny island nation with

---

the Brigade often visited me. The fact that I was a North American enabled me to bridge a cultural gap in my explanations of what was happening in Cuba.

11. Fernando was Nguyen Phuc (1930–1982), the head of the Voice of Vietnam in Cuba. I taught him English three days a week for several years and we became close friends.

12. The Vietnamese patriots would defeat the United States on April 30, 1975, just days after this letter.

such a strong residue of colonization, 90% black, strangely remote and isolated but with an unmistakable people's culture breaking through British and American penetration, African speech patterns, etc.). Here, in Caracas, where I'm "holed up" at the elegant Anauco Hilton, the experience is a bit heavy with press conferences, receptions, interviews. And the Congress itself hasn't even started. But it's also been interesting discovering how the women here think and feel, meeting with the Socialists and others, just getting out in a different world and soaking it all in.

Yesterday, visiting the family of a comrade in Habana, I was able to see a *población*[13] for the first time, walked way up the steep side of a hill covered with what they call *ranchos* here, the homes of the miserably poor. Not as bad as many places I've been because most were brick or cinderblock with real floors. This is a product of the wildly uneven oil development. What I did feel was a violence in the air, worse than almost anywhere I've been. The frustration of young men, especially, evident in their loud exclamations of rage. The women seem always to be waiting, anguished. This particular comrade was in prison four years and then expelled from the country: Antonio, maybe you remember him, the brother who takes care of Domingo.[14] When my friend who brought me to the house suggested to Antonio's mother that he might be coming back one of these days, she began to cry and said: "No, no, no. Oh, God knows I long for him, I want him back, but not if he has to go to prison, not if he has to suffer like he did before. I'd rather never see him again and know he's living and working in Cuba." It broke my heart.

---

13. What impoverished marginal areas were called.

14. This was Antonio Castro, in Cuba caring for another Venezuelan revolutionary named Domingo León, who had been paralyzed from the waist down in a shoot-out.

I'll be back in Habana on the 29th. Write! Love, struggle, M.

La Habana, Cuba—July 30th, 1975
"Year of the First Congress"

Oh, Jane, how beautiful to find that little square package yesterday out on our back gate, stuck between the grill-work bars. At first, the return address and Mazatlán postmark threw me. Who do I know in Mazatlán? But as soon as I saw a whole page of your strong handwriting—one of the few handwritings I always recognize—I knew it was from you.

The other night, about two weeks ago, I was coming home from militia duty late at night. I was standing at a bus stop waiting for my bus (our car crashed, is hopefully being repaired) when I met an old friend who used to be a designer at the Book Institute and now works with Rostgaard at OSPAAL.[15] Navarrete is his name, I don't know if you ever met. We got to talking and all of a sudden on a whim I opened my billfold where I always have a picture of you and the round mural. I pulled it out and said: "Look, this is a friend of mine who used to work at OSPAAL." I told him about you and the mural and gave him the photo to take to the people at the design department there, to remind them of you and the beautiful work you are doing. A nice moment.

We haven't had water for a while, have had to haul buckets from the street. This adds another dimension to the housework side of my life. And I'm fat, fat, fat, desperately wanting to lose weight but obviously not wanting that enough, because I don't.

15. Alfredo Rostgaard (1943–2004) was a Cuban artist. OSPAAAL was the Organization of Solidarity with the Peoples of Africa, Asia, and Latin America, an entity that did educational outreach around the liberation struggles taking place in the developing world in the 1960s–1980s.

The kids are home for vacation now and I must say all four are growing into the most extraordinary human beings. Sometimes I sit back and can't explain, even to myself, how I have been blessed with them. Gregory just came back from a bicycle trip to Camagüey, with five friends from his school. It was their initiative, and the school lent them the bicycles, knapsacks, tents, gave them food, medicine, and a letter saying they're from the Lenin.[16] They took an interesting route, going south and returning north, had great adventures! Gregory is 14 and the others are all between 18 and 20 so his body is nowhere near their more developed ones. But he kept up. The trip was a trial of endurance at times, but they all finished!

Sarah graduated from sixth grade with a blazing 97.3 average. She has her fingers crossed for the Lenin in the fall. Ximena finished fifth grade with a fine 91.6 average and will do 6th grade either at the *beca*[17] where she's been or maybe get into the university's experimental high school called Felipe Poey, where Ana has been accepted to begin first grade in September.

Meanwhile, they're all enjoying their vacation. We wanted Sarah and Ximena to go to Mexico for two weeks come this Friday, but still no word on their exit permits so they may not be able to make the trip. If the permits don't come through, they'll probably go along with Annie to Pioneer Camp. Ximena has a boyfriend now (she's 11!) who plays the guitar and drums,

---

16. The Lenin School was an exceptional high school for students who qualified with the highest grades. It had five thousand students, who had the use of modern labs, beautiful art, every sort of sports facility, and a specially selected teaching staff. There were also factories and fields, where the students did manual work in conjunction with their studies. One such school was created in each of Cuba's original six provinces, and when the country split up into fourteen provinces, more were built. Sadly, with the economic problems of successive decades, these schools have fallen into disrepair.

17. Boarding school.

has his own musical ensemble at the children's section of Teatro Estudio. All three girls are in the choral and guitar groups there. It meets on Saturday mornings. The kids write their own songs. Love, M.

La Habana, Cuba—November 5th, 1975
"Year of the First Congress"

Dear, dear, Jane, sister, comrade:

I feel kind of *quemada*, as the Cubans would say, burnt out. Not entirely, because I'm functioning all right. I come and go, do all the work I have to do, attend to this and that, am present for Gregory, Sarah, Ximena, Ana. And the strange thing is, I know if I could go to Varadero[18] right now, if I could get away, rest, be somewhere tranquil for a few days, I'd come back and feel the same. Nothing would have changed. Because it's not a physical tiredness. It's something else.

It's too much death, the deaths of people I've loved intensely. It's Roque.[19] It's Chile and Nicaragua and Mexico and Colombia and Angola and Laos and Portugal and Lebanon and the Spanish Sahara. It's so much death and Franco living on. It's my own life, not doing enough in this struggle, this struggle which is my major reason for living. It's my loneliness and my anger. It's my job situation which remains exactly the same day after day, month after month and year after year. I have no *contenido de trabajo [work content]*, none at all. I have this huge need to write but somehow without the sense I could just do

18. Varadero Beach, about an hour to the west of Havana, is a popular resort destination for foreigners as well as Cubans.

19. Roque Dalton (1933–1975) was a poet, political analyst, and revolutionary from El Salvador who returned to his country to take part in its armed struggle and was murdered by members of his own organization.

that, that it would be justified. It's asthma and not being able to breathe. It's weighing 30 pounds more than I should.

I needed this letter from you . . .

Did I tell you that about three weeks ago I was given the "Ho Chi Minh" medal? It was a total surprise and one of the most moving things I've experienced. They called me at work and told me that the UPEC[20] wanted me to attend a ceremony on the night of the 15th but they didn't know what it was about. They said they would tell me on the morning of the 15th. The 15th of October is the anniversary of Nguyen Van Troi's assassination—the young patriot who tried to kill McNamara—remember? That morning, they told me to be at the Havana Libre, in the *Salón de la Solidaridad*, at 8 p.m. About 100 were given the medal but I was the only foreigner. All were somehow connected to the world of culture or the press: artists, singers, painters, writers, theater people, dancers. And Haydée Santamaría, Melba Hernández, Alfredo Guevara, Santiago Álvarez.[21] The ambassador of the Democratic Republic of Vietnam spoke, followed by Ernesto Vera, president of the UPEC. It was a very emotional ceremony and, although I certainly don't deserve recognition for doing less than what's necessary, it made me very happy.

20. Union of Cuban Journalists.

21. Haydée Santamaría (1922–1980) and Melba Hernández (1921–2014) were the only two women who participated in the attack on Moncada Barracks in 1953. Santamaría was the director of Cuba's preeminent cultural institution, Casa de las Américas. She took her own life in 1980 at the age of fifty-seven. Alfredo Guevara (1925–2013) was a filmmaker, gay man, and founder of the Cuban film industry. Santiago Álvarez (1919–1998) was a filmmaker known for his documentaries, among them *79 Springs*, about the life of Ho Chi Minh. The three were revolutionaries whose political commitment was imbued with independence and imagination.

An interesting thing also happened that night. Naturally, I arrived on time. Except for the Vietnamese, no one else did. I was sitting there, looking at the podium and speakers' table, above which were Ho Chi Minh's words: NOTHING IS MORE PRECIOUS THAN INDEPENDENCE AND FREEDOM, in Spanish of course. I began to fixate on the white letters of the word *PRECIOSO*, and my mind went back to Roque, to a conversation he and I had about that word around 1971, I think. *Precioso* in Spanish doesn't exactly translate to precious in English. Our discussion was also about Ho. And you know, Jane, that was something else that was wonderful that night. It was the first time I've thought about Roque without his death weighing me down, tearing me apart.

Roque and I had an extraordinary relationship. When I think of it now, I am filled with gratitude. We met in Mexico at the beginning of 1964; he came to our *Encuentro de Poetas* in February of that year. After we both moved to Cuba, we were judges together at the Casa de las Américas literary contest in 1970. Throughout those years we also did a lot of other work together. He helped me translate Vallejo.[22] I helped him too. Our ideological discussions were probably what taught me most during that time. They were long and clear and always began at the beginning. I worked with him on *Miguel Mármol*, his long oral history of the Salvadoran revolutionary.[23] He helped me with my book about Cuban women. When I discovered

22. César Vallejo (1892–1938), Peruvian poet who went to Spain during that country's civil war and lived in Paris until his death from malaria at the age of forty-six. He was one of the great poets of the Spanish language and, because of his inventive syntax, is very difficult to translate.

23. Miguel Mármol (1905–1993) was a Salvadoran revolutionary, one of the founders of the Communist Party of El Salvador, and a participant in that country's 1932 peasant uprising. Roque taped a series of interviews with him that resulted in the book *Miguel Mármol*.

> Rugama's[24] great poem about the moon, Roque incorporated it into a theatrical production he was staging with Teatro Estudio.
>
> We were lovers too. And when that part of our relationship ended, nothing changed all through his years in Cuba, Korea, Vietnam, and until his death. This is the first time I've expressed any of this in words. All my love, M.

During my years in Latin America, I increasingly provided an informational bridge for people in the United States and elsewhere to help them understand what was going on in places such as Cuba and Nicaragua, places that were ignored or intentionally distorted in the U.S. corporate media and on the nightly news. I kept a diary and sent carbon-copy pages to friends, who shared them with their friends. And I made several trips to the United States and Canada, meeting with diverse groups of people and lecturing to many different sorts of audiences. This bridge role became an important part of my identity and the writing I was doing.

> Toronto, December 11th, 1975
>
> Dearest Jane:
>
> After a great many ups and downs, plans and more plans, this trip finally got off the ground on November 11th. I traveled to Toronto via Jamaica. The trip has been deeply good so far, productive in all sorts of ways, tremendously educational for me, very exciting and also frustrating in that the schedule has been very heavy. Too often I feel I am just getting to know a place and wham: I'll be on a plane heading to the next stop. This trip was organized by The Canadian Women's

24. Leonel Rugama (1949–1970) was a young Nicaraguan revolutionary and poet who died at the age of twenty fighting against the Somoza dictatorship.

Educational Press (they published my book about Cuban women in English) and LAWG (Latin American Working Group) that does educational work around Latin America. Other Canadian groups—CUSO, SUCO, Miles for Millions, the B.C. Labor Federation, Voice of Women, Congress of Women, development education groups, INDIRA, Oxfam, etc.—also supported it, either providing some of the funding or through people contributing their time and effort. From the beginning, the organization and efficiency of the women in Toronto who launched the whole thing has been spectacular: Sheila Katz, her sister Helene Katz, Janice Acton, Donna Bobier, Margaret Gahlinger.

The first week, five days really, was mostly given over to orientation in Toronto, with a few activities in that city such as a big public meeting (some 800 attended), panels, workshops, a film, etc. This was followed by a party and reading, at which I read some of my own poetry as well as some by Latin American poets in English translation. Then there was orientation about the rest of the country, what the political/social/economic scene would be in each place. Then we started westward, accompanied by Donna from Women's Press and Margaret from LAWG. We traveled mostly by plane, with books and literature and a new Cuban documentary on women (a 50-minute color film produced by ICAIC that the Cubans lent me for the trip).

Heading west, we hit Sudbury, the largest nickel mining production in the world, open pit mines. Multinational control and corruption. The city sits in the middle of sulfur-ridden country that resembles the chemically and electronically devastated liberated area of Quang Tri, Vietnam that I visited in 1974. Then Winnipeg, lots of different audiences at different events: Liberation Bookstore, the two universities, an assortment of Chilean refugees. A good deal of television coverage, including making videos for an organization called FOCUS to use in the countryside.

From there to Regina. Biting cold. Snow blowing off the central plains, good organization and many lectures and film showings. On to Edmonton, where the leftwing Christians were very much in evidence. Tremendous interest and evidence of class struggle at some of the meetings. Vancouver, on the west coast, was a tremendous experience, a city not unlike San Francisco—physically as well as socially and politically. There I spoke at the two big universities, a junior college, to the Chilean community, with an invited group of women community leaders, union people, and just last night at a big public meeting.

By the time we were a week into our travels, we began to see the hour- or hour-and-a-half flights as our only breaks, in terms of rest and relaxation. Often, arriving at a new city, we'd be whisked right from the airport to our first event. From Vancouver, we flew back east. Then it was Ottawa for a few days and then Quebec. In Quebec the experience was quite different, much more profound really, due to a much higher political level. Throughout that province, Helene accompanied me and did the translating from and into French. We spent a few days in Montreal but concentrated on small mining communities like Rouyn, Chicoutimi, etc. That was an incredible experience for me, among the best on the trip.

After Quebec, it was the Maritime provinces: New Brunswick and Halifax: also new and totally different experiences. And then finally back to Toronto. The last night, or what was supposed to be the last night, was in Hamilton.

Some of what I took away with me was 1) discovering that Canada is Canada and Canadians are Canadians. This may sound strange, but growing up in the United States my vision—at least my unconscious emotional sense—of Canada was that it is some sort of extension of the US. Of course, in recent years, if asked I would probably not have said this. I realize how much cultural imperialism operates in a northern direction as well as to the south. 2) Sharing Cuba and the Cuban revolution, specifically what it's meant for women, with housewives, workers, intellectuals, immigrants, students, Chilean refugees, and others. 3) The three hours I spent with Laura Allende in Vancouver. We had a whole morning together, talking, or rather I mostly listened, and she talked. 4) Getting to know Quebec, even superficially, especially the day we spent in Rouyn. Quebec is really a part of the Third World inside Canada. The struggle there, which is much more developed than in the rest of the country, is a class struggle but with aspects of national liberation.

Politically, there was a strong pro-Chinese feeling in leftist communities across Canada. Stronger in some areas: Vancouver, Quebec, Halifax. At times this seemed quite sectarian and sometimes, by extension, it also took the form of anti-Cuban sentiment. Those provinces with NDP governments (the New Democratic Party, which is Social Democratic) felt quite different from those with conservative governments. In Fredericton, New Brunswick, the almost total absence of an awareness of the rest of the world was frightening; I didn't see a single poster alluding to Chile, Vietnam, or Angola. In Quebec, on the other hand, I saw a militant solidarity with those struggles almost equal to that in Cuba.

Well, I've wanted to give you an idea of the tour. Much love, M.

La Habana, Cuba—January 16th, 1976
"Year of the XX Anniversary of the Granma"

Dearest Jane:

Angola: I've been sending you diary pages and press clippings from here. So, I think I've answered most of the questions you pose.[25] Cuba is aligned with the Soviet Union in terms of the Sino-Soviet split and sees China's foreign policy as playing into the hands of imperialism and fracturing the Socialist camp. I think Cuba perceives this to be the result of a power struggle within the Chinese Party. I wonder what difference, if any, Chou En Lai's death will make. It's frightening. Here in Cuba, almost everyone has a brother, father, husband, friend, or work colleague in Angola. There must be some 10,000 Cuban troops in that country now. The solidarity is strong and concrete, and you see evidence of it everywhere. For a more complete Cuban line on the Sino-Soviet split and other issues, see Fidel's Central Report to the First Party Congress under the foreign policy section. I think the section on self-criticism is also very revealing and the most honest statement I've seen from a political leader.

Robert, in case I haven't mentioned it, has been living apart from us for about a month. Both of us are feeling better, I think. The children are okay, although I know they are struggling.

Love, M.

---

25. In mid 1975, at the request of Angolan president Agostinho Neto, Cuba sent tens of thousands of troops to help liberate that country and defeat South Africa and its apartheid policies. Fidel Castro cast the Angolan campaign as a righteous response to the fact that Africans had been kidnapped and brought to the New World, where they'd been forced to help develop the very nations, Cuba among them, that kept them enslaved.

La Habana, Cuba—July 21st, 1976
"Year of the XX Anniversary of the Granma"

Dearest Jane:

I have your long, wonderful, welcome letter written between the end of May and beginning of July. Got it yesterday. It really came at a good time. I need the contact with people I love as much as I love you. This situation around my job—which I now see is much bigger than that—has me very depressed.[26] I have done so much over the past few years and now find I can't lift a finger. In your letter you mention needing to cry. I've always felt it very important to be able to cry, to release tension, and even wonder if there isn't something wrong with those who can't. But lately my relationship to the act of crying is a new, and terrifying, experience.

I cry all the time. I'm not exaggerating. It's hard on the children and so I have taken to walking alone, often along the *malecón*.[27] I feel as if there is nowhere that I can call my own; crying at home would upset the kids and Antonio.[28] So, I go out and walk, sit on the low sea wall and look out at the sea to try to release the tension I feel. The other day I was doing this, happened to look down to my right and there was a young white man sitting on the sand masturbating while staring up at

---

26. Without explanation, I was let go from my job at the Book Institute. I tried to find out why, but my efforts were unsuccessful. The Cuban government continued to pay my salary, and my work was occasionally accepted by Cuban publications—which further confused the situation. Several friends were also warned against visiting my home. Try as I did, I couldn't find out why this had happened to me. After much frustration, I was finally given an explanation and something of an apology: My feminism and the fact that I hosted friends from other countries whose politics didn't always coincide with the Cuban line was too much for Cuban officialdom at the time.

27. Seawall.

28. Antonio Castro and I lived together for a few years after Robert and I separated.

me. I got up, walked two or three hundred feet farther along the coast and again tried to be alone. And within a matter of minutes the scene was repeated, this time with a young black man who wasn't sitting but standing. So, I just went home, feeling there was nowhere I could be myself and let my emotions out.

This whole thing with my job. I have been fired from the Book Institute, although no one has used that word. I have tried and been unable to find out why. I continue to draw a salary but have no idea how long that will last. And this has paralyzed me. I am clear that this has nothing to do with the revolution per se but comes from one or more individuals in positions of power. I will always unconditionally support the Cuban revolution, but I am miserable.

Another thing that stood out in your letter was your mention of racism—the way your mural was so clearly attacked because it portrayed people of color. In the past few years, I too have been very conscious of racism, although my experience here in Latin America is different from yours in the States. Here it's mostly about the marginalization of indigenous people, my experience in Peru, then Vietnam, and here in Cuba (where it is directed at Black Cubans although there is more consciousness and an attempt to combat it). Latin American exiles I know also tell me stories of having faced racism in places like Sweden. My own experience of French colonialism. The realization that racism, like sexism, is an evil we must work tirelessly to eradicate.

The other thing you bring up is the issue of children, wanting to have one and getting older and thinking about it more. My children are a central part of my life. They have taught me more, given me more, loved me more, and drawn more love from me than anyone or anything else. And in four totally different ways. I think it's good to have a father around who cares, one with whom you have a solid relationship. But it's not completely necessary and perhaps could be put aside. I don't know if my own experience could be helpful to you, but I can tell you that Gregory was my happiest baby. And that was 16 years ago in New York, a city that didn't yet have daycare centers or other services, and at a time when single motherhood was looked down upon—at least by those of my social class. Having Gregory was a beautiful experience. And I've always thought that he benefitted by the lack of tension in his first years. He had lots of father figures, and mother figures too.

Tomorrow Agostinho Neto arrives in the country. I plan to go out and wait hours if necessary to receive him. The last time I did that was for Pham Van Dong. We just got the news from Argentina about the death of Santucho and seven others in the ERP leadership, a terrible blow.[29] And the fascist wave in Latin America is one of the worst things we are experiencing now. Who could have imagined, say in 1946 or '47 that in less than 30 years fascism would rise again in the world?[30]

Well, enough of all this. I love you and need your letters. Maybe I'll call you one of these days, though I can't really afford that. Maybe you'll be seeing Gregory and Ana and Robert; he didn't know for sure but might go to the coast before the kids return. Sarah and Ximena leave for Mexico next Monday.

---

29. Mario Roberto Santucho (1936–1972) was an Argentine revolutionary and guerilla combatant, founder of the Partido Revolucionario de los Trabajadores (Revolutionary Workers Party) and leader of the country's largest Marxist guerilla group, the Ejército Revolucionario del Pueblo (People's Revolutionary Army). He and his comrades were killed in a shootout with the army.

30. This statement seemed legitimate at the time I wrote this letter. Since then, of course, waves of fascism have risen and been beaten back periodically. History repeats itself, and since it is systematically erased or skewed by those in power, we are destined to make the same mistakes again and again.

And all four kids will come back at the end of August. I miss Gregory and Ana, just as I will miss Sarah and Ximena, but love it that they are having these great experiences. No more for now. Love, M.

La Habana, Cuba—November 1st, 1976
"Year of the XX Anniversary of the Granma"

Dearest Jane:

Your letters always help. This October 7th one helped a lot. The letter and the photos, the clippings, that sense you always manage to transmit of being there and then what there is really like, as well as simply your solidarity and love and strength. Today is November 1st, which means that tomorrow is the election in the US. I imagine Carter as the winner.

October has just ended, and October is always heavy for me. Heavy and beautiful and painful all at once. A feeling no words have yet been invented to convey. For as long as I can remember, October has had a special significance for me, long before I was conscious of why, long before I knew anything about the Russian revolution and the importance it would have in our lives. Gregory was born in October 1960. In 1965 I put the name *October* on a book of my poems. I look at that book now and its pages seem to be slipping, falling, picking themselves up again. More recently, October began to be the month of the living dead: Che (1967), Tlatelolco (Mexico) in 1968. Turcios Lima (1966) and Miguel Enríquez (1974), Dagoberto Pérez (1975).[31] This year that sense of death came right up to the edge

31. Ernesto "Che" Guevara (1928–1967), Argentinian doctor who joined Fidel Castro's rebel army and fought in Cuba, held important posts in the country's revolutionary government, and then went on to fight in Congo and finally in Bolivia, where he was killed on orders from the CIA. On October 2, 1968, a thousand people were shot down on orders from the Mexican government at a plaza called Tlatelolco. Luis Augusto Turcios Lima

of the beach and licked our toes: Miguel on the 5th, then the news that Antonio's father had died the day before, and finally the terrible CIA sabotage of a Cubana plane in which 73 people plunged flaming into the sea, 57 of them Cubans—the Cubana crew, national work heroes, and a group of youngsters on the country's fencing team. Now October has ended.[32]

It's raining today. The car is broken. I have taken three buses and walked a long way, through Miramar and then Vedado. Finally, the hot summer is finished, and it's been cool for several weeks. I love the rain and grayness. I was thinking how much clearer the architecture of a city looks when it rains. No sun to get in the way. Buildings stare back at me, very delineated, very present. Architecture has always been important to me. I've never had a desire to make it, to be part of creating it, just to look. I have a whole series of architectural images in my mind, and I pull them out and examine them from time to time. Niemeyer Drive in Rio de Janeiro (that was 1950!). The old Sullivan buildings on New York City's Lower East Side (1960). Santiago de Chile, Lima, Paris, Hanoi, Caracas, Toronto, Vancouver, Montreal. I wonder why I think the sun gets in the way of seeing buildings, but the rain doesn't. The rain and gray skin of sky seem to bring everything into sharper focus; the images become more intense.

All my love and struggle, M.

(1941–1966) was a Guatemalan army officer who became a revolutionary leader and died in an automobile accident. Dagoberto Pérez Vargas (1947–1975), Chilean revolutionary and member of that country's Movement of the Revolutionary Left (MIR), was the oldest of five siblings in the Pérez Vargas family; all but one gave his or her life in the struggle for liberation.

32. Cubana de Aviación flight 455, en route from Barbados to Jamaica, was brought down by a terrorist bomb attack on October 6, 1975. It was later proven that the CIA had orchestrated the attack.

This period in Jane's life was characterized by her relationship with Tony Chávez, a man she met and fell in love with and with whom she had her only child, Río. Tony exerted a powerful attraction on Jane and, although she recognized that his addiction to cocaine and heroin caused him to lie, steal, and be incapable of becoming a reliable partner or father, she broke with and then returned to him over a period of several years. I think color and class guilt kept her in the situation, as well as physical attraction and her desire that her son have a father.

San Francisco, December 20th, 1979

Dearest Meg:

I hope this gets to you, doesn't matter when. Sent a letter to Nicaragua, in which I explained a little of why I've been so terribly out of touch. Now it's a matter of finding some political direction in this morass and to secure myself in work that's meaningful, that builds for the future. It's been the most difficult experience in my life trying to live with a junkie, someone who was off it but still has the same street mentality. I wouldn't be with him if there weren't beautiful things too, a sense of comfort when we're together. But when we're apart, I can't trust. So, I'm facing the end of something I can't face the end of. This year will be different because it has to be. Amazing how focused one person can be, and there is a whole world out there with millions of people. Nicaragua was such an uplift, and we will only see more. But when here? When will the contradictions exist for people to do what must be done? All I see here are drugs and alcohol. And it's getting worse.

Meg, you have a very interesting function, an international flexibility that always roots you somewhere, though not rooted in the sense of growing out of some one place. I always wanted to be rooted somewhere, but maybe I have to realize that my roots are broader than immediate community. I need your communication, Meg; I want to share again. Let me know how you are, and about Nicaragua and your family. Love, much love, Jane.

La Habana, Cuba—October 19th, 1980

Dearest Jane:

This has been a difficult year for me. Mostly bogged down by persistent depression. Almost no poetry. A feeling of terrible tiredness most of the time. I managed to finish the book on Nicaraguan women, though, and think it's the best thing I've been able to do. It will be out in January from New Star as *Sandino's Daughters: Testimonies of Nicaraguan Women in Struggle*. For the first time, my own photographs will accompany the text. Another Vancouver house, Pulp Press, will publish the anthology of Cuban women poets I put together over the past year, before leaving for Nicaragua, but I don't have an exact publication date yet. And a new book on Cuban women—coming out of those lectures I brought to the States two years ago—will be out next month from Smyrna Press in New York.[33]

I've mostly been doing photography. Built a tiny darkroom here in Cuba, and even with the lack of paper, film, and just about everything else, managed to keep working and learning.

Pretty wonderful news is that the Mexicans finally saw fit to give me back my passport! That just happened a few days ago. I have a desire to "come home," have been thinking of what I might be able to do to earn a living in the US. Any ideas?

No more for now, but a big hug. All my love to you, and to Tony, and to the new human being, Margaret.

---

33. *Women in Cuba: Twenty Years Later* (New York: Smyrna Press, 1980). Cover and photographs by Judy Janda.

Santa Cruz, California—September 1st, 1981

Dearest Margaret:

My wonderful baby Río is now a year old. We've been moving around since he was two months, settled for now in Santa Cruz, a laid-back resortish town an hour and a half south of San Francisco. I had to get away from the madness of loving Tony, a junkie, get distance from that intensity. Tony and I have a deep bond with each other and it's only right that a child would emerge from that, but the bond is also dangerous. He has been too unwilling to change his ghetto habits, and I was naïve about so much. He got back into heroin after we moved in together and his use (which I never actually saw but experienced the effects of deeply) pushed me into another bout of PID. We had lived together about six months, '78–'79, both working at the Neighborhood Arts Paint Shop when I got sick again, had to quit work and went into extensive acupuncture and Chinese herb therapy. Gave up all coffee, alcohol, high protein and processed foods and then, about ten months later, got pregnant. After eight months of living together, after I had begun to get better, Tony went into Centro de Cambio, a drug rehabilitation house in the Mission community. He did well, was great leadership there as he is everywhere when he's connected to the good parts of himself, and then came out in December '79. I was a fool, believing he was "better," not understanding the nature of heroin addiction, and he moved back in with me into "our" apartment. That December I got pregnant. A real miracle.

In September I'd had a laparoscopy and laparotomy to remove scar tissue from my tubes. That and the herb therapy worked. My body was made receptive to the new spirit. And, as I knew, the new spirit has been just that—the renewal of Jane. All during the pregnancy I worked full-time downtown at a commercial design studio in the financial district. Package design, design for marketing. I hated the work, but it was good for picking up professional skills and for the money.

Meanwhile, Tony had dropped out of City College, where he'd gotten in despite not even finishing the ninth grade and was back into the junk. As you can see, I have no typewriter.[34] It made for a difficult pregnancy. He got into an architectural draftsman trainee program which placed him two blocks away from my work downtown. But he can't function in that atmosphere of upper class and upper middle class educated white people and he dropped that when he was asked to work for Centro de Cambio, the drug program, as their graphic artist. He dropped that a few months later.

I couldn't break with him during the pregnancy. I just couldn't do it. I kept thinking the baby he wanted so much would set him straight. Two months before my due date we began a mural-on-panels project which would be the backdrop at the tenth anniversary of the Chicano moratorium against the war. That was an effort to mobilize Chicanos against the draft, to build Chicano militant unity again. We painted the panels in our house, nights and weekends, four other artists coming over when they could. I had developed preeclampsia and was told to rest, so I quit work a month before due date. But I wasn't able to quit work on the mural. Tony needed me to push him, I see now. They were all depending on me, and I was the one physically least able to work.

The weekend before the moratorium we were about to finish up the panels, late Friday night after the others went home, I climbed down the ladder and went into labor. Río came three

34. Like many of Jane's letters, this one was handwritten. In this case it was because Tony had pawned her typewriter.

weeks early to tell his mother it was time to pay attention to him. Tiny Río developed jaundice and had to stay in the hospital for six days after his birth. I stayed three days, as long as medical paid for, and then went up every four hours to feed him around the clock until he came out. Living only two blocks from the hospital made this possible.

The birth was wonderful. I had no birth classes but my karate training which had showed me how to breathe through pain got me through. And the wonderful midwives. Tony was there off and on getting more and more loaded but managed to be there for the pushing and Río's emergence. Río's name came five days later, for the blood of the living earth and for Diego Rivera, political art, the murals, and for my family and his father's family: Río Diego Norling Chávez. No hyphenated last name because too much to carry around.

Tony left the night I came home from the hospital because I was so mad at coming home to the stereo missing and in the pawn shop. I couldn't even go to the hospital to have our baby without the stereo being moved out. He was on a bad run. So, friends came to stay with me and take me to the hospital. When Río was a month old, we were sued for eviction by the landlord because I didn't pay rent. I was not going to be able to keep that apartment by myself on disability payments. Besides, too much pain.

I picked up my things, stored them, and went to stay with Gail in Oregon for five weeks. Then two weeks back in SF staying at different places, and eight weeks with my mom and dad over Christmas. That was wonderful, gave them a chance to bond with their new grandson. Then SF for a couple more months, then Santa Cruz where I had a job waiting for me. Stayed with friends till I found this place where I've been now two and a half months. I couldn't be better.

Now a year later, a year away from living two systems, my old self is returning. The old drive to create, the need to create in other ways beside Río. Over this recent time, a better relationship has developed with Tony. We have seen a lot of each other, him venturing down here to the country and me bringing Río up there to build ties with his grandmother, aunts, cousins, etc. Tony has been wonderful with Río, Río very attached to him, which is scary, but I don't think there is anything better than the child and father loving each other.

Tony is doing well now, but better than that I am doing well. I am not so desperately needy of him. The positive break took place in my moving. I realize my goal in life is not to build a family, the way I had been believing the past four or five years. My life's work is to be a political artist, to put my skills at the service of revolutionary change and simultaneously raise a healthy new person to carry on. Strong in myself is how I feel.

The only weakness I feel is the terrifying love for Río, weak in the sense that if anything happened to him, I would be completely devastated. Meg, I would like to hear from you on that. I am not worrying for now about whether I break off from Tony and leave room to develop another relationship, or who will father Río best, or any of those questions. Things changed when I stopped breast-feeding so much and my body was more for me. Getting the art out is what needs to be done. Río is fine, in fact he is a wonderful baby. He is a great character, and strangers stop me and tell me how expressive his face is. I love hanging around with him. He's in childcare for about seven hours a day with a woman from a farmworker family who watches children at her house. She teaches them things and Spanish is spoken as much as English. The only thing that bothers me is that the TV is always on and now that

Río is a year old, he's getting interested in it. So, I'm considering moving him to a center because maybe there he'll receive more stimulation. At the sitter's he has older kids, and the center is just about all white which is what this area mostly is. Anyway, I've put aside the question of another child for the time being.

Now I'm doing a few freelance jobs. Had one doing illustrations and graphic stuff for the Migrant education project of the Food & Nutrition Services Agency here, a non-profit progressive organization that does food-related distribution and education. The job ended when the Department of Education stopped the funding in July. I'll be operating their print shop when I finish these jobs. I did four posters for them and various illustrations for use in nutrition education classes for Migrant kids and families. Santa Cruz county a strange combination: north county is the town, which is surfer, retirement, university, tourist, resort. South county is agricultural. You can guess the racial breakdown.

I loved the photos you sent a year or so ago from Nicaragua. You amaze me with your drive to constantly expand your capabilities. Please tell me how you had four children and did anything else. I never knew love like this—how do you have a second child after the first? A single mother and child have such an intense thing. When Tony's around I feel myself being drawn away from Río and I don't like that. I feel much more capable of being a real friend to you now, Meg, which I don't think I've been for a long time. The creation of this child took precedence over everything, I realize in looking back, and that meant this life with Tony that took me from much of me that I love: you and other friends.

Love, Jane (and Río)

Managua, Nicaragua—September 7th, 1981

Dearest Jane:

You know, Jane, in a very general sense I knew some of what you have been going through. I intuited, somehow, the problems with Tony, the struggle to emerge as Jane, even the motherhood. Someone had told me you had had a baby. What I didn't know were the details. I don't know what could have happened to our letters. I have received none of yours here in Nicaragua, and from what you say it seems you have gotten none of mine either.

Río is fantastic! What a beautiful baby! Don't worry about him being small. The sizes and weights given as normal are very deceptive. The range of normalcy is certainly much broader than American doctors would have us believe (undoubtedly to con us into buying their syrups and pills). So much of what you say about you and Río sends me back to that time with Gregory in New York so many years ago (21 now!). I was alone with him and that allowed me to be so very much with him. I am reliving those feelings here in Nicaragua with Ana. It is clear to me that the relationship between an adult and a single child is qualitatively different from that between an adult and several children.

The move to Nicaragua was decisive. I had thought about coming to the States but the real possibilities there seemed too vague—legal as well as how to support myself. And so, I opted for here. I gave each of the kids a choice: to come with me or stay in Cuba. The three older kids chose to stay, which I think was the right decision in each case. Ana was too young to give her that option. Of course I miss Gregory, Sarah, and Ximena terribly. It seems we have each entered a new phase in our life.

Originally, I had planned to work for the Women's Association here, in promotion. But when I arrived, I found that their funds had been cut, along with those of all the mass organizations and that they must now depend on volunteer labor because of the economic crisis. So, I took a job at the Ministry of Culture and will work with the Women's Association in my spare time.

The first few months were hard, having left such a "set" life in Cuba, having to battle with all the problems of capitalism again: finding a place to live, getting Ana into school and helping her adjust. But it all feels better now. You'd love it here. There is so much enthusiasm and so much opportunity to paint murals. Art is central to this revolution.

There's also a terrible press for time. No days have enough hours. I will soon be working on a new book about the class struggle inside the Church, how Vatican II has changed the meaning of faith for many Catholics. It's wonderful to feel your presence once again. Be well. Take care of yourself. Write. All my love, M.

Santa Cruz, California—January 1st, 1983

Dearest Margaret:

May this year bring needed advances for all and may it open new lines of communication between us, closed down by my negligence. How are you? I would love to be saying this in person but short of that, Miranda[35] is practically my eyes, ears, and heart anyway.

It's been so long, I'm not sure what to say. I see your books in the stores here in Santa Cruz. They continue to be necessary windows out to a world that seems so far away from this one. This area has a small core of politically minded people and a large core of surfers and no-minded people. To the south is Watsonville and the Salinas Valley, where the population

35. Miranda Bergman, artist and close friend of Jane's who worked on many murals with her.

is mixed Mexican and Chicano and Filipino, most of whom aren't aware of much outside their valley, just trying to feed their families.

I'm working on a mural at a senior center in Watsonville. Part of the agency I've been working for since I got down here two years ago. Miranda is bringing you the posters I did, and some other things. This is the first large scale mural since the history mural in SF. And the first mural that is not "overtly political" in style or content. In the main hall they serve a noon meal to an ever-growing number of low-income elderly people. Actually, the place itself is political in that it is run by Chicanas and serves white, Chinese, Filipino, Mexican, some Black, is completely bilingual and bicultural, with many of the white people taking Spanish classes. When racism happens, it is so obvious and strange because it comes from 80 years of habit and not at all from the surroundings people find themselves in. The fact that all these people enjoy taking their meals together is political, and the agency teaches about the political nature of nutrition in this country, etc. Today is the monthly "government surplus" cheese and butter giveaway. Through this agency, I've been able to do work that's satisfying from a humanist perspective, trying to maintain social services against cutbacks.

The mural magazine is taking a stronger stand politically. It's growing, getting better. Many people rely on it for info about public art going on internationally. It's still mainly Tim Drescher and me getting it out, supported by a group of local artists. I think it's the fifth year at two issues a year. Partially funded by National Endowment for the Arts.

Mainly I've been trying to keep afloat, keep jobs coming in. I'm a contractor, not on a salary anywhere, and am seeing the difficulties of being a small business. Actually, I've come to like it. When called (which is about seven to ten days out of the month), I drive one and a half hours to Sunnyvale in the heart of Silicon Valley to work for IBM, inking engineers' drafts of computer parts, pasting up parts of operator's and technician's manuals that go with the machines. I never see the whole manual, only fragments. I get paid well compared to Santa Cruz pay scale for graphic art, twice as much. Most of the month I work for Food & Nutrition, doing such projects as the mural and visuals for slide shows or nutrition aimed at immigrant families (part of the state's Migrant Education Project). It is kind of an odd stretching of one's skills and frame of mind. And there is a physical transporting, too. To get to the computer world, one must make the drive over the Santa Cruz Mountain range. Coming home is always clean air and redwoods and ocean. The drive in the other direction, to Watsonville, is the heady agricultural air, brown people in the fields. In one direction it's money and white professionals; in the other, it's subsistence level and brown.

I've come to terms with this because I have to do it this way to pay the bills for an apartment large enough to have design and layout space. Which does get mixed up with Río's togs and Tony's socks. Tony has been with Río and me for a year and a half now and all is going pretty much as I had wanted. He's working for a technology company (these are springing up around here, moving over the mountains from Silicon Valley) making disc drives for computers. We do have a good interaction of minds and emotion, especially now that he has grown into his 32 years. Women seem to grow up by 20, men when they're well into their 30s. In this country, anyway. It's just the usual problem of not respecting my work enough, not respecting that I need separate workspace at home because my job is at home. And taking up too much emotional space. But as far as paying the bills, being a father to Río and his other two kids, you couldn't believe he was the junkie he was a couple of years ago. Why did I continue to give him chances? I don't know. I guess I believed he could be the person he is now. Our best friends in Santa Cruz are a couple, two women. Aunties to Río. I think that's a fine balance.

I don't know how you have been able to give so much to four kids and still deal with men. I guess I'm concluding that I won't have another child. To have to work, to want to work as an artist, to care deeply about people and changing conditions for the better, and to be a good mother—I don't see how I could have more kids. I'm 36. If I'd wanted more, I wouldn't have had three abortions. But I'm saddened too. At least Río has a sister and brother (11 and 12) who consider him their very own, whose mother considers Río one of the family.

Your kids must be so deep into their own separate lives by now. I have the picture of Annie in Nicaragua over my desk. I love it. Time seems to be slipping away so fast. You have a whole other sense of time over there, I imagine. Do you think you will be coming up here in the future, near or far? It would be so good to see you. I don't know if I'll ever get down there, not for a long time. I send with Miranda my deepest love, and I want you to see my kid someday.

Actually, he's waking up now. My morning—4 a.m. to 6 a.m.—has ended. Love, Jane.

Santa Cruz—May 1st, 1983, Workers Day

Hello Margaret!

Very excited that you're coming here. Got word from Jack Levine that you'll be up in June. He was so thoughtful to call me and tell me of his visit with you, give me a picture of you, tell me how you are. I had hoped you would have gotten my

January 1st letter, intended to go to you with posters and more things with Miranda Bergman. The trip never happened, so I send that letter now with this one. That letter explains a little about my long absence from correspondence.

I want to see you in San Francisco for sure, but also am wondering if you can fit in a trip to Santa Cruz. Casa El Salvador and *Matrix*, the local women's newspaper, would sponsor you. There is a huge women's community here that would love to just lay eyes on you. Your books move very fast, are in curricula at the university (University of California, Santa Cruz).

I hope your trip to Canada was successful in what you set out to achieve. There's so much to talk about. I only hope we will have adequate time to make up for my five years of silence and to reflect over the ten years that we've known each other. El Salvador, the CIA in Nicaragua, are knives turning in my heart. How much pain must people endure? It's astonishing how numb we can be here, we who call ourselves makers of change, who believe our hearts are big.

I want you to meet my kid. He doesn't know it, but he wants to meet you too. And I can't wait to see you. Love, Jane.

[postcard with a photo of my four children on the flip side]

Managua, Nicaragua—May 16th, 1983

Dearest Jane: It's wonderful to have both your letters, bringing you back into my thoughts. I had put your name on a list of people to be invited to a Conference of Artists and Intellectuals on Central America which will be held here in Managua July 12–18. Can you come? If so, please contact the consul in San Francisco as your name is on the list but the address that he has may be an older one. Things are good. Ximena has joined Ana and me here. I am working hard against the Contra war. The writing and photography have suffered some, but they will come back. I am 46 now. Not all that much time left. Your life sounds good. Would love to know Río. The picture is of my kids last summer. I hope to see you soon. All my love, M.

Santa Cruz, California—June 20th, 1983

Hello Meg:

I am disappointed not to be able to make the July Conference of Artists and Intellectuals. I look forward to reading the reports. It sounds like exactly what I need.

But! I am planning to come there to paint a mural in September. Miranda and I were asked to paint a mural in a daycare center. Over the last couple of weeks this has become a burning drive in me—as well as the obvious act of solidarity the trip represents, it is a goal for me as ME. The fact that I even hesitated about going shows where my thinking has been at. Río is going to come with me. He'll have just turned three. I don't want to leave him for the three weeks or so, don't feel comfortable doing that. I do worry about safety, of course, as the situation changes daily.

Jane didn't go with Miranda to paint that mural in Nicaragua. The hesitation that plagued her from her earliest years intervened. And her drawn-out relationship with Tony also got in the way. In November 1983, she finally broke with Río's father for good. It was a major step, and clearly very difficult. On the nineteenth of that month, she wrote Tony a six-page typewritten letter. I don't know if she ever gave it to him or, if she did, whether he read it; perhaps it was more to explain the previous five years to herself. Tony himself died of AIDS not many years later.

Jane's farewell letter was filled with her still conflicted feelings. It contained phrases such as: "This morning early I dreamt of the soft brown skin of your neck and shoulders, and I was kissing that skin and could taste and feel it on my lips. . . . I live now in relation to you, in a state of joy that the ugliness and fear is over, and sadness that the somebody I was loving so hard is gone." Then: "It overwhelmed me to realize you used me not only for money and a home, but to create a character for yourself in the eyes of other people. The murals I painted you said you painted. The mural project in Nicaragua you said you had been part of. The cars I and my family bought you said you bought." And finally: "I don't miss the coming home to a cold apartment with no you and no stereo. Today I can finally come home without fear, with the confidence that I know what to expect. The question for me came down to this: if I was always holding you responsible for my not doing enough artwork or writing or staying connected to people, then what was wrong with me for being with you? Once I got to work on that, everything came into focus. What was a creative and responsible person like me doing with a maniac drug addict?"

In a personal journal also written that November, Jane wrote: "Margaret validated me. She came into my life again at the most critical moment and validated who I am. Buffed up the ragged edges, drew out the buried sensibilities, checked off the good points, illuminated the Jane that has to be. It deepens each day, the knowledge of what I am now capable of doing."

I read this now and feel humbled and grateful that I could help Jane emerge from those years of self-destruction and subjugation.

Managua, Nicaragua—December 20th, 1983

Dearest Jane:

My last days here before my return to the States. Your letters, the note, the longer collective letter, and the letter to Tony came the very same day as the mural was inaugurated. It was kind of magical! I picked up the mail but didn't have time to read it until I got home that night. I had been doing a long interview with Ernesto Cardenal in the morning and it ran over—my last for the book on writers[36]—and then had to dash to the wall because I didn't want to miss the inauguration, and Miranda had asked me to translate for her—she was nervous but beautiful. And of course I wasn't going to miss the chance to take pictures.[37] I asked Ernesto to make a special effort to be there and he was, which was also nice.

So it wasn't until that night that I had a chance to read your words, and they gave me tremendous strength. Jane, you give me much too much credit. You are strong and important to so many. Don't forget that. This is a difficult period but if I hadn't come along, it would have been someone else because, as you said in your letter to Tony, you are a survivor. Surviving means finding the you within and using it. The letter for Tony is extraordinary. I think it will speak to many. You shouldn't feel that you may be exposing him; he is beyond that.

I love you, Jane, M.

[excerpts from my journal of December 15 that I enclosed with the above letter]

Two truckloads of Honduran army people entered Nicaragua yesterday, attacking La Reforma, a village near Somotillo

36. *Risking a Somersault in the Air: Conversations with Nicaraguan Writers* (San Francisco: Solidarity Publications, 1984). Jane did the cover.

37. During the years of the true Sandinista revolution, Nicaragua encouraged the painting of murals on many walls. Miranda Bergman and a small group of women traveled there to paint a mural on the children's library in Managua's center. All these murals were later painted over by successive conservative governments.

and five kilometers inside Nicaraguan territory. Meanwhile, Mexico insisted, in a meeting with Kissinger, that the US respond to Nicaragua's peace proposal.

I have gathered the bulk of my poetry written since 1982, only about a dozen poems, and I'm going over them: changing, tightening, reworking in some cases. I sense the beginnings of an order to my life, with all the changes.

Ernesto is finally back from his US trip, and we spoke on the phone today. One of the reasons among many that I must stay until next month is to initiate and complete my interview with him, the only one missing from the new book. I had tried to do it before my trip to Canada and the US, but he was off to the States himself. We kept missing one another. I'm back now and so is he. I'd been speaking with his secretary for several days to make sure we set a time before he must travel again. Today when I got to work, I had a message from his office and when I called back Luz Marina said: "The Father wants to speak to you."

He was saddened by my leaving for good—he'd heard in California. He begged me: "Stay in Nicaragua. Stay and come back to work for the Ministry of Culture. Please, Margaret, stay." I was incredibly moved. All the years of our friendship came back: Mexico, Solentiname, reading together, *El Corno.* His loyalty and solid friendship. But I can't stay. I've made a decision I'm sure about, although it is difficult and complex. But while everyone here has been supportive of my move, Ernesto is the only one who's responded in this way. The interview is set for Monday morning. He promised to give me as much time as I want and need.

Another moving experience was lunch today with Michael Czerny. Michael is a close friend, a Jesuit from Toronto. Whenever I'm in that city I spend some time with him and whenever he's here likewise. He got into town a few days ago and will be here for four weeks. Before coming he said he went with a close friend to a Trappist monastery, a sort of retreat that he and this friend do once a year. Generally, at a Trappist monastery there is little speaking. Michael says the monks and visitors speak a maximum of a half hour daily. But he and his friend had decided to try something different: bring two copies of the same book and read out loud to one another. The book they brought was my *Christians in the Nicaraguan Revolution*. Michael's description of the experiences he and his friend had with the testimonies in the book was very moving to me.

Michael said that in particular the section on Solentiname was interesting reading out loud at a Trappist monastery so like the one Ernesto himself left after a year at Gethsemane, Kentucky (with Merton).[38] So much of what's in the book reflects what both Merton and Ernesto wanted to escape or change in the community they contemplated, and that Ernesto ended up founding alone on that remote island in the Great Lake of Nicaragua. Merton's sudden death didn't allow him to be part of that. It is also a reflection of the current struggle within the Church, that is playing itself out on such an incredible stage in Nicaragua today.

In Eduardo Galeano's *Days and Nights of Love and War* I read: "'We're flying over your country,' Eric said. I said: 'Yes.' Eric fell silent. And I thought: Will this land of mine remember me?"

Santa Cruz, California—January 11th, 1984

Dearest Margaret:

I am going to assume you are back in this country when this gets to you since I'm mailing it to Albuquerque. Thank you

---

38. Thomas Merton (1915–1968), Trappist monk, political activist, and novelist, who planned on leaving the monastery and founding a contemplative community with Ernesto Cardenal but was prevented from doing so by his sudden death.

for sending the journal pages and poems again. They mean so much to me. Keep me alive in some way. I do tend to get isolated but hopefully that tendency is changing.

I am now absolutely unemployed. The work at the marketing support services company is suffering its January slowdown and I have nothing paying in the way of community art. I am about to work on the flyer for Solidarity Publications, which is good timing because, if nothing else, I have time now. But it's been an opening up time, and an investigation of different directions I can take. Have actually been considering making paintings and selling them.

I am happier at 37 than I have been since I turned 28. And a hell of a lot healthier. I was just so happy last Friday, my birthday, for no other reason than myself. It is truly a new year, a new beginning. I can feel my strengths and am not panicked at living my worst fear: zero income and no partner. Because of course Tony was no partner; we were a sick society's worst product—people locked in self and mutual destruction. Time takes memories away, and the mind and soul are filled with new growth. It's amazing how age has little to do with growth. It's all circumstance.

I must get going. Have wanted to write to you for a long time. Excitement about your return fires somebody way up here on the coast of the Monterey Bay, and I can't wait to see you in the desert because I've been wanting to go there for a long time. Enjoy your homecoming! Much love, Jane.

Santa Cruz, a new spring—March 21st, 1984

Dearest Margaret:

Isn't it about time I wrote? I ask myself. Your journal pages are my life at night, my news, my entertainment, my conversation, my communication with other adults. I have a typewriter now to respond with, thanks to one of the women at the collective I work with. She said I could use her typewriter until I had the money to buy my own. (Of course I could never keep a typewriter. It always went to the pawn shop.)

I got the best job for me Santa Cruz has to offer. Graphic artist in the only collectively run political printshop in the area. Great people, perfect work environment in the sense that it is like working for myself but with the added backing of marketing people and camera and cooperation. Nine of us turn out packed full days of work that are about ¾ community and anti-nuke and political and ¼ straight commercial. We reserve the right to refuse jobs that are reactionary. Love, love, Jane.

Santa Cruz, California—November 13th, 1984

Dearest Margaret:

Plans are being made to move to Berkeley. The question is whether to get a place for Gail and Miranda and me and the two kids or move into and rearrange the house they are living in now. There have been good steps forward. In spite of all, I made enough money at an outside job to get this typewriter and a new color TV. I love this typewriter. I would love the TV more if it were programmed to tell the truth. Love, Jane.

Friday, February 8th, 1985

Dearest Margaret:

Have carried your writing around in my soul for all this time. My heart quite raw and I feel everything you say deeply. Some things make my chest thick with my heart going to burst. About missing your kids, the terrible treatment Ximena received at the hands of our border protectors, the terrible images that force themselves into your consciousness, Doris

Tijerino's daughter—oh god, how could that be!—the rippling effect of pain.[39]

Your university hassles are grim indeed. At least you truly give and get from the few classes you do have. I thought about you as I visited Cornell and then Syracuse, where I met with the people who put out the calendar that includes my work and who are co-publishing and distributing my International Women's Day poster. I felt like you must feel on the road, the guest of honor at innumerable potlucks. The whole group turned out to meet me and I had the opportunity to find out what life was like in upstate New York. I like them because they love my work, among other reasons. It was nice to hear someone wonder why I don't go crazy when in fact I'm feeling so borderline that way these days. I know my routine is difficult, but my god, I am so privileged! I am not very resourceful in figuring out ways to support myself precisely because help has come my way when I have needed it.

I really miss you, Margaret. The visit was so whole, that weekend. It felt, hey, normal. I thank you for the many plugs. It was an enriching time for me. It pointed me well in the direction of taking stock of what I have done so that I can move on in clear directions in my work.

Speaking of work, my job is so much better since the guy I don't get along with has been in Nicaragua. I work well with two people in terms of creativity, getting the jobs through the

39. My daughter Ximena, now living in Mexico City, came to visit me in Albuquerque. At the U.S. border she was cruelly harassed as a way of getting at me. One official demanded she sing the Mexican National Anthem. On January 21, 1985, Doris Tijerino's preteen daughter, María Doris, died along with thirty-nine other victims when a Cubana de Aviación plane went down in Costa Rica. Also dying in that accident was Sandy Pollack, secretary of the U.S. Committee for Peace and a great friend to Cuba.

shop, in terms of my learning the things I was weak on—pricing, paper, dealing with customers. The difference is amazing. This will work well until July, when I will leave for Berkeley. Right now, I am investigating schools for Río. Isn't that something—I have to "get Río into kindergarten!" In the Berkeley school system, there is an alternative school, emphasizing the arts and language, new approaches to teaching, etc. which is where I want him to go. I'll probably have to rely on his Spanish surname to get him in. What the fuck.

Your vulnerability. I was aware of that part of you from long ago, the asthma, but somehow the sheer volume of your production overshadows your person at times. That's unfair, hero worship. Your writing about the white spots[40] brought to my understanding the short-circuiting, the crack in productivity where the pain of what you've seen is pushing through.

I want to thank you so much for the best pictures anybody had taken of me, equal with the one Gail took last summer. That one of me laughing and sort of biting my lip is how I like to see myself. I actually look involved with the photographer as opposed to looking like I'm running away. My usual way is to just stand there and wait for it to be over with. I don't know how to sell myself into the camera any more than I can visualize myself in the mirror, even while I'm putting all this makeup on my face, looking right at myself. Your picture shows me that I have changed a great deal, and I like that I have a record of the change that I can hold in my hand. Love, love, Jane.

---

40. Upon my return to the States, still fragile from my last months in Nicaragua and the first of my immigration case, my mind would momentarily go blank during lectures. I described this as seeing white spots, places where no words were. As I adjusted to the transitions in my life and learned to deal with them, the white spots disappeared.

Santa Cruz—Saturday, June 22nd, 1985

Dearest Margaret:

An unusual night here. Alone in the house with the typewriter due to unexpected gift of Río's absence. As usual, you in my thoughts every day. I have had a large ending of things here, a clearing of unnecessary activity to prepare myself for my real work. A few months of ridding myself of unwanted roommates, unwanted job, of visiting my family which indicated a turning point in our relationships, of completing of my life in Santa Cruz.

I quit work at Community Printers one month ago. I went immediately to New York to see my family. The last week I have begun to feel myself again. Have begun to relearn how to think for myself. An ongoing goal is to never again be enslaved by a 40-hour-week job. By that I mean to work for someone else all those hours. I fully anticipate continuing the amount of work I do but the nature of it will be different.

I see that you never had the problem of being silenced by demands on you made by people for whom only you were responsible. I have been reading *Silences,* in which Tillie Olsen has put into words exactly what I have been grappling with in myself.[41] You had plenty of problems, but never the problem of *being silenced.* You produced despite the work interrupted, deferred, relinquished. And you raised four children well.

I love you and will talk to you soon, Jane.

Albuquerque, New Mexico—November 1st, 1985

Dearest Jane:

Back from Washington where we filed the suit and on to Tallahassee early tomorrow morning. Your letter came and

41. Tillie Olsen (1912–2007) was an American author identified with the first wave of feminism and a working-class literature. Her book *Silences* was first published in 1978. It single-handedly revolutionized the literary canon.

made me so happy. Between Washington and Tallahassee work, teach, love, live, write, make some pictures, and generally try to hold my life together.[42] So this will be shorter than I would like. The case is beginning to be terribly demanding. Between yesterday and today I have personally answered 131 letters. What we really need is a full-time coordinator at CCR in New York, because there are literally hundreds of individual or small group efforts happening across the country and unless we can coordinate them to a certain extent, I'm afraid my energy and that of many others will be dispersed, lost. So, we need to do some serious fund-raising in order to pay someone to handle that. What you and others in the Bay Area seem to be pulling together sounds very good. I would love to be able to come out for one giant fund-raiser, poetry reading, art show, whatever. I think we could do something really creative. This case is important, especially for people who have no reference for the Fifties (like almost all my students!).[43]

I love you a lot, M.

March 11th, 1986

Hello dearest Margaret:

It's been a long time, yet I think of you always. The momentum of this important case builds, yet there is you, YOU. The somebody that's just somebody, brushing her teeth, brushing her hair, and thinking about how to guide the next 24 hours. Like everybody else. But everybody else does not have to think

---

42. I was traveling a lot to speak about and raise money for my immigration case.

43. CCR organized the case, giving leadership to the more than twenty-five defense committees that were established throughout the country and also taking initiatives from them. These efforts raised the quarter million dollars needed to fight the case. My three lawyers—Michael Ratner, Michael Maggio, and David Cole—defended me pro bono.

about how to present themselves in a court of injustice. Not everybody else has a one day in their life like that you will have in less than a week. My heart pounds for you. My breath catches when I feel you in courtroom clothes having judgment passed on you. I see you sitting there. The testimony should be fascinating. I wish I could be there.

We are gathering momentum and are in contact with CCR. Are mapping a strategy for "when she wins . . ." or "If she doesn't win." "When she wins" will include a push to invite other writers, García Márquez perhaps, and a broadening of focus to include writing in general.[44] "If she loses" is a bit clearer and a lot harder. Much more I want to say, but this has got to go into the mail immediately to get to you before you go.

Loving you deeply, always, and working for you too, Jane.

Berkeley, California—May 23rd, 1986. Full moon.

Hello dearest Margaret:

I'm pissed at the Syracuse Cultural Workers group for rejecting my/our piece for the upcoming calendar. I did what I and others consider a really fine work: a colored pencil version of one of your photos. I jammed on it to meet the deadline and sent them explicit directions about how to present the whole thing. The visual art on top and on the page below a section of your poem "Under Attack." Under the calendar grid would go info about you and why your case is an example of cultural repression. In the back of the entire calendar, in their resources section, would run more info specific to your case, how to reach CCR, etc.

44. The Colombian novelist and Nobel Prize winner Gabriel García Márquez was among several dozen internationally acclaimed intellectuals who were denied visas to the United States because of the same ideological exclusion clause of the 1952 McCarran-Walter Act under which I was being prosecuted.

The person I have dealt with most from that organization, Dick Cool, is the person who encouraged me to do this piece. He and I had spoken about a Malcolm X piece by me which would go into the calendar or as a poster, and I submitted a sketch. A month later, at their final meeting about contents of calendar, he called me and said that he and Jane Creighton felt the Elaine poster inappropriate for the calendar and would I do a piece about you instead.[45] So I did just that—conferred with people here, you, and got going on what I thought would be good in terms of what would look good on a wall for a month, what would be an exciting combination of your and my work, and what would be good politically about who you are, and some aspect of people in Latin America speaking through you.

The five-person collective of diverse backgrounds who were selecting pieces for inclusion rejected my submission in favor of a silkscreen about Nicaragua which included the words "*no pasarán*." Our support group is pissed, and they want to make a poster out of the piece and an entire poem of yours. The question is marketing, as always. Where, how, who, etc. I know it's hard for you to visualize but I'm sure you will love it. I do. It's that thing Miranda and I talk about on the Jack & Lisa tape,[46] the taking of your work to another discipline. Reaching out further with each application of media.

I am so looking forward to seeing you again. Time moves so fast. We are working on gigs for you that weekend in

45. Elaine de Kooning (1918–1989), who was an Abstract Expressionist painter and close personal friend, took one of her 1960 portraits of me, had a high-quality poster made, and donated one hundred copies to be sold to benefit my case. This was just one of many such gestures by artists.

46. Jack Levine (1942–2010), a lawyer turned photographer and good friend, was making a film about my case. He and Lisa Maya Knauer did many interviews and quite a bit of filming, but finances kept the film from being made.

September. I hope this summer will give you the time to get back into the creative self who makes art because it must be made. How much to give and give and give. And you know, we do really receive what you give. People are moving with your efforts. It's not going nowhere.

I remember how good you make me feel. I never forget you, not for a minute. There is no person like you in my life—who is not in my daily life but who I never stop thinking about. You continue to bring out the best in me because you continue to see the best, no matter how hard I try to deflect it. Love, Jane.

September 30th, 1986

Hi Margaret:

Lovely talking to you last night. You sounded so much better than I've heard in quite a while. It was also a good connection to be talking to you as we went into our evaluation and coordinating meeting. Six of us met over dinner and laid out the national tasks to accomplish, what each of us is capable of doing, and what we need to do on the local level. We set up a meeting to bring in the 25 or so people who said they wanted to work on the case. Looks like we made about $4,450 from the weekend. Close to what we made last time for about a fourth of the work. We're sending $2,500 to CCR. The rest goes to minimal bill-paying. So, we have some left for duplication of info packets, mailing, etc.[47]

Jane Creighton called. The Center for Investigative Reporting just pulled out of their commitment to renting the

47. Fund-raising was an issue throughout the almost five years of my case. After I won, CCR estimated that fighting the case had cost around a quarter of a million dollars, not counting our tax dollars that went to the government's side of the case. Most of this was raised by the defense committees and most came from small donors. I wrote a personal thank-you to each of them.

National Committee space for an office. Shit! You expect shoddy treatment from a landlord, but from a progressive organization? They made a verbal commitment and then pulled out the day before our moving date. We'll try the Women's Building.

I so much look forward to coming to your home in early December. Sort of like a tent, the year has a point where it is highest, held up by the pole, something to be seen and excited about from a great distance.

I love you very much, Jane.

[hand-written on the flip side of a small painting by Jane]

12/86

Dearest Margaret:

No words to say how important the stay with you was. You know it. I feel you, your house, that land so deep in my heart and soul. And I was glad to be on hand for such an enriching turn in your life.[48]

Much love, Jane.

January 26th, 1987

Hello dearest Margaret, and Barbara too!

I miss you both tremendously. It would be wonderful to just be around each other again. Writing takes such effort for me. But too much time has gone by since we last spoke. This friendship has lived through so many years of sporadic communication from me. I can't let those silences interrupt the flow again. Because of course for me this writing to you, Margaret, is writing to myself.

48. Jane came to Albuquerque for my fiftieth birthday, which coincided with the beginning of my relationship with Barbara Byers, the woman I have loved and lived with now for thirty-nine years.

I am remembering that Rini[49] said I always had a home with her in Pilar. That was part of what I felt when I was visiting you, although I didn't remember then. Pilar now belongs to Rini's niece who lived there at one time.

For my birthday I was given *In My Mother's House,* the story of Communist activist Rose Chernin told by her daughter Kim. I am finding it fascinating.

Ericka Huggins was the intake person at the East Bay School for the Arts open house where I took Río to sign up for music/movement classes. I took one look at her and told her I drew pictures of her in the early '70s. She said: "What for?" in the pleasantest way. I told her because she was a symbol of strength for many women in those times (she was a leader in the Black Panther Party and was memorialized in the poster of her reaching her fist up high and shouting). She said she would love to see the pictures.

Give my love to your parents, Margaret. Miranda and I got wonderful letters from your mother. I wish them well. I can see your father now, picking up the newspaper.

Much, much, love, Jane.

Albuquerque, New Mexico—March 27th, 1987

Dearest Jane:

The buttons are terrific![50] What a great surprise to find the shoebox full in our mailbox today. I gave the first one to my mom and dad—small compensation for what this case has put them through.

---

49. Rini Templeton (1935–1986) was a U.S. graphic artist, sculptor, and political activist. She made hundreds of black-and-white sketches that she donated freely to the causes she supported. She lived for many years in the small rural community of Pilar, in northern New Mexico.

50. Jane designed buttons that said KEEP MARGARET RANDALL/ DEPORT MCCARRAN-WALTER. We sold them to benefit my immigration case.

Nothing much to tell since I'll be seeing you soon. We've told everyone that we're going away this weekend, but we're really holed up here working, working, working. Trying to get everything done before my next weekend's trip to Potsdam, NY, then the Bay Area, and finally Hartford for the job interview.

Ximena called from Mexico to tell me she loves her job but has quit school. Psychology proved not to be what she wanted. She wants to study literature or history of art. Ana has also revised her near-future plans. She is in New York, and instead of returning to Nicaragua as she had planned, has gotten a job there and wants, as she says, "to turn over a new leaf, start from zero." She sounds more together and happier than when she left here, which is a relief.

I'll be sharing the podium with Audre Lorde in New York on May 10th.[51] I'd been invited to speak for an event being held by the Nicaragua Construction Brigade and thought the occasion might provide a context for doing something to help the NY committee get off the ground. I am thrilled to be reading with someone I admire so deeply.

For the interview at Trinity, I am designing a course I call "The Popular Culture of Language" and having a wonderful time hunting down texts and making them fit together in a way that makes sense. Designing a course strikes me as being something like making a sculpture or perhaps building a house. The whole depends on the quality and positioning of the parts. Now that I've had a few years' experience doing this, it

51. Audre Lorde (1934–1992) was a Black feminist writer, professor, philosopher, poet, and civil rights activist. Her work continues to be profoundly influential.

feels easier. Whether or not I get the Trinity job, I will have created a good course.[52]

Barbara and I are beginning to walk in the early mornings. It gets light much earlier now, and though it's still pretty chilly before the sun is fully up, the light is breathtaking.

The folks in Eugene are having a large women's event, with Ursula Le Guin,[53] Isabel Letelier,[54] and me. They plan on producing another one of those lovely photo-posters they did the last time I was there. I'd been searching for an appropriate image to send them (making me long for the darkroom!). Finally selected two: the two young Nicaraguan women with the young daughter of one of them and the stone angel in the Havana cemetery. Will be interested to see which one they choose.

Love, M.

Berkeley, California—August 12th, 1987

Dearest Margaret & Barbara:

Through the journals, I follow your lives, loving you each day, yearning to be there. That last poem is magnificent. Maybe I understand it better and quicker, like the way I like to paint, placing the images in just such a way as to throw them into

---

52. I did get the job at Trinity College in Hartford, taught there for a year and then one semester each for the next nine years. It turned out to be a good fit for me, but having to separate from Barbara for five months out of the year was painful, and in 1994 I retired from teaching altogether.

53. Ursula Kroeber Le Guin (1929–2018) was an American author. She is best known for her works of speculative fiction, including science fiction works set in her Hainish universe, and the Earthsea fantasy series.

54. Isabel Morel Letelier is the widow of Chilean ex-foreign minister Orland Letelier. He was imprisoned and she was under house arrest in Chile following the coup of 1973. Her work on his behalf gained his release and the couple moved to Washington D.C. It was there, in 1976, that he and an associate were murdered by a bomb placed under the family car as it was parked on Washington's Embassy Row.

brilliant color or contrast, but always to clarify. I guess I need things spelled out in poetry and "Under the Stairs" is just such a lovely clear set of pictures. Makes me cry, which things seldom do.

I am so glad the Trinity job finally came through, although you must be going crazy pulling everything together to go. How wonderful to have Sarah there with you. How I would love to meet her as an adult. Please say hello to her for me. I remember her from so long ago.

Our big mural, it's a long wall. Again. We've been back on the wall a week and a half now and the old feelings of pride, contribution to community, joy in orchestrating visual art on a grand scale, all come flooding back with each supportive comment from passers-by. I had forgotten how much foot traffic comes past that long wall, and of course the street is a four-lane rush hour urban route. Exhausting, with the traffic, the constant conversations, wind, San Francisco fog, and the simple standing and walking, bending, pacing, holding up of painting arm for seven hours. The team is Miranda, Arch Williams, me, and an assistant, a wonderful young woman from the community college the wall is part of.

I love you two women. I send energies for your move to go smoothly and for the nine months to be the best. Don't worry, Barbara, you'll do great. You will. You both form such a solid base for each other.

Much, much, love, Jane.

Hartford, Connecticut—October 22nd, 1987

Dearest Jane:

What a wonderful surprise. Yesterday it was so dark and gloomy here you couldn't remember whether it was day or night. I kept reminding myself it was early afternoon. I was at my office on campus, just getting ready to walk back to the apartment. The English department secretary called up the stairwell: "Margaret, you have a large package!" and I came bounding down to find your familiar and beloved handwriting, slightly smudged from the rain. I knew it must be some of your art but couldn't remember what we had talked about you sending. I was secretly hoping it would be the picture I bought. When I brought it home and opened it with Barbara our surprise was multiple. It's so wonderful to have those particular posters cheering up these glum walls! I know I told you that we didn't bring any of our artwork east. Just one frame with the six photos of the kids (including Laura) that I have hanging in the bedroom. Barbara has a lot of her work on the walls, some in frames, most just tacked up with stick pins. She has been working a great deal and people here seem to appreciate her work in a way that didn't happen back in Albuquerque. But aside from that, the walls are pretty bare, and we miss our art. Now I have the two vertical posters where I work and the International Women's Day one in the bedroom. Thank you!

You know Readers Feast bookstore also has the Syracuse Cultural Workers posters up and your *Leche Materna* one is right in front of you as you enter the store. It's a real meeting place here in Hartford with a nice restaurant and hosts lots of good events. So, I'm sure hundreds, maybe thousands, of people see the poster there. Every time I go to the store, I think of you and your work.

Jane, the appeal hearing was the day before yesterday. Guadalupe González came from El Paso and was, according to Michael and David, even more crazed than she was the first time around. The board, in silence, listened to both sides. David thinks it would be important if people would start writing letters to Nelson again, this time talking about the fact that the administration itself recently came out against the sole clause that is being used against me and that I'm the only person since 1953 who has been accused and charged exclusively under that clause. Write asking him to drop the case against me. Do you think the Northern California Friends could get a mailing out to people asking them to do this? Apparently, it could be helpful.[55]

Otherwise, things continue more or less as always. I want to see the mural sketch! I love you, Margaret.

Berkeley, California—December 19th, 1990

Dearest Margaret and Barbara:

I have felt unusual these months. Quite simply, I no longer feel depressed. The lightness in my body and spirit is different from every sense of myself I've ever had previous to this. I have felt happy before with my achievements and have felt "in love" before, and wonderfully happy with loving friends and seeing beautiful places and things before my eyes. But I have never before felt so strong in foundation, so present, so outward in my interactions with people, from clients to longtime friends to "strangers." I have been participating in a dance class three times a week. My body feels developed and strong in the way I felt when I was doing martial arts before the whole Tony involvement, only gentler and more confident of my place on earth. I feel softened and rooted like prairie grass. Now at 43 I feel like a rounded-out human being.

Interesting that the healthiest man I've interacted with yet comes into my life now, introduced by the cancer. What excites me is not so much *him* but myself. I am enjoying myself and he

55. We were appealing my loss in El Paso. Guadalupe González was the government attorney who litigated against me. Alan C. Nelson was the head of the U.S. Immigration and Naturalization Service at the time of my trials.

is helping me do it. I've never had a man who's helped me be me. He wants to do things that make my life easier, that contribute to the development and output of my art, that ease the stress of the single mother, that give me better paying work (which he is in a position to do). I have a sense that, however this relationship develops, this man is there for me.

I know some of his track record. He was absolutely wonderful around his partner's death. Nori was a political artist for years yet was able to run a profitable graphic design business in Chicago. They moved here a couple of years ago, whereupon Nori found breast cancer. We got to be friends in our women's cancer support ground. When her cancer metastasized, we got to know each other more deeply. During that time, I met Lawson, and she would tell me how wonderful he was being for her. I could see it. When she died, she left many of her clothes and all of her graphic design materials to me. I have inherited many assignments that would have gone to her.

My therapist wanted me to be wary of needs Lawson might have for a partner right after his partner's death—the sort of needs that would cause the end of a relationship after he moved out of the grieving period. But he and I are moving together in some relation much less proscribed. We are knowing one another in a way that belongs to us alone but is supported by all the reasons which brought us together.

Supporting ourselves sometimes feels so fragile. I am so infuriated by your not having a teaching job there at the university. You, of all people. I get scared about the future. As I listen to the results of yesterday's humongous election, I get really scared about how much influence money is able to buy and how much people want to go to war and chop down all the trees.

Much love, Jane.

Lawson is Bob Lawson, a union organizer with a long history of working for justice. Jane and he consolidated their relationship and married. They are together to this day. In Lawson, Jane found the person she could love unreservedly, and Río got a father dedicated to helping him develop into the healthy person he became.

Albuquerque, New Mexico
January 11th, 1991

Dearest Jane:

I am beginning to allow myself to feel the sadness of my imminent departure for Delaware. Barbara and I start driving on February 1st and she will return home on the 8th. When the time for these departures is close, I tend to get stoic and feel that the only way I can confront them is by pretending it's all right. But it isn't all right that I can't get a decent job here in Albuquerque and so must leave the woman I love for such lengthy periods each year. I'm seeing that I must acknowledge this and grieve it—then just go off and do it. Barbara should be teaching by next fall and then we can reevaluate. Even if we must cut way back, we must end these separations.

Love, M.

Berkeley, California—July 29th, 1991

Dearest Margaret and Barbara:

Lawson and I talk about living together. He has his house, I have mine, and they are a mere eight blocks away from each other. That proximity helped propel us. Now the three of us stay either at my place or his, with a night or two a week when we stay separately when I need to work or when the shlepping gets overwhelming. I never experienced how I could live in partnership with a lover *and* maintain my own selfness. This relationship affords me that opportunity. I will always need my own studio space. One plan is to keep my place as office and studio. I like the idea of having a separate building in which to work. Especially living with two men (let's not forget Río's 11-year-old self).

[postcard with photo of three clay storyteller dolls by Mary Trujillo, Cochiti Pueblo, New Mexico]

Albuquerque, August 6th, 1991

Dearly loved Jane:

It was wonderful to have your great long letter, to have you close and communicating again. I'm so happy for your life with Lawson and Río, the three of you, and the sense that this is a relationship that encourages you to keep yourself, your art. So important. How I would love to see you. How can we do that? Things are beginning to settle and calm here, which we badly need. People's Park sounds sad.[56] Everywhere I see that terribly complex struggle which isn't at all straightforward like those we used to know. How difficult the world is getting. And how much more important that we continue to do our real work. I love you. Love to Río and Lawson too, Margaret.

Berkeley, California—November 25th, 1991

Dearest Margaret:

It seems my life and the world around me is whizzing by so fast, something which seems like it happened a day ago happened weeks ago. What a complex combination of things we who believe in freedom must sort through. In particular, your writing on Cuba and Nicaragua, and analysis of your own participation in this distance in time—I found fascinating. MADE

56. People's Park in Berkeley has long been the scene of popular struggles against corporate America for a place to gather, protest, perform.

ME THINK. Writing about socialism and feminism is the most important thing you can do. I can't wait to read the essay.

The journey from being a person who would try for a family with someone like Tony, through fighting cancer, to the sense of wholeness I feel today, was a step-by-step process, the destination of the steps at any one moment of which I was mostly unaware. Changes, changes. I look at the world around us, am moved to tears by something every day, moved to rage at the sheer inequity of it all. Such as the pile of burned cars on a lot in West Oakland which caught my eye—the cars which were removed from the burned area in the hills, but which were dumped in someone else's neighborhood, a poor people's neighborhood. But I am deeply happy. Not the surface happy that a new love brings, but the thorough understanding happiness that solid loving trusting companionship brings.

Albuquerque, New Mexico
May 21st, 1992

Dearest Jane:

These are barbarous times. Even before, during and since Rodney King, but certainly the acquittal was a catalyst. I was still in Hartford when it came down. There was rioting there, and in New York City (although they tried hard to keep it out of the news) where I had to go overnight for the 25th anniversary of NACLA. Strange to see and mingle with so many mostly men from the old New Left. Nice in ways, especially, to reconnect with people such as Jon Frappier, whom I hadn't seen in years. But such a different sort of energy than I'm used to.

Then up to Buffalo, also just for one night, where it felt good to share in the victory over Operation Rescue. A win once in a while feels important. My friends Liz and Bobbi had been out on the lines every morning from 3:30 on and it had been going on for twelve days. At Trinity we (meaning a few professors who do more than talk about these issues) tried to support our students in whatever they felt they needed to do about the verdict. Unfortunately, nine women decided that a "freedom fast" was the way to go. They stayed out on the quad for three days and nights, not eating. I spent some time with them, feeling that any sort of action means something for those kids, but was disappointed that was the direction it took. But then, who knows what is most effective now? We are so lacking in a movement, in a cohesive organization that can bring us together. Perhaps you don't feel this in the Bay Area, but I do here.

My father, at this point, seems mostly lucid. He has forgotten how to add, subtract, and tell time. Barbara and I are doing all his banking. He asks a dozen questions, almost daily, to try to understand what's going on. But mostly he seems to trust us (something I never felt before—he never told me anything about his finances). And he frequently tells us how grateful he is that we've taken over. He can't get many words out and it seems a memory thing, like just not being able to call the word up. He won't talk on the phone now because of this and doesn't like being around lots of people because he's afraid he won't be able to express himself if they speak to him. On the other hand, he still has rich conversations with us once in a while. I guess we all need to be patient and see how it goes. My mother, understandably, is frustrated and upset, also intensely angry and doesn't handle things well. She continues to interrupt my father all the time, not allow him to finish sentences, "helps" him in other inappropriate ways. But then, she's been doing a version of this throughout their married life.[57]

---

57. It gradually became apparent that my father was suffering from dementia. He continued to worsen, eventually was confined to a hospital bed, and died two years later.

Jane Norling at different points in her life. In one, she is standing before her segment of the Balmy Alley mural, San Francisco, California. All images by Margaret Randall.

Interesting that you should have mentioned hearing Blanche on KPFA. She and Clare are coming in today around noon.[58] They'll be here for Barbara's birthday/graduation celebration and stay on for five days. That should be nice; I love them both a lot. Blanche's book is stunning, and it seems it will finally bring her the attention she deserves. They say it will get onto the *Times* best-seller list this week in ninth place!

Others are also coming from out of town for the party. Wish you and Miranda could be here. I've decided to do all the cooking. Should be fun.

I'm working hard to finish my long essay on feminism and socialism (really on feminism and revolution). It's now called *Gathering Rage: The Failure of Twentieth Century Revolutions to Develop a Feminist Agenda*. I know, I know, much too long a title. But at least the first part is nice, don't you think? I want the book to have a smashing cover because I don't much care for the *Monthly Review* covers. Barbara may try to work something up. I also have a new book of poems coming out and I used a piece of art I've had for a long time on the cover, a tapestry made by a Chilean woman. It looks terrific.[59] All this means I'm working long hours, except for these few days I will take off to be with Barbara and Blanche and Clare. I am also preparing for the Nicaraguan field work, which means figuring out how I can do what I need to do in a relatively short period of time: a month and a half. I don't yet have all the money for that project,

58. Blanche Cook is a feminist historian, biographer of Eleanor Roosevelt. Clare Coss, her longtime partner, is a poet and playwright.

59. This was *Dancing with the Doe* (Albuquerque: West End Press, 1992). The Chilean woman who made and gifted me the tapestry I photographed and used on the cover was Coca Milán.

but I have enough that I am going ahead, hoping the rest will come.[60]

Speaking of money, as of today I have $1,150 for Barbara's gift, which is a summer to paint without having to work. I figure I need $2,000 for that so I think I will make it. That feels good. Again, thank you for your contribution.

It's beautiful here now. It's been a wet spring and everything is in bloom: those little white desert roses, the Apache plume, and the cacti are heavy with fruit, their blossoms to open soon. I often think of you when we walk.

Much, much, love, Margaret.

Albuquerque, New Mexico—August 5th, 1992

Dearest Jane:

In Nicaragua and since my return, I thought of you so often. I knew you were moving in with Lawson or had just moved, and I kept wondering how that was going, how you are adjusting to this big change in your life. And in Río's life. And of course, in Lawson's too. I hope this whole period has been and continues to be good for you, Jane. That this new life will be filled with light and air and creativity.

High points of my trip were the renewals of two important relationships. The first with Víctor Rodríguez who is one of the young poets I was so close to in Cuba. He and his wife and young son have been living in Managua for the past four years. We ran into one another fortuitously, at a forum at the Jesuit University to protest Nicaragua's new anti-sodomy law. The

60. This fieldwork was for *Sandino's Daughters Revisited*, a follow-up volume to *Sandino's Daughters*. I did get the money I needed and was able to complete the project. The book was published by Rutgers University Press in 1994.

other extraordinary reconnection was with a woman named Gladys Zalaquett. She and I also go back to my early years in Cuba, when she and the man she was with at the time were Sandinistas temporarily living in Havana. Gladys and I reconnected after the 1979 victory and saw a great deal of one another during the time I lived in Nicaragua. But then we lost touch. Lifetimes have intervened for us both, but ours is one of those relationships in which, no matter how much time has gone by, you simply pick up where you left off. It was emotional for us both to realize that we've moved in similar directions, engaged in similar struggles, have similar questions. She will be returning to Chile (where she was born and grew up) within the year. Her daughter Ana (named in part after my Ana) begins medical school in Santiago this fall.

Jane, I think of you a lot. I hope this finds you well, settled and working and loving. Love, Margaret.

Albuquerque, New Mexico—May 23rd, 1993

Dearest Jane:

After thirteen years, I was finally able to return to Cuba in April-May. I took a group of North American feminists down to visit with Cuban women and explore the gains and problems of the revolution, especially as they affect women's lives. It seemed important to do this now, when so many of our social experiments are in shambles and Cuba is one of the only places where a people's government remains in power. I had no idea what I would find. Many of us are currently involved in complex discussions about the failures and losses of socialism—where we went wrong, what may be salvageable. I decided that one of the best ways to find out was to visit a country that still has a Socialist government. What I didn't expect—and it was a tremendously energizing experience—was the lift the trip gave me. A lift that has motivated much good work since.

It was a marvelous trip. I had tried to prepare myself for the type of situation our press (even our progressive press) exploits when it writes about Cuba at all. What we discovered, instead, is an island nation with a revolution almost 35 years old in the midst of a traumatic economic crisis. Bicycles are replacing automobiles; teams of oxen are replacing tractors. But the Cuban people retain their amazing and very creative spirit of resilience. In fact, an important culture of resistance has emerged.

Almost every family has its garden of fruits and vegetables. The government is beginning to distribute multi-vitamins to every man, woman, and child in order to stave off the incidence of optic neuritis that has broken out. Grandmothers are supervising the growing and processing of traditional medicinal herbs. Family practice doctors live and work in the communities they serve. People continue to build their own homes with materials provided by the State. Cuban children go to school. Universal health care is free. You don't see people begging, as you do in the rest of Latin America, nor is there the problem of homelessness we have here. Cuba has recently modified its AIDS protocol, making it optional rather than obligatory that persons with HIV live in special sanitoriums.

Nor, of course, is everything "perfect" or easy. We found Cubans open and willing to talk about their problems as well as their successes. The level of discussion was exciting. This first women's trip was really wonderful, so much so that Global Exchange and I want to do more. So, we have planned another for December 17–26 of this year. I hope you will consider going with us. I think you would be energized by seeing Cuba after all these years. We want to limit the group to twenty or less and commit ourselves to at least a third of those going being women of color. The cost for the ten days, Miami to Miami, is $1,200. Some partial scholarships will be available.

Although this is in the planning stages and the itinerary is still being worked out, I can tell you that we will be hosted by the Federation of Cuban Women and, while in Havana, stay at their guest house which is in the middle of the city and accessible to all points of interest. We will be visiting with women construction and factory workers, a family practice doctor, women artists, lawmakers, and professors. We will visit a day-care center, talk to people in public health, and investigate such topics as sex education and AIDS. We will spend time in one of the provinces as well as in Havana, and cultural activities will be part of our agenda. There will also be a considerable amount of free time in which we can go off and explore on our own.

Much love, Margaret.

Albuquerque, New Mexico—October 18th, 1995

Dearest Jane:

Thanks so much for finding out about the Tina Modotti show for us! Barbara is off school from February 10th through 25th. Maybe we could drive and spend a week in the Bay Area during that time. It would be great if I could get a paid gig, as I need those badly. I'd also love to do a benefit for whatever you think needs it: political prisoners, AIDS, women and cancer, peace. I can't think offhand of academic contacts, though I imagine there must be some at Berkeley or San Francisco State. I haven't read my poetry at either place since the seventies.

Did I tell you that Alice Walker is coming on our 1997 river trip? We are now complete at twenty. Two women from here had to cancel, so my old friend Dorothy Abbott from

Tampa was thrilled to sign on; she was first on the waiting list. It's a good group of women. We're all excited.

I was in San Antonio last weekend for the book fair. My reading went well, and I got to hear lots of other good poets and fiction writers. But I'm glad to be home now and back to work. Fall is so beautiful here. Much love, Margaret.

Albuquerque, New Mexico—December 28th, 1996

Dearest Jane:

I so wish we could fly off to Berkeley and share in your birthday celebration. Fifty years! It's a special time. Maybe because we are conditioned to thinking in terms of these chunks of time: years in units of tens, half a century. But surely also because a half century marks a turning point. You have lived for fifty years. So much experience, learning, frustration, creation, longing, fulfillment of different sorts, and hard lessons too. By fifty most of us have settled into the life we have chosen. Are well on the way to learning how to make those choices work for us.

I will never forget meeting you so many years ago in Cuba. One image, particularly, the one of you sketching in the parking lot of the *supermercado* at the corner of K and 17th Streets. You were so light and ethereal, immensely talented, exciting for me to begin to get to know you and count you as a friend. I took to you immediately, as I remember.

And then there were your letters about a lonely beach in Mexico, adventures of many kinds. You returning to make your own history in the US. I continuing to make mine in Cuba. Much later there were many other stories, your amazing drumming, the unfolding of those extraordinary murals. Especially those murals. I will forever return to the memories of my visits to the Bay Area and you taking me to see them, one by one.

For me, your letters have been one of the great joys of our friendship. How you can write! Your descriptive powers are brilliant. All through those painful years with Tony, that time I stayed with you in San Francisco, later the visit to Santa Cruz, and finally the almost tree-house quality of your quarters at Gail's. Of course, Río, his birth and childhood and own struggle to become the beautiful human he is now. Your choice of Lawson, ultimately how right that choice has proven to be. The terrible shadow of your struggle with cancer, your courage and victory there.

When I think of our friendship, I cannot refrain from thinking of my immigration battle and your consistent support of that, even to sacrificing your own valuable time and working way beyond any realistic idea of duty to head the Bay Area defense committee.

When I think of my own fiftieth birthday, my thoughts go first to you and your presence at my celebration. Our walks in the foothills, "Jane's Ridge" (which we still mention every time we hike there), your huge generosity of spirit in being able to incorporate and accommodate my sudden coming together with Barbara as an unexpected aspect of that moment. It was so important to me to have you there to share in all of it. Fifty, for me, was indeed a turning point.

Since then, my life has been so much more of a piece. I have felt more whole, more centered, more able. More compelled to make choices and easier in my ability to follow through on them. Deeply fortunate in having Barbara with whom to share my life, in seeing my children moving into their own choices, in producing work that seems to mean more, in having the space and support to think and feel and act upon the issues I care about.

Dear Jane, many more precious years of love and work and health and art and friendship and sisterhood. Margaret and Barbara.

Berkeley, September 7th, 1999

Hello dear one:

Intense times for the Puerto Rican political prisoners, evaluating Clinton's "offer."[61] Apparently, they'll make a decision this week.

Went to a lively Local 2 demonstration yesterday. Hotel and restaurant employees of the major downtown SF hotels and supporters in full force took over Powell Street in front of the St. Francis Hotel, preventing Labor Day tourists from riding cable car halfway to the skies. Local 2 is absolutely great, SF at its best—energetic Filipino hotel maids in uniform, Chinese waiters, chefs wearing tall hats, bartenders of all stripes, openly gay workers, black, white, people speaking Spanish. All with glorious smiles as they engaged in civil disobedience on an unusually sunny day in SF. One hundred thirty-eight people were removed by police in a peaceable way, each cheered warmly by the gesticulating crowd.

And me without my camera. But I carried a sign and raised my voice. And saw the sort of paintings I want to make. THESE PEOPLE. Not the exhorting strained face of demonstration so much as the wildly diverse smiling gesturing people, the cops among them, the weird skeletal pale white

61. On September 8, 1999, President Clinton offered clemency to sixteen imprisoned members of the Armed Forces of National Liberation (FALN) who had been convicted of sedition and were serving long prison terms, on the condition that they renounce their use of terrorism. After some consideration, all accepted the offer. This issue pitted Hillary Clinton against her husband; she stated that she thought he should rescind the offer because of their delay in responding.

billboard models in the background. Oil painting class has begun, and I'll work on a portrait. I want to capture the quick expression I see in a person's face at a glance.

Love, Jane.

[undated letter from Margaret to Jane, on the occasion of Jane's fiftieth birthday]

Jane, from years now dimmed, sitting in some park or parking lot, with your sketchbook on your lap. Looking up and out and then down again, your artist's hand tracing a human stance or gesture, a rise or curve of land. Jane, producing some of the covers for Margaret's books that Margaret has loved the most. Jane, taking us through Haight-Ashbury and the Mission, offering a running commentary on those extraordinary murals you helped bring into being. A pivotal part of all our histories. Jane, your own face, breaking into that slow smile ending in full-flowing laughter, engagement. Jane as first witness to Barbara's and my love. Jane, your rhythmic palms on the drums. Jane ushering us into the sacred space of your studio, sharing recent pastels, their intensity burrowing into us and staying. Jane over the years, spilling your profound powers of observation and insight onto pages of letters/journals—your particular way of seeing the world which has become so much a part of our own. Jane mother of Río, Jane partner of Lawson, Jane fighting cancer and winning. Jane turning fifty and flowering. Jane, we love you and value you in our lives. Here's to the next fifty years!

11

ROBERT SCHWEITZER: OUTRIDER INHERITANCE

ROBERT SCHWEITZER WAS BORN in 1950. It was the aftermath of World War II. Intent on reviving a peacetime economy and creating jobs for the men who had returned from the front, U.S. corporations and conservative influencers were encouraging women to retreat back into the home sphere. To that end, a host of homemaking gadgets were being advertised, designed to make housework seem glamorous. The decade would be regressive in many other ways as well, with Senator Joseph McCarthy's anti-Communist witch hunt, the execution of Julius and Ethel Rosenberg, a stricter anti-immigrant policy, and serious censorship in education and the arts.

Robert's parents were unusual, especially for the times. Their names were Vita and Edwin. Neither had gone to college. They met at the furniture store where they both worked. They appreciated music and art, had human-centered values, supported progressive political positions and sophisticated ideas about child rearing, and were morally coherent in ways few people are. I wouldn't only say that Robert is an outrider—original in his thinking, solidly against the status quo, calm in his demeanor, and fierce when necessary—but that his parents were, as well. In many ways he inherits his outrider condition from them.

Robert and I met in the mid-eighties. By then he was a curator at the Everhart Museum in Scranton, Pennsylvania, and offered me a retrospective exhibition of my photography, the first time anyone of his stature had recognized my work in that genre. His concept of curating a show was unusual and embracing; he asked many profound questions about my images and produced a lovely catalog. We became close friends, and over the years have had many meaningful conversations about photography, art in general, and its connection to social change—just the sort of conversation that belongs in this book.

But there was a problem. Robert suffers from extreme dyslexia and writing is tedious for him. For this reason, our most interesting back-and-forth has taken place in person or over the phone, while our letters—with some notable exceptions—have contained only brief questions, plans for visits, and other mundane content.

I decided to deal with this lack of written correspondence by asking Robert if he would mind my interviewing him about his childhood home life, how he became involved in the world of art, and his other life choices. To my surprise, he consented and, despite his difficulty writing, sent me long and detailed answers. He has retired to a small island off the coast of Denmark, and I live in Albuquerque, but email facilitates our exchange and it, along with the few letters where Robert discussed pivotal issues in detail, made this chapter possible.

And so we began:

M.R./ Robert, you have always spoken so lovingly of your parents. These days, when so many acknowledge horrible family secrets or childhood abuse, your early home life impresses me as having been an exceptionally happy one. Can you tell me about your childhood and young adulthood, who your parents were, what your relationship with them was like, and how you believe they influenced the person you are today?

R.S./ To understand who my parents were, I'd like to talk about their families and the influence that my grandparents had. My grandfather Schweitzer's death has had a lasting impact on my life, especially with respect to my travels when my parents were still alive. I think I've told you that I was an exchange student in Bogotá, Colombia in the summer of 1968. I returned to visit my Colombian family there in the summer of 1970, and before leaving home I remember being at my grandparents' house. I gave my grandfather a kiss and said: "I'll see you when I get back," and he, in a low voice said, "I hope so." I hadn't given his response much thought until I returned to the States, planning to stay with a college friend in Miami, but as soon as I arrived at their home they told me I needed to call my father. My father told me that my grandfather, his father, had died the day before. So, I got on the next plane back to Scranton to be at my grandfather's funeral. And it was then that my grandfather's last casual comment came back to me.

When I was in Colombia the only way we communicated to the States was by mail, and of course it took days for the letters to arrive. I realized that if anything had happened to my parents when I was away, that news would never reach me until far too late, a reality that I couldn't handle. So, from then on, whenever traveling anywhere outside the country, I always checked in with my parents every other day or so, with a quick call to make sure everything was ok back home. This was before cell phones, so I needed to be near a pay phone if I wanted to be able to make the call.

Later, in Europe, that wasn't as much of a problem, but in Latin America, and especially in Chiapas, it would prove to be impossible at times. When I went out to Oventic, where there were no phones that I knew of, I would only stay a few days (while others would stay for more than a week at a time). I feel that some friends there saw this as a lack of seriousness on my part, but for my sanity I had no choice. And later, living back in the Scranton area, I bought my first cell phone so that I could always be able to receive a call in time of need, or make a call to check in; by then my parents were in their late 70s and 80s. One funny story: soon after I bought the cell phone I was at a meeting and put my phone on the table. When I went to see my parents afterward, they asked why I'd called but didn't speak to them. I was a bit confused and asked them what they meant. They said that their phone rang (my first butt-call), and they heard me speaking, along with a number of other people and waited for me to speak with them, my father listening in for the first ten minutes, and then my mother for the next ten before they decided that I wasn't going to speak to them and hung up. That is the devotion of my parents, and a sign of the times with cell phones.

I believe I mentioned that my father's parents were poor, right from the start, and when I asked my father what the depression was like, he said that he began to see others in the neighborhood begin to struggle and live as he and his parents had done all his life. My dad's father worked as a part time butcher and helper in two different small local grocery stores in north Scranton, and lived in that neighborhood, where he and my father were born, until his retirement. My father told me that his mother took in laundry, and baked bread that she would sell from their home.

One weekend when I was home from college my German grandmother (my father's mother) asked me about how I was doing at school and if I enjoyed it. In response I mentioned the name of the woman I was dating at the time. Her last name was clearly Jewish and my grandmother, a devout Lutheran, said, "That's nice," adding that we had a lot of Jewish blood in our family. This was the first time I'd heard that. As the conversation went on, I failed to go back and ask my grandmother to tell me more about our Jewish heritage, and later thought I would ask her when I returned over another weekend. But my grandmother died soon after and we never had that conversation. I knew that my grandmother's maiden name was Singer (her father was also a poor shoemaker) and then, as I did some more research into her side of the family, learned that her grandmother's name was Frank.

My Italian grandfather would often tell me stories, (sometimes while squeezing a rubber ball; before I was born, he had a stroke that drastically changed his life, including having to change from being right-handed to left-handed, among many other issues). I would sit at his side, listening and asking questions. He had a most interesting life, arriving at Ellis Island with his mother and younger brother in 1896, when he was six years old.

His father had set up a shoemaking practice in Dunmore, next to Scranton, and he, his mother, and brother were among the first to arrive in the States. Tragically his father died four years later when my grandfather was ten. His mother spoke no English, he was in school, where the teacher said he had to change his name, which he did (the entire family followed in the same manner). I often said that he was forced to take all the beauty out of his name, going from Francesco De Clemente to Frank Clemens (a direct Anglicized version).

But the story that I want to tell here relates to his graduating from the Wharton School of Finance (as it was called then), something not to have been expected given the early years of his life. I never actually found out from him how he was able to pay for it, or even get in. And one of the most interesting parts of the story is that he didn't "go to" Wharton, it came to him. During a brief period, the University of Pennsylvania tried to establish a satellite school in Scranton, and this is when my grandfather attended. He became the class historian, and he gave me his only copy of the book that he wrote. It had photographs and short biographies for each student, and for the professors. Nearly everyone in the class but my grandfather was what they used to call a WASP. The graduating class was almost entirely male; there were two women among 25 or so men.

These were the people from whom my parents came. I was truly blessed to have had the parents that I had. I was never punished. My mother would always talk through any issue (misbehavior) that other parents would generally scold their child for, or worse. And I was never sent to my room as punishment, or even the more modern "time out." Later in my 20s when I asked her about it, my mother told me that my room was just that, my room, and it should always be a place where I would feel safe, never to be confused or identified with punishment.

I remember that at times I would go to my room on my own, never being told to, so I could have my own space to think through whatever I might have felt bad about. And I was never struck or spanked by either of my parents. My mother was generally the one who would sit me down to speak with me if there was anything that I may have done wrong, since my father was at work much of the time, but he also took the same approach, especially in later years.

I remember when my nephew and niece were living with my parents after my brother and sister-in-law divorced.[62] *I returned from Washington D.C. where I was teaching at a daycare center to help my parents take care of the kids who were five and six years old. My brother and his ex-wife couldn't care for them. The children lived with us for two years, after which my sister-in-law said she was ready to take them back. My mother had told my nephew that he should change from his good school pants before going out to play, but he didn't and tore them. When he came back inside my*

62. In all the years of our friendship, I had never heard Robert mention his brother and was surprised when he appeared in this conversation. Donald Schweitzer is eight years older than Robert. He joined the navy right after high school and they didn't see each other often after he got out. They aren't close politically, nor in their cultural or social experiences over the years, but they care deeply about each other as brothers, and Robert tells me that in their old age they have begun to communicate occasionally via Zoom, something he says he thinks would make their parents happy.

mother sat with him at the kitchen table and asked him if he now understood why she'd asked him to change into his play clothes before going out. She hoped that he would listen to her the next time, or just do it on his own. At one point I remember my nephew saying to my mother "Why don't you just spank me?" And my mother said: I would never do that, hitting you would not help you understand what you did and why you would need to think about it, and do differently the next time." This was in the mid-1970s and was consistent with my mother's way of engaging with me in the 1950s. I have few friends my age who could tell a similar story.

My mother's sense of my room being my own can also be illustrated by a time when my father had just painted it blue, and after the paint dried and my bed was put back against the wall, I went in by myself—I was about five or six at the time—, got up on my bed and began to draw a ship on the wall. When my mother came in, she didn't say: "Your father will be angry because he just painted it" but got on the bed with me and talked about what I was drawing. She asked if the blue wall made me think of the ocean. I remember that experience as if it was yesterday.

And I never ever heard my parents raise their voice at anyone, certainly not at each other or me.

When I was in my late 20s or 30s, I asked my mother about Miss Hahn, the woman who owned the apartment house where we lived until I was two. She lived above us on the second floor. I know that we are not supposed to have memories of the time when we were still crawling, but I had a body-feeling memory of trying to crawl up the stairs to her apartment, a very vivid and safe physical memory, and asked what my mother might remember about it. She told me yes, she saw me attempting to crawl up the stairs and instead of pulling me back, got on her hands and knees over me to protect me, to let me continue to try. I did make it to the top. I then realized why my memory was so strong, and why I felt safe. I could, as she told me the story, immediately feel my mother's body above me. And some 60 years later, on the last night of my mother's life, I didn't want her to choke while lying on her back, so I raised her on her side and laid behind her to keep her in place. She died leaning back into my body. Afterward I thought how my body, trying to protect her in her last moments, was like her body over me in my very early years, supporting my independence and curiosity.

Around the age of five, my mother began to teach me how to cook, sew, do my own laundry, and even clean the house with her. I realized later that she wanted to make sure that I could be independent and self-sufficient, and I am so profoundly grateful that she did. It has forever impacted me in a positive way, enabling me to feel comfortable on my own, never "needing" anyone to be a replacement mother to me. And allowing me to enter my various relationships over the years, never wanting, needing, or expecting my partner to do the "woman's work." That concept never occurred to me. In my relationships we always shared every chore, and I always did my own laundry and ironing. Of course, we would always share in the cooking and washing the dishes.

I would say that my father was more at ease relating to me beginning in my early teens, than when I was very young. He was always warm and caring, just not as involved as my mother in my earlier years. I do remember how my father would try to teach me how to play tennis, but since I was left-handed it was more difficult. He kept at it, though, and I did learn a lot from him. We also had a ping pong table in the basement and would play together. My dad won many medals in high school and afterward for playing both, but always managed to make it possible for me to stay in the game and improve. He also taught me how to swim and tried to teach me how to ice skate. He was great at so many sports, including basketball when he was younger, and he and my mother were both avid and award-winning bowlers.

My father, along with working at the first furniture store where he started as an elevator boy, and at the second where he retired as general manager, also ran the toy department at Christmas. As a result, my parents almost always were able to get me all my "wants" for the holiday. I remember one year I asked for a dollhouse, and there it was under the tree on Christmas day. I played with my one neighborhood friend a lot, and she had a dollhouse, so I also wanted one for when she came to visit. As you might expect, most young boys in the '50s, asking for a dollhouse, would have their fathers, and most likely their mothers, say: "Doll houses are for girls, not boys. Here, have this gun or truck." I often think back to that dollhouse, and how arranging the furniture in different ways gave me an early experience in curatorial practice, and why I have always enjoyed designing an installation in my adult years. I am so deeply grateful that my parents let me follow my instincts at a young age.

My father was in the navy, in the Pacific, during WWII, along with his two brothers who were also stationed there. One was in the army, the other in the marines. The one in the marines was among the first scouts killed during the "waste the enemy's bullets" invasion of Iwo Jima. This devastated my father. This was the brother who was the poet and writer in the family, the one my dad told me with tears in his eyes he never really got to know because he was into sports and out of the house most of the day. And then this brother was gone.

For me, though, it was my father's horror at the bombing of Hiroshima and Nagasaki that showed me his deep morality. Having lost his brother to the Japanese, many might have thought that he would relish revenge. Just the opposite, he never forgave Truman and cried whenever he spoke about the bombing or the subject came up in conversation. And he cried rarely. He said that war should never occur, but if and when it does and it becomes a necessity to defend oneself or country, it is between the military to fight and take the losses, and civilians should never ever be the target. He would be furious with what's happening now in Gaza.

I was in Venice when the Twin Towers came down and managed to call my parents within hours, I remember my father saying he was so angry that the news anchors kept saying it was the worst attack on a civilian population in years. He said: "No, the worst attack on any civilian population was by us when bombing Hiroshima." He was also against the war in Vietnam from the very start. And later against the Gulf War, aid to the Contras, the Iraq war, the invasion of Panama, and all the other long list of our country's imperialist endeavors.

I've already mentioned that my brother and sister-in-law divorced when I was in my senior year at college. My sister-in-law insisted on being paid what she felt she deserved. She wanted close to half the value of all they had. My parents, for the sake of their grandchildren, worked to come up with the money. I was just about to start my final semester at American University and my parents called to see if I could find a college loan to help out. At the time, the only one I could quickly and easily get would be a National Defense Act Loan, and when I called to tell my father about it, and mentioned that it would require me to take a pledge of allegiance, he quickly said: "You didn't do it, did you?" I hadn't. My dad was relieved and said that they would find another way to come up with the extra money for my sister-in-law. Years later, during the Gulf War, at my father's 50th class reunion he refused to stand and pledge allegiance to the flag. That raised many eyebrows among his classmates, but he told them that it was like defending Bush's war, and he wouldn't show any sign of agreeing with that.

My parents' independence started early. As I mentioned, they met at the furniture store where they both worked in the early 40s, and the romance soon took hold. But the fact that my mother was an Italian Catholic and my father a German Lutheran made their relationship totally unacceptable to my Italian grandfather. He went so far as to send my mother's brothers to threaten my father, try to make him stay away from my mother, and insisted that my mother not spend any time with my father. Months later my mother began to throw some of her clothing out her bedroom window when no one could see her, gathered them together and took them to a friend's house on her way to work so she would have enough clothes for their honeymoon. They signed their marriage license in another county, my mother using a slightly different first name for her father so he wouldn't be alerted. After they were married and were at the bus station in Scranton, heading into New York City for their honeymoon, they called my grandfather to say they'd gotten married and were already in New York. Of course, he was furious and demanded that my mother return home and have the marriage annulled. But she told her father it was final, she would never leave my father. The marriage remained a huge strain for both my parents afterward, with my mother eventually being allowed back in her parents' home but not my father for many, many more months. It was only after my brother was born in 1942 (almost twelve months to the day from when my parents were married), and since he was my Italian grandparents' first grandson, that the ice began to slowly crack, but still my father was very much an outcast. When my mother's mother died suddenly a few years later, my father and grandfather finally began to communicate.

After college, when I returned to Scranton (actually Moscow, Pennsylvania, where our house was and where I grew up) to help take care of my nephew and niece, my parents asked me what I wanted to do after graduating. We hadn't discussed that all through my time at college, as I changed majors often and they always said all they wanted was for me to be happy. I said what I really wanted to do was start a commune in the countryside, where we would have a free school and gardens. While at AU, in 1970 or '71, I'd had the enormous good fortune of hearing and speaking with both Ivan Illich and Paolo Freire. This was right after Pedagogy of the Oppressed *came out in English. I had read it and later would also read Illich's* Deschooling Society. *Those two books and the two truly compassionate and brilliant individuals who wrote them had a lasting influence on me and how I would later approach my studies and work.*

When I mentioned to my parents, who had just paid a good deal of money to put me through school, what I wanted to do, instead of saying. "After all that expense you want to start a commune?!" they said, "How can we help?" The commune never came about, but with their help I did explore the possibility further, and I still have the plans I made for it, including a design for the building, and a multiple-page outline of how the school would function.

Instead of the commune, my parents helped me build my stone house, and they came every weekend to work in the gardens and we'd have lunch together. My mother actually started organic gardening when I was growing up, back at our house in Moscow, and she loved to plant, care for, and harvest the various vegetables which she canned and later also froze. When I became a vegetarian at the age of 19, my mother began to try new recipes with the vegetables we grew. We ended up with a large garden, close to an acre in size. And since in 1969 there were hardly any vegetarian options in the grocery stores or restaurants, my mom became very creative and loved experimenting with new recipes or inventing ones of her own. I remember my father's favorite menu option at the time was veal parmigiana, but after I explained to him how they treated the calves, he stopped eating it. He never became a vegetarian, nor did my mother, but they were always supportive of my decisions and choices.

M.R./ Robert, I am astonished at the scope of your response. Despite your difficulty in writing, and your repeated insistence that you don't feel you belong in this book—"My life just isn't as interesting as the others you've chosen," you always say—you've managed to provide me with a real sense of your childhood, how unusual and enlightened your parents were, and the ways in which that gave you a solid foundation for who you are today. I'm curious about the dyslexia, though. I know it wasn't well understood by educators during your youth, and that it remains deeply distressing for those who suffer from it. And I remember when the exhibition of my photography at the Everhart opened, and Barbara and I drove from Hartford to Scranton to see it, we had your instructions but kept getting lost. Finally, utterly confused, we called you. You apologized profusely, explained that you suffer from dyslexia, and finally provided us with directions that worked.

R.S./ I was in my mid to late 20s when I first realized that my reading and writing problem was called dyslexia. I was riding with some friends in a car and after reading a billboard from the car window asked: "What was . . . ?" My one friend said I'd mixed up the letters and told me the word. A few weeks before this, I had watched someone talking about dyslexia on TV, I believe it was on

60 Minutes. *That was the first time I'd heard the term. Putting together what I had heard on the program with what had just occurred in the car, I said: "So I am dyslexic!" And I soon came to realize I was profoundly so.*

Going back, long before this revelation, when I was in second or third grade, I remember the teacher asking me to stand up and sight read from a story in one of our readers, and soon into the first or second sentence I read "red horse" for "red house" and all the other children laughed. I can't remember what the teacher said, or anything else from that moment. But I knew then that I couldn't read like the other children. I never wanted to read out loud again, and still don't. What saved me at the time and for many years afterward was that I would readily raise my hand to answer the teachers' questions, which they appreciated, and nearly always had a good answer. I became much more engaged verbally.

For the most part I'd managed to avoid reading anything that I hadn't already read over more than once to myself. But when I was in college, I took part in a seder. Everyone at the table was to read one paragraph from the Torah. I can't remember which day of Passover it was but given the direction in which we were reading I counted the number of people before me and went down to the passage that contained, for almost anyone, numerous unpronounceable names. I read the paragraph that would be mine over and over in my head. But then the person to my left decided to read two paragraphs, including mine, leaving me with a paragraph I hadn't looked over at all. I can remember the sweat on my forehead, and how slowly I attempted to read it, with minor mistakes.

It was of course in my writing, then and now, that my dyslexia was most evident to others. Remember that at this time, from early grade school through college, I had no name nor understanding for what my issue was. And no one seemed to be able to tell me.

In high school and college we had those little blue books we were to use when answering test questions or for turning in a short essay, and mine were always filled with red circles. Early on I developed an almost unreadable penmanship, and that was intentional: to try to cover for my inability to spell. If I was pretty sure that there was an i in the word, I would put a dot above the scribble at some point, hoping that this would be enough. It worked sometimes (or maybe I was just lucky and got it right at times), but most often not.

So, misspelling was a major issue then, and still is. Even some of the most common words, ones I use every day, I need to look up to be sure I have them right. This lack of trust in what you write follows you forever. Fortunately, today, word programs on the computer and on the internet provide you with red highlighting of misspelled words, but not always. If you write "form" when you meant "from" (which happened more than once while writing this response) or "tow" when you meant "two," there is no red highlighting on most programs because both are also words. So, I still miss many mistakes, and even rereading something I have written more than once, there are some that always get past me; because in my head I know what "I wanted to write" and that is what I see when rereading. It can take a day or two before reading something I wrote once again before the mistakes register in my brain: an embarrassment that I have come to live with, but one that still frustrates me.

One of the worst, and most embarrassing examples of my misspelling, before the computer, while using the little blue books, occurred during my first class in political science, when the professor gave us an assignment to write what we believed a conversation would have sounded like between Dubcek and Brezhnev.

This was after the summer of 1968, following the Soviet invasion of Czechoslovakia. I had a copy of Dubcek's Blueprint for Freedom *and felt it would give me better insight into his way of thinking, and that my paper should be one of the better ones. There were about 50 students in this class, and when the professor was handing back the essays, he began with the paper that had the lowest grade and worked his way up. The last paper in his hand was mine and I was really excited. But as he held up my blue book, he said: "Although this appears to be a well-researched paper and deserves a high grade, I will only give it a B because not only was Brezhnev misspelled on the title page, but it was also misspelled seven different ways throughout the paper. At least you could have been consistent!" Later, another professor told me that I had to find a proofreader to go over any papers I would turn in. Fortunately for me, Matt, my roommate throughout college and still my closest friend, took on that task and was great at it. And it often provided him with some laughs when he came upon some of my "best" misspellings.*

Sentence structure, punctuation, grammar, etc. are also issues I've never been able to conquer.

I have dyslexic hands as well. I have noticed that when typing quickly I will type one word twice. It's the second typing of that word that should be there, but I fail to type the word before the second word, thus repeating the second word twice and having to go back and type in the first word, if this makes any sense. It seems that living with dyslexia is not a fixed reality but is still playing new games with my ability to write.

In addition to writing and spelling, my reading suffered greatly from an early age. I was still quite young when my mother responded to a woman at the Met who asked how I knew so much about Egyptology, by saying that I "read a lot." When I was interested in a subject I would try to read as much as I could, but it took me a very long time to get through a few pages. I had some great old issues of National Geographic *back then, and with the illustrations and captions, I was able to make my reading experience a little easier. And when it came to reading assignments in high school, and even some in college, I would most often only have time to read a portion of the book assigned. I would try to figure out the ideas in each book by reading those few pages, clearly missing all the interesting details, and that's how I was able to bluff my way through high school, even, at times, impressing the teachers with my understanding of the subject. I still rely on that method from time to time.*

One summer day, when I was in the galleries at Marywood, I noticed a teacher and a group of high school age (or slightly older) students. She was talking with them about a temporary exhibition we had. I went over to her when the students were on their own and asked her about the class. She told me that they were in a GED program, which is what I had expected, given it was summer. I asked if she thought the students might like a short tour of the art storage area for The Maslow Collection, explaining what it included.[63] *She said yes and then asked the students. It remains one of the most meaningful discussions with students I ever had.*

In the collection we have a large major work by Chuck Close, Phil III, *1982.*[64] *Technically this is a unique work made using small pieces of hand-made paper, but it is categorized as a print since it's in a multiple edition. There were many reasons why I focused on this work, including the very interesting and complex problem-solving manner by which it was made. But most significant to me was that I wanted to include three "conditions" of the artist's life, one of which I shared. First was the creative way he developed and used technology to be able to continue to work and paint from a wheelchair after a sudden spinal collapse in the middle of his career radically altered his life. The second was that he had "face blindness" but that his subject matter in almost all his work were portraits and how he would grid the information in a photograph based on color or tonal quality, and then grid a large canvas and paint that information*

63. The Maslow Collection is a family-owned contemporary art collection. Robert worked for Marilyn and Richard Maslow beginning in the mid 1990s, helping them catalog, shape, and consult on its future place in the community, becoming its curator, and eventually also aiding in securing a permanent place for it at Marywood University in Scranton. Richard and Robert became close friends. Richard Maslow died in March 2024, at the age of ninety-two; Marilyn died in 2016.

64. I should say that Close was later accused of sexual misconduct by an assistant, but this wasn't known to me at the time.

in the smaller squares to make the larger work. Both exercises involved overcoming significant obstacles.

The third condition, the one I told the students I shared with him, was that he was dyslexic. I turned to the students and asked if any of them were also dyslexic. Over half raised their hand. We then talked about the difficulties that dyslexia presented to them and to me when trying to keep up in school, and that I was glad to see that they were now getting their degrees within a more understanding and helpful environment. I pointed out that even though I had dyslexia, as did Chuck Close, we had both been able to participate in society in ways that were meaningful to us. And I hoped that this could also happen in their lives, maybe in work settings that were less traditional but in which they would feel comfortable. The students and teacher all expressed how appreciative they were to have taken part in the discussion. I could have retired then, as far as I was concerned.

To sum up, some of the side effects of dyslexia, for me and I know for others as well, include having a very difficult time remembering names after being introduced, and not being able to distinguish lyrics sung when the music is loud and played with multiple instruments. Dyslexia has been a challenge in my life from the very beginning, and for the first 20-plus years put me in a position where I had to find ways to adjust to a condition I had no name for, and no sense of others having the same experience. It also created some obstacles I really haven't been able to overcome. For example, when I've had to write longer essays, as I attempted to do for "Rayuela/Hopscotch." I didn't have the luxury of focusing on the essay since I was responsible for every aspect of the exhibition, and repeatedly got sidetracked. In the end, the result was acceptable but not what I'd hoped it would be. With dyslexia, personal disappointments are frequent.

M.R./ I am grateful for your willingness to go into such informative detail about a condition that is still clearly painful in your life. Thank you for that. Now I'd like to move on to an area in which you've been immensely successful, often introducing concepts before their time. I'd like to know how you got into the art world and developed the skills that allowed you to become a highly original teacher and progressive curator of art. When and how did you first get interested in art? When and how did you realize that studying and curating it would be a major part of your life?

R.S./ As with most young children, I loved to draw from a very early age, and my mother always encouraged me. She would draw with me and we'd talk about my drawings. In first grade the teacher asked some of us to make a poster for a PTA meeting and when she saw me pick up the pencil in my left hand, she said, almost reflexively and somewhat under her breath: "I forgot, you're left-handed. You wouldn't be creative enough." Because my mother had been so encouraging, instead of believing her I questioned all my teachers from then on. As I think back on the experience, it may have been one of the more important moments in my education, although it could have been just the opposite if not for my trusting my mother more than the teacher.

In high school I challenged my social studies teacher when he marked an answer wrong on a test that I felt had been right. He said if I could get up in front of the class and successfully defend my reasoning, he would give each of us who answered in the same way a better grade. I did, and the teacher accepted my reasoning. He later told me it was the first time he had ever changed a grade in this manner.

I did the same when I was in college, when the psychology professor (a Skinnerian, actually Skinner's former assistant) was explaining how superior Behavioral Modification was, illustrated by a study he was citing that said 70% of the participants changed their behavior. I quickly stood up in the large class and said: "That sounds good, but if it was such a great method, why didn't the other 30% change their behavior?" He seemed caught off guard and then admitted that in a follow-up question session regarding another study, when the participants who changed their behavior were asked about why they felt that they had, they said they began to understand what was "expected" and followed along, while the others, who did not change, didn't recognize what was expected and did not change theirs. I stood again and said it sounded more Existential to me. I didn't know much about Existentialism but knew I didn't trust Behavioral Modification.

But back to art. When I was about eight or nine years-old, my mother and I began going into New York with my father and staying there for a few days. While my father was attending trade shows during the day, my mother would try to make sure that we visited the Museum of Modern Art, the Guggenheim, the Whitney, and the Metropolitan, at least three or four of them each trip. Going through those museums, I remember we spent time with works by Henry Moore, Alexander Calder, Alberto Giacometti, Barbara Hepworth, David Smith and others. Finally sculpture, more than painting, interested me most.

And I remember vividly that it was at MoMA that I saw and "felt" for the first time a Rothko painting. I just stood there, captivated, unable to move. I know that at the time I had no understanding of what a transcendental experience was, but later that became the most accurate term to describe the response. And I remember that my mother patiently stood alongside me as I took in the experience, and eventually leaned down to ask what I was seeing and feeling. All I could say was that it felt as if I had entered the painting, and that I really liked it.

Dialogue was important to my mother and would become so to me as well. I have often thought back on that moment as the one when I seriously became interested in art. Soon after that experience at MoMA, when I was 11, I created a small museum in my parents' attic that included my collections of stones, fossils, seashells, and even some Egyptology "artifacts" I created. All the items were catalogued and presented on shelves with labels. This was one more stage in what would eventually lead me to my curatorial practice.

When I was just turning 16, my mother and I were at the Everhart Museum in Scranton on a Saturday. I looked through a slightly opened door to see people in the process of making plaster casts of their sculptural works, originally created on an armature using plasticine clay. I told my mother I would really like to take that class if possible. The teacher was in the room and my mother went in and spoke to her about my interest.

The teacher's first reaction was one of surprise, since I was seeing the messiest part of the total process; and she was also leery about accepting someone as young as I was into the class, which was traditionally for adults. But after asking me some questions, and feeling encouraged by my responses, she agreed that I could take part in the next session starting in the fall. The teacher, Hope Horn, was the most well-known and important of the artists in the region at the time (which I learned afterward), as well as a teacher of both painting and sculpture at the museum. At this time, I had just decided to drop out of the art class in high school. I had gone to a few classes at the beginning of my first year at the school, but when I saw and heard how the teacher ridiculed a few of the students, saying that they were not creative enough to be in the class—which reminded me of my experience with my first-grade teacher—it immediately told me this was an environment where I didn't want to be.

I ended up studying sculpture with Hope at the Everhart for two years and would return when I was home from college to visit and help out. For the first two years we worked from live models, first a figure study, and then the bust of another model in the following session. At the end of the second year, I "moved up" to working in wood, my choice instead of stone. I was surprised after my first year when Hope suggested I submit the bust that I had done into a highly regarded regional art exhibition, which that year was held at the Everhart. The regional took in artists, nearly all of them professionals, from northeast Pennsylvania and southern New York, and hundreds submitted. I felt that I would have little chance of being juried in, but the experience would be good. Then, much to my surprise, my work was accepted. I believe that I may still be the youngest person to have been included in the regional over the many years it took place.

As a bit of irony, I went to the opening with my parents, and there was the high school art teacher who, when she saw me, said: "Robert, I didn't know that you had an interest in art." Before I could respond she went on to say she had submitted two works, and even though they weren't accepted, she was honored to know that the juror from Temple University had seen her work. I remained silent. A short time later I noticed that she came to my piece in the exhibition, and in great surprise (shock) turned, looked over at me, and then came and asked how, where, and with whom I'd done the work. You only get a few moments like this in your life.

Prior to taking classes with Hope, when I was about 12, I remember I saw the art curator in one of the galleries at the Everhart and asked him what you needed to do to be a curator. His advice was to study art history, which would have been a very traditional response, especially before the advent of the curatorial studies majors that began to emerge at some universities in the late 70s and became more common by the '90s. I initiated, oversaw, and taught a course at Marywood in curatorial studies from 2008 to 2017 when I retired, within their Arts Administration Major.

All these early experiences stayed with me through my college studies but were not at the forefront of my thoughts or interests. They would resurface a few years after graduation. This is not to say that I did not study art in college. I did study both art history and studio art, but they were not my sole focus. I created the interdisciplinary course in Contemporary Community Studies that became the major with which I finally graduated. And it would be almost seven years after leaving college that I merged the approach formed in my major with my curatorial practice. During those seven years I continued to work in early childhood education, eventually becoming the director at one center. I also built my stone house in the country during this time.

I will jump to the end of those seven years, to the moment when I approached the art curator at the Everhart, the same one who was there when I'd asked about what I needed to do to become a curator years before. I'd written a proposal for creating a position of curator of education. This new museum profession was in its infancy in 1979, but I felt it would be a great entry point for me combining my interest in new approaches to teaching and the collections at the museum. Carl, the curator at the Everhart at the time, said he was very interested but right then he was preoccupied with a difficult situation that had surfaced with some of the outside board members. He said we should schedule a meeting in a few weeks. Sadly, he wasn't simply stressed; he died of a heart attack a few days later there in his office at the museum.

The Everhart hired a new curator/director to replace Carl, and soon after that I asked to meet with him. I explained that I had written a CITA grant. This was a federal grant in the 70s that provided funds to institutions enabling them to hire unemployed workers at a low pay level to fill new positions that the institutions would be interested in continuing after the grant monies ran out. The grant I'd written was for a position that related to creating new approaches to working with the museum's collections that would engage various members of the public, primarily school groups, in discussing a wide range of subjects connected to works in the museum's collection. The Everhart was established in the early 1900s as a more general museum, more like a mini-Smithsonian, with collections in natural history, art, science, and ethnographic artifacts. What I proposed would integrate these collections in a range of meaningful discussions. All the grant needed at this point was his signature and the approval of the county commissioners for it to go into effect. The new director welcomed the idea, and the position came into being.

I won't go into all the programing or small exhibitions I created and curated that were part of my overall project idea, but I will say that my approach with larger groups of visitors, especially students, was to open up a dialogue with those in the group "around a topic of their expressed interest" and as we moved through the museum's collections identifying works that helped make our discussion more visible and interesting.

The discussions were never scripted but moved into and through areas generally initiated by a student's comment or question, after I had presented an open-ended question on the topic they came to consider. The docent program that existed before I arrived always worked with a specific script and only had a few topics it was prepared to offer. For me, there was almost no topic that the teachers would come up with that I couldn't see a meaningful way to relate to the collections. The teachers embraced this opportunity and my approach to expanding the students' learning experience. I did hundreds of such programs over the years.

My position as curator of art and education included my responsibility for the ethnographic collections at the Everhart, and I had the opportunity to do some groundbreaking work with them as well. I almost immediately removed the Peruvian "mummy" and Jivaro "shrunken head" (later determined by the Smithsonian to be a tourist replica) from the galleries where they had been installed for at least thirty years. I did this in 1980, when the ethical questions regarding museums exhibiting human remains were only beginning to be discussed. It was ten years later, in 1990, that NAGPRA *(the Native American Graves Protection and Repatriation Act) was passed, and it has taken years for museums to comply. Without any available help at the time, we began to search for a way to both authenticate and to eventually repatriate these remains. The Peruvian mummy was authentic, and by the time I left the museum in 1991 they were still trying to make arrangements for its return.*

Sadly, I remember that soon after I'd removed these remains (I also removed what was purported to be an Iroquois "False Face Society" mask, among other artifacts), on more than one occasion, when I was up in the galleries, I would see someone talking with the guards and soon turn and point to me. And I knew what the issue was. The individual would come over and complain that I had removed their favorite objects, things they'd been coming to the museum to see since they were a child. It troubled me that these would be their favorite objects in the museum's collection. But I would ask them if they believed we had a right to exhibit human remains from another society? And they would usually say: "Sure, they are already dead." At which point I would suggest that, instead of going to another culture to find dead bodies to exhibit, maybe we could go to the local cemetery and dig up a body there, one buried a long time ago or maybe a more recent one for comparison. They would look at me astonished, and say that would be sacrilegious, entirely disrespectful, or just horrible. Then I would tell them: "I guess now you understand why I removed the mummy and the shrunken head."

When any group, often adults but sometime students, asked me for a tour of the ethnographic galleries I would begin our discussion with a question: "What are your expectations? What do you believe you will learn through the experience?" And the responses would always be something like: "To know more about the people who made the artifacts, how they lived, their beliefs." I would try to explain that what they would learn would basically be more about our society than those who made and lived with the artifacts. They should consider that at the core of what they would see is the fact that we believe that we have both the right and the power to take from another group of people objects that had very real meaning to them, a meaning that I couldn't adequately or with a clear understanding relate to the group. And that we not only took the objects, but felt we could truthfully present them, tell their story, without any input from them at all.

And I would ask the group what they would think if we were to give these same people objects from our lives, if they felt that they could create a meaningful exhibition using our material in their community, or if they would even have any interest in doing so? Just before going in, I asked them to look with open eyes, recognize that what they were about to see and experience clearly had, in most instances, profound meaning in the lives of those who made and lived with the artifacts, but they shouldn't try to invent some specific story that would only do a disservice to those from whom these artifacts were either purchased through trade or stolen. I wanted them to try to shed their colonial past.

Part of what I brought to the curatorial practice, based on my studies in contemporary society from an anthropological point of view, was based on a thematic approach that considered the possible and potential meaning and function of curated exhibitions that arose from a broad range of ideas, issues, and concerns. I worked to present new artists, or reconsider established artists, often within a non-traditional context, that introduced new or different ways of thinking about their work, as was becoming the practice at that time by a number of other colleagues. And some of the broad themes that I focused on when inviting artists to participate in group exhibitions included: artists responding to established structural formations within our culture, such as "Art and the Dialectic Process" in 1987 that featured Joseph Beuys, Hans Haacke, Jenny Holzer, Alfredo Jaar, and Louise Lawler; or, also in 1987, artists focused on environmental concerns with "Artists and the Land," that included Betsy Damon, Harriet Feigenbaum, Robert Smithson, and John Bromberg; and when installing the exhibition "From the Collection of Sol LeWitt," I *explored the meaning and function of context and how it affects (at times even determines) the way we see and consider meaning in any object or situation. Certainly, Marcel Duchamp in the early 20th century, and Sherrie Levine, Louise Lawler, and Barbara Kruger in the later 20th and early 21st centuries, to name just a few, made context a central theme in their work, but examining, in a self-reflective manner, the exhibition itself as a context, and how that can, and most often does, impact the way the viewer thinks about the artists and their work from then on was less frequently addressed through and within an exhibition.*

In each of the group exhibitions I curated, I would initially propose a rational for bringing the individual artist's works together within that thematic framework. But, to the best of my ability, I would always make sure that I wasn't using the work to further a theory or interest of mine with which the artists wouldn't feel comfortable. This is also one of the fundamental principles I would impress upon the students in my curatorial classes, one of respect and honesty. To ensure that artists fully understood and approved of being part of an exhibition, I would as often as possible work directly with them through the planning stage right up to installation. I wanted to make sure we could work together to clarify and explore aspects of whatever theme I had proposed.

When it came to exhibitions of individual artists, after seeing their work in an exhibition in another venue and feeling strongly about it, I would ask if it would be possible for me to arrange an exhibition at the Everhart. But I added that, given the existing schedule, it would most likely not take place for about two years. And I would say that, although what I was seeing then was something I felt was significant, it's not necessarily what I would expect to see from them in two years. I wanted to trust the artist, and not become an obstacle to the new ideas or approaches that may come to them over the years leading up to the exhibition I wanted to present. With one artist in particular, what I initially saw was a group of prints. And the exhibition that took place two years later involved three massive installations that were both personal and historical; they related in part to the struggle of exploited immigrants working in the early coal mines of northeastern Pennsylvania. It was exceptional and received the most positive national review in Afterimage Magazine *that anyone could have hoped for.*

You'll probably remember that for the exhibition of your photographs we also discussed a wide range of issues that provided me with a much clearer and more meaningful way to both discuss your work in the catalogue and on the gallery text panels, and in the way that I installed it.

I wanted to create a possible new/or different reading of the works of well-known artists, to break their work out of the pigeonholes that often limited the way the viewer thought about them.

For the Sol LeWitt exhibition I also created a small installation of ephemera related to the artists and their work in a separate exhibition on the museum's lower level to give greater context for the visitors to whom this work was new and unfamiliar. I should talk more about ephemera. It's use in the mid-80s wasn't common to help contextualize the works being presented, although now, certainly since the 2000s, it is appearing in many more museums, from MoMA to the Reina Sofia in Madrid.

Over the years I had kept much of the ephemera from exhibitions I'd seen long before working at the museum, and of course much more after I became a curator. By the late 90s, my ephemera collection was growing to such a mass that I needed to find a way to catalogue it and make it more useful to me in my research and teaching. So I began a website I called Left Matrix, that initially contained short essays and photographs related to my political activities in Chiapas, along with some other material on the Havana Biennials, and experiences and observations in other parts of Central America. And then in 1997 or '98 I added what would become the largest section to my website, the one that acted as my inventory and searchable, cross-referenced, catalogue for the various works in my ever expanding ephemera and catalogue collection, a site that would enable me to access the works in my collection wherever I was in the world, by linking on to my website.

With this online catalogue I designed a way to cross-reference certain related material in my collection pertaining to the artists, including in which exhibitions they appeared with other artists. Basically, what I established was a way to search within the website that opened up many paths for cross-referenced searches, such as starting from the page with the list of all the exhibition catalogues in my collection, click on a catalogue of interest which would take you to a list of all (or most) of the artists in the exhibition and then from that page you could link to the page of any of the artists (those represented in my collection, of which there were over 475) where you would then find all the ephemera I had in my collection related to that artist, everything from their individual catalogues to early exhibition documentation and photographs, and also, in some instances, small works by the artist, including artist's books. On that artist's page there were also links to all the catalogues I had (over 500 group catalogues) that included that artist. I also added the ability to check and cross-reference from each artist's individual page by following the links for all the listed periodicals, albums, art books (about 200 in total) where the artists discussed in these texts were also listed for further cross-referencing. And there was much more, to the point that there were over 2,000 internal links, and many more thousands of photographs. It obviously took some time to build.

It wasn't until I was doing a Google search regarding one of the artists I had in my collection that I began to see my website appear in the group of other sources, and at times at the top of the list, even above MoMA. I was somewhat shocked, because I did nothing to promote my site at all. In fact, I was still thinking of it primarily for my own use, a tool I could access from anywhere. I later found out that it was being used by other curators and students for research worldwide, with additional links to my webpage from numerous institutions totally unknown to me.

It was while I was taking care of my mother that a student from Goldsmiths University in London emailed, asking if she could work with my collection. I then realized that it was being used by students in the most prestigious program in curatorial studies in the world. I told her that it really wasn't practical for her to consider working with my collection, given that she was in London. But just after my mother died, she contacted me again and said she could come to the States, since she had finished her studies at Goldsmiths.

I'd sold my stone house when I was taking care of my mom. After she died, I realized that I would need to purchase a home and leave the apartment where my mother and I had lived in her final years. Since I only once had a loan, very early in my life, and didn't want to have another, the only way to pay for a house was to sell parts of my ephemera collection, and I knew that many items in the collection had greatly increased in value over the years. So, when this former student from Goldsmiths called again, I said that the timing wasn't good because I was beginning to organize parts of my collection for sale. Within a few hours she called back and said that she needed to tell me more about her and her family. Her father and mother had one of the most important collections of contemporary art in Portugal, actually one of the most important collections of late 20th and early 21st century contemporary art in all of Europe, and her parents wanted to consider adding a large part of my collection to theirs. They did, and in the first major exhibition catalogue of their collection in Madrid, the purchase of my ephemera collection was mentioned at the very beginning, marking it as the foundation for their developing ephemera collection. Not just museums, but collectors were now recognizing how the addition of highly relevant ephemera added much greater context and history to the works they have in their collections. I still have a small part of my ephemera *collection, mostly related to artists with whom I have had a strong personal connection.*

I believe that context always informs what and how we see works of art and think about them afterward. This belief informed an exhibit I curated called "Rayuela/ Hopscotch: Fifteen Contemporary Latin American Artists." The idea for the exhibition originated in a discussion with the professors involved in teaching Latin American Studies at the University of Scranton and Marywood University. That is why it involved fifteen artists who either lived in or were from Latin America. But for me, this posed an initial conceptual and context-making problem. I didn't want visitors to believe what they would be seeing was "Latin American Art," as if all the works existed in, and expressed, some common unified Latin Americanness.

Because I wanted to set an alternative stage for the reading of the works in the exhibition, I stated in the catalogue that the title came from Cortázar's book Rayuela/Hopscotch, *the choice I made to both relate to literature being taught at the universities, and more importantly for the organization of the catalogue and exhibition design, to open up multiple possibilities for relating to each of the works. Although those works would be fixed in place for the exhibition, they were not thematically arranged, but as best I could, non-thematic, so that they had the chance to "speak for themselves" without comparison to other works near them or in proximity in the galleries. I also wanted the viewer to consider in what other manner they could they have been presented, following the multiple possibilities established by Cortázar as to the ways his book could be read. I also stated that I wasn't implying that by exhibiting these artists, each of whom had a direct connection to Latin America in one way or another, was representative of Latin American Art in general, a concept that is fundamentally flawed. I remember you also dealt with this in the essay you wrote for the catalogue in this exhibition, where you spoke to the ongoing dialogue between the North and the South as exemplified by* El Corno Emplumado. *And context was also clearly a central element in how we discussed and presented your photographs, both in the catalogue and in the exhibition I curated at the Everhart.*

M.R./ Oh, Robert, that show! I can't tell you how much it meant to me that you paid that sort of attention to my photography. Although I consider myself first and foremost a writer—a poet—photography has been an important part of my creative life. I'll never forget the care you took in designing a meaningful retrospective of my images. You titled it "Photographs by Margaret Randall: Image and Content in Differing Cultural Contexts," and after almost a quarter century in Latin America it felt to me like a visual expression of my coming home to the United States. My sensibility, artistic and otherwise, was forever altered by life in the Global South, but the transition was complicated. I now had new cultural references mixed with the old. While in Cuba and Nicaragua I'd photographed people—particularly women—often dealing with the pain of war. Once home I was more interested in landscape—my beloved New Mexican high desert—but also continued to photograph women engaged with experiences of changing identity. You understood all this, at times better than I did. In the beautifully designed and executed catalog you produced for the exhibit you wrote:

> Margaret Randall refers to herself as a chronicler. Her commitment to the authentic voice arising from those who have been silenced in culture and history is central to her writings and photography. The individual in relationship to the ideological/cultural context generates the discourse on issues such as domination, emergence, transformation, reconciliation, and struggle for justice and dignity. Photography can function to chronicle the moment, the historical present.

I am also forever grateful for your ongoing support of my photography, which didn't end with the Everhart exhibit. You have always been so generous. I remember your driving a series of my photographic prints across the border to Canada for a gallery show you'd arranged in Toronto. And then there were those few days of deep communion when you traveled to Albuquerque to go through hundreds of loosely organized proof sheets and help me make choices for a possible book. That book never materialized, but, again, I learned things I hadn't realized about my own process, my particular eye. Our friendship has been educational for me in so many ways.

I believe that everything you've told me so far about your life and work has its roots in your passion for education: how your parents rejected outmoded ideas about bringing up children and developed an alternative model that shaped you from your earliest years, how you yourself focused on education as the logical entrance point for young people to know themselves and the world around them, and how you developed your own innovative ideas that you've practiced in venues as diverse as day-care centers, college classrooms, curation, and museum outreach programs. Can you expand a bit more on this?

R.S./ You're right, it all starts with education. And my teaching method was non-traditional from the beginning. Although I did use slides (and later PowerPoints) along with videos (and at times other types of recordings or albums), the students were not expected to remember each image I introduced. I didn't believe in tests or quizzes but would ask the students to keep a journal of thoughts on what we discussed during the time in class, and I said I would "look at" but not read them. I told them I thought if they believed I would read them they would try to write them "for me," and attempt to come up with what they thought I wanted to see. I told them I hoped the journal would be theirs for years to come, and when they looked back at it, they would find their thoughts and impressions, not something meant for their teacher. The students also had to write a paper on a subject of their interest that we'd covered. I knew each student would find one or more topics and artists that resonated with them, and this is what they should focus on for their paper.

As for grading, on the first day of class I would announce that as of then, everyone had an A. I said there would be no competition, and it would be hard to lose the

A unless they didn't attend regularly and fulfill the few assignments. I wanted them to relax in class and feel free to express themselves at any time. I told them I thought tests and quizzes only added stress and inhibited rather than enhanced the learning process. Marywood insisted that all faculty teach to "the curve" but I told them if they wanted me to teach, they shouldn't expect that from me. I never did teach to the curve. Nearly all my students managed to keep their A to the end of class.

Since I approached each class as a way to introduce new artists and concepts, we would spend a good deal of time discussing what was presented, all of which was very time consuming. About mid-way through the last course I taught in Contemporary Art I introduced an additional assignment: I gave them a list of artists to look over and research on their own, and pick one from that list, or in the process of researching they might come upon another artist who interested them, and for the last two days of class I would make time for each student to do a presentation on the artists they selected, and to explain why they thought I should have included that artist in the class. I think you can see how following through on this assignment I was also able to see how well they understood what we had been discussing, while at the same time allowing them to decide on those artists they found most interesting.

Those last two days were the most exciting of the class. Students would say: "I can't believe you left this artist out," or 'This was the best part of the class." If I was to teach the class again, I would include that assignment earlier on. One student, some years later in a Facebook message to me, asked if I would now read the first pages of his journal, and I said I would be honored. He told me he didn't clean it up, so the grammar and spelling would be off, but he wanted me to read it. When I finished, I was in tears. He said the journal had changed his life! (He is now a successful and established artist himself.)

M.R./ Robert, you've mentioned attending art biennials worldwide. Could you expand on that experience, and what it's meant to you to be able to view so much contemporary art in those diverse locations?

R.S./ Through the late 80s until the mid-2010s I'd begun to attend a number of art biennials. The first was in Havana in 1989, and I went to four subsequent ones there. The experiences I had in Havana, the artists I met from around the world, most of them Cuban or from other Latin American countries, opened a whole new world to me, one that would lead to my teaching courses in contemporary Latin American art at Marywood and the University of Scranton.

From 1990 on, I also spent more time in Europe attending Biennials in Venice, Berlin, Prague, Istanbul, Tirana, and in Kassel, Germany for Documenta, along with others in Santa Fe and at the Whitney Museum in New York City. I also attended the Munster Sculpture Project and Manifesta along with a number of other individual and group exhibitions in Europe. Each of these experiences, conferences, and the artists and curators I met, added significantly to what I could bring to my teaching.

M.R./ So much of the important work you've done as a teacher and curator is closely linked to your deep involvement in the struggle for social justice. And you've been involved in that struggle in several countries. Can you tell me how you first realized class and other differences, first saw them as something you wanted to help change? Can you speak now about your early political awareness and the first movement with which you were involved?

R.S./ I have mentioned that my father was against the Vietnam War from the very start, but I was a bit more conservative than he was during my high school days, due mostly to the influence of the social studies teacher I mentioned earlier. And it wasn't until I was an exchange student in Bogotá, Colombia in the summer of 1968 that I moved quickly to the left.

M.R./ Nineteen sixty-eight was such a pivotal year for so many, with the uprisings at Columbia University in New York, May in Paris, and the Mexican student movement, which impacted my own life so deeply. It's interesting, in this respect, to hear that your consciousness was raised in Bogotá.

R.S./ I should also mention that my father rarely spoke about politics in the house. It wasn't until I became more active that he not only spoke up more in support of those issues with which I was involved, but actively took part in nearly all the local demonstrations I organized in the Scranton area, including coming out on a cold morning in late December 1989 to join us in an event to protest the U.S. invasion of Panama. At the time he was undergoing daily radiation for prostate cancer, something I would also go through many years later. I had said to my dad that it was far too cold and that, because he was weakened by the radiation, he should stay home. But when we gathered at the county courthouse that morning his little VW pulled up and he got out all bundled up to join us.

But back to my time in Bogotá. I remember that when I was an exchange student there I attended high school for a short time. I'd already graduated from high school but wanted to have the experience. The first day a few of the students wanted to show me their history book, especially the chapter covering how the U.S. stole Panama from Colombia. It included a very evil looking caricature of Teddy Roosevelt. That certainly wasn't the "history" I was taught in high school in the States. From that moment on, I realized how and why "history" was written, by whom and for whom. By the time I entered American University, just after my return to the States, I knew that political science, the major I'd had signed up for, wasn't for me. I dropped it and began considering art as a major. From art I shifted to anthropology where I created my interdisciplinary major, Contemporary Community Studies.

I was clearly not interested in following a traditional anthropology major, but I liked the vantage point that anthropology provided, of looking at a culture with the critical, more open focus that anthropology offered, unlike sociology which in most instances works with the accepted norms within society. But at that time anthropology was almost exclusively interested in "the other," "primitive" societies. My approach to integrating anthropology, sociology and psychology to form a major we called Contemporary Community Studies, using Erich Fromm's The Sane Society *as a foundational text, turned the study and view towards the society within which we lived, with a critical, more open focus than anthropology offered.*

Since this was fall 1968, and American University was in Washington, D.C. I didn't have to go far to go to take part in protest actions against the Vietnam War. By my second year at AU, having met a new Quaker friend, Mark Looney, who came from a family steeped in anti-war activism, and on his initiative, a few other friends and I, along with Mark, started a group on campus: AU Peace Through Non-Violent Action. We worked with national organizers to help house those coming to the capital for major protests, held teach-ins, presented workshops in non-violent training, had an office for draft and vocation counseling in the student life building, and much more. I was active in each of these areas. I can remember at one teach-in I was given three films on the effects of napalm bombing. I screened the first and, after showing it, said I had two more but that, from my standpoint, if you were not convinced by the horrors shown in the first film, I doubted that watching two more would change your mind.

Every morning, we leafleted at Ward Circle, the major intersection of Massachusetts and Nebraska Avenues that passed through one end of campus. Many government workers traveled to work along Massachusetts Avenue from their homes in southern Maryland. One morning we created quite a scene when the car in which Melvin Laird was riding tried to get through on his way to the Pentagon.[65] *He must have found an alternate route because we never saw him again.*

65. Secretary of defense under President Nixon from 1969 to 1973.

Robert Schweitzer at different points in his life. In the one taken out of doors, he is visiting the author at her home in New Mexico. All images by Margaret Randall.

Most days when we were leafleting, those passing by would just open their window a crack to take the papers we were handing out, if they even did that. I believe those in the cars felt they needed to do so to keep us from harassing them further. But everything changed on the morning of May 5th, 1970, following the student massacre at Kent State the day before. On that morning, so many people who had just opened their windows a crack the day before rolled them down, some with tears in their eyes. They eagerly took our information sheet. It took the loss of four student lives to finally open their eyes, something the loss of over a million North Vietnam citizens and tens of thousands of U.S. soldiers hadn't done. From that day on, we felt the change that was slowly taking place. The major demonstrations increased in size, with many more adults involved, not just primarily students.

While I was a draft counselor, I was able to help numbers of students with getting medical deferments and applying for Conscientious Objector status. But I also realized that our phones were being tapped. During one call I received, it was so obvious that it was clear they wanted us to know that they were tapping. The caller sounded like a younger woman, who said that she was desperate to get her father to Canada and wanted me to tell her over the phone how to do that. About every 30 seconds I could hear a faint beep in the background. I told her that I couldn't discuss any options over the phone, and that her father was more than welcome to come to the office to see me. Which of course he never did. On another call I was on, from the French press, when the subject of our "secretive" (within the U.S.)

bombing of Cambodia came up, the call was immediately cut off.

AU was often tear-gassed by the D.C. police as "practice," especially just before a major demonstration. And interestingly, the tear gassing got more of the student body involved, folks who hadn't been active prior. I took part in every major demonstration in D.C. from 1968 on but was never arrested. I was tear gassed often, though, including so heavily during one demonstration near the South Vietnamese embassy that I couldn't see. And I remember how someone working in a hotel, just alongside where I was standing, took my arm and brought me in and helped me wash out my eyes. This act of kindness by a stranger who easily could have locked the door to keep any of us out was so greatly appreciated by me, and it expressed such a needed level of decency amidst the chaos of those times.

If I remember correctly, I had turned my draft card into my Congressperson in 1970. Soon after, I went to see him in his office in D.C. But when I arrived his assistant immediately took me into another room, scolded me and demanded I take back my card. Of course I refused and told him that the blood was on his and the Congressperson's hands, which only made him angrier. Weeks later I received a letter from my local draft board with a "new" draft card, this one with Conscientious Objector status. I can't remember just when, but I had filled out the papers to apply for C.O. status long before this, turning them into my local draft board in Scranton, but had never had a hearing with the board, which was a requirement. So, receiving this status without the hearing came as a shock.

I wrote to them that I wouldn't accept the C.O. status, that I was still a student, and that if they wanted to go further, I would see them in court. I don't really know why they did nothing more, except possibly they didn't want to have a court case in Scranton, especially with the son of a family that was respected, and because I had strong backing in my C.O. papers from other highly respected community leaders.

From the mid 70s to the early 80s my political activism slowed down, at least in the larger public sphere of rallies and organizing. I certainly remained aware of what was taking place, primarily in Latin America. The coup in Chile, through which Pinochet destroyed the hopes of the Allende government, was supported by Henry Kissinger and was one of the events that kept me focused on U.S. policy. After the Chilean coup, I also remember attending one of the first concerts that Inti-Illimani gave in NYC at Avery Fisher Hall.[66] *This was March 1979. There were guards outside, and the event wasn't highly publicized for fear Pinochet's henchmen might try to assassinate the musicians. It was only months later that Orlando Letelier was murdered by Pinochet on U.S. soil.*

It wasn't until after the Sandinista Revolution in 1979, and the rise of the Contras with the support of the Reagan Administration, that I again began protesting in

66. Inti-Illimani is an instrumental and vocal Latin American folk music ensemble from Chile. The band was formed in 1967 by a group of university students, and it acquired widespread popularity in Chile for its song "Venceremos," which became the anthem of Salvador Allende's Popular Unity government. After the 1973 coup and until the restoration of democracy so many years later, the group remained outside the country, touring the world to raise awareness of the situation in its homeland.

the streets and in the press. I was working at the Everhart by that time, but fortunately the director and I shared similar political views, and although he wasn't an activist, he was supportive of my activities, and I was given a bit more flexibility regarding my hours and the days I might want to take off.

29 March 1989

Dear Margaret:

It must be because I write so infrequently, that as I approach the moment, I feel such an overwhelming flood of thoughts that it is somewhat paralyzing. I received your draft of the essay "Woman to Woman, Our Art in Our Lives," and upon my first reading I felt within a floodgate of thoughts, concerns, and past dialogues reoccurring, vivid ones which would have so greatly benefited from the inclusion of this essay. In one context I think of the art history classes in which I would introduce women's art as the vital and necessary expression that could (and eventually would) break down the dominant, male, construct which has forever "legitimized" the incorporation of form/expression in the art world. Initially most of the students, both men and women, would challenge my statement, a challenge I would always consider significant and healthy, since it would be an active element in further discussions. By the end of the semester most of the students would have begun to develop a clearly stated, well thought out personal point of view on the issue.

As for now, Amy[67] and I are off to Mexico and Nicaragua on Friday and will probably not be in touch with you again until

67. Amy Weigand. She and Robert were partners on and off for several years, in the mid-eighties until the mid-nineties, and remain friends, having participated together in many political actions in the United States and abroad. She is a lawyer.

the latter part of April. I trust all is well with you and I look forward to reading whatever journal notes arrive when I return.

As always, the struggle continues—and we are together! Love, Bob

14 June 1989

Margaret:

I have made inquiries and sent information to two exhibition spaces in the Hartford area and will call them within a week to discuss the possibilities for an exhibition during the time you will be at Trinity. I also spoke to Belena Chapp in Delaware, and she appreciated you sending the slides—she continues to be interested in making an exhibition happen when you are there. I will continue to do what I can.

I also appreciate you sending me the three recent prints. I am personally drawn to the incredible unity of place and time/space in your work—the present moment and the awareness of past: certain and uncertain. If space carries an oral history, you have chronicled it.

I have enclosed a few black and white images from our most recent experience in Nicaragua. These represent the first black and white photographs I have ever taken—I normally use photography/slides only to visually back up or stimulate discussion during a presentation.

I hope you like them; both are from Condega—one is at the school (now with 350 students in the morning session and another 350 in the afternoon) that Amy and I helped to build.

We are preparing to turn the bookstore into an exhibition/information center to celebrate the 10th anniversary of the Sandinista Revolution. I had hoped to be in Nicaragua for the celebration, but that didn't turn out to be possible—maybe later in the year.

I am presently trying to put together an exhibition for early next year to focus on the much-discussed issue of "the other." I do not want to present an exhibition of/about the "marginalized other" (typically done by the white male critic/author) but generate an exhibition of/by primarily Central and South American artists who are creating work that points towards the "dangerous other" (white-male-establishment-authoritarian-imperialists). Love, Bob.

[undated, but its content shows this letter to be from the end of August 1989]

Margaret:

I am sure you are receiving 100s of letters such as this—please add this to others as we each express our love, respect and solidarity—*la lucha continua*!

Amy and I were having dinner at the bookstore and for the first time in a very long time we were not listening to *All Things Considered* (a friend was outside the bookstore when I arrived to open and we began to talk, then Amy arrived, the discussions continued, and the radio was never turned on).

Suddenly the phone rang (I suppose phones always ring suddenly—there is hardly ever a warning) and it was a friend from a neighboring town who I see only about four or five times a year. With great urgency in his voice, he said: "Do you have All Things Considered on?" My reply was obviously "No" and he said: "Turn it on—Margaret Randall is speaking, and she just won her case!" Within seconds we were listening to your voice and realized it was true. We expressed every positive utterance with the hugest of smiles on our faces and a few tears mixed in.

That evening when I wasn't making calls to tell friends, friends were calling us to tell us they had heard the news—this went on for hours and continued into the next day. You have touched so many people here, most of whom you have never actually met, but they all care and celebrate with you.

It was SO good to hear Barbara's voice that night—to be able to reach her and in so doing you also meant so much to me. I am sure the calls never ended then—we wanted to be among them. As I told Barbara, the first thought that came to my mind (with fresh images from your most recent journal notes) was that I could see you holding your grandchildren in the country of your birth and then being able to return to the countries of their births—a right you have been so wrongfully denied for the past five years.

Within an hour after calling you, we had a new sign in the Voices Bookstore window expressing that same feeling.

In solidarity. Our love, respect, and support will be with you always! Bob and Amy

August 5, 1992

Dear Bob:

Well, I am back from my month of field work in Nicaragua. And, as promised, here's a letter. In some ways it seems as if I've been back for weeks. In reality, it's only been six days (six days?!), but—as you know—time does very strange things when you move your body from one world to another. Early last Wednesday morning I was standing in the middle of the crowded, very hot, confusing Managua airport, thinking hard about leaving that place once again. I thought about the time I'd spent there: excellent in terms of work accomplished, constantly painful in the sense of how I felt each day. The city itself had become ugly to me: sprawling areas of ragged open land, now filling with the shanty towns of the many ex-Contras who have returned. And I wondered: Was Managua always this ugly? Was it this ugly when I lived there? The destitute areas were much the same. The destruction of poverty overlaid upon the destruction of war in turn overlaid upon the destruction of the 1972 earthquake: all that was also the Managua I knew in the early eighties. But it was also absolutely different. Perhaps hope became a tangible part of my previous image. In ways I now find hard to articulate, revolution filled those empty spaces back then.

In the airport that morning I also thought about the 50% unemployment rate (government-conceded figures), the fact that food and other basics cost approximately 10% more than in the US, the terrible problems my friends who are Sandinistas have had getting or keeping jobs. And I thought about the dispersal of the FSLN itself, the splits and fragmentations, the corruption brought on by an acquisition of power on the part of some of the higher echelons of the party. The betrayals and corruption that emanate from the misuse of power are mind-boggling, appalling.

Then, as if pinching myself to make sure I was awake, I remembered the Plaza. Going with 50,000 others to Revolution Square on July 19th. They were celebrating the 13th anniversary of the revolution as if the FSLN was still in power. It was extraordinary, like old times, Visually, if one didn't know what had happened since, it might have been July 19th, 1981 or '82. You knew the FSLN had lost, you knew this is a different era, a game played by different rules. And yet there they were, tens of thousands of Nicaraguans, their red and black flags flying, many of the youngsters with their faces painted or other signs of struggle kept alive. We sang, chanted, screamed. I left after the official celebration but many people and whole families stayed there all day, eating, drinking, celebrating. And I remembered Dora María Téllez, towards the end of the very long interview I did with her, telling me: "You know, Margaret, Nicaragua is a very surprising place. We mustn't forget that. Anything can happen and will."[68]

So, there I was one Wednesday morning in the heat of the Managua airport and with all these feelings and images swirling about in my head. And six or seven hours later I was in Albuquerque, being picked up at our local airport by Barbara, retrieving my luggage in perfect efficiency, driving along the clean open space of State Highway #556 towards my mountains and home. Even going through immigration and customs and the change of planes in Houston hadn't been enough to ease me from one world into the other. Too quick, too easy. I was home, surrounded by the physical "bounty" of my trip: computer disks containing transcriptions of close to thirty interviews with Nicaraguan women—surprising interviews, powerfully feminist, questioning everything, challenging everything—a carefully-wrapped lead-protected bundle of film, 35 rolls of it, a month's worth of badly hand-washed clothes I was eager to feed to the washing machine. And so many memories.

Now it is early the next Wednesday morning. Although there is only one hour's difference between Managua and Albuquerque, I still feel uncomfortable in the temporal

68. Dora María Téllez is one of the important figures of the Sandinista struggle, and one who has maintained her honesty and commitment. She fought against Somoza, then served in various positions in the Sandinista government, including Minister of Public Health. She broke with the FSLN when it went bad and continued the struggle for justice. When Daniel Ortega and Rosario Murillo grabbed power, they harassed and eventually imprisoned her for almost two years. She was one of several hundred political prisoners released and banished from the country in 2023. Currently, she is living in Spain, writing a memoir. I interviewed Dora María for *Sandino's Daughters* and again for *Sandino's Daughters Revisited.*

transition. Of course I came back to great mountains of accumulated work. The amount of mail alone is staggering. I wanted to develop my film as soon as possible, for I knew my audio material was excellent and wanted to find out if my visual material measured up. I spent a few days trying to pace myself, attending to what I considered priority business first, fitting in what I wanted to be doing in bits and pieces around the edges. I did develop all my film and made contact sheets of my images, plus prints of a few pictures I wanted to send to friends right away. That was exciting, because my images are everything I hoped for and in some cases more. I also printed out my interview transcripts and notes, more as a reminder of the work ahead than anything else. I now have these piles of "raw material" sitting on a large table in my studio, a constant visual reminder that I have exactly six months to make this book happen. And I organized my studio—clearing out havoc in preparation for the discipline of daily work.

What more to say about Nicaragua? Perhaps I am loath to say too much right now. For the book is already writing itself in my head. I can tell you that the fragile, and in many ways artificial, power of the conservative government is showing more cracks every day. The last week I was in Managua there were outbursts of fighting in the streets almost daily and every night. Young people forced to take early retirement from the army and begging for retirement benefits against police trying to keep order around their demonstrations. University students marching by the thousands, demanding 6% of the national budget be given to the schools. Transportation workers (buses or what pass for buses, and taxis) were on strike for four or five days. And from the countryside there was news of even greater upheaval. In the north sporadic fighting continues to rage.

I confronted the usual shock one experiences when returning to a place one has lived—inevitably, there are those who died without your knowing, those who are out of work, those who once held high level government posts now selling hot dogs or used clothing in the streets. I'm sure you felt this when you were there. It's hard. And everything one finds to do somehow seems like mere band aids.

So, I came home filled with experience, memory, the need to assimilate and articulate a great deal. I look forward to the coming months in which I hope to move through this challenge. I also came home to the publication of a new little poetry collection, *Dancing with the Doe,* which West End brought out here in Albuquerque.

An immediate demand, in terms of work, was that the page proofs of *Gathering Rage: The Failure of Twentieth Century Revolutions to Develop a Feminist Agenda* were waiting for me to look over. As you know, this book started out being a 30-page essay. It grew and grew, over a period of a year or more, and I finally "finished" it upon my return from Hartford this spring. To my surprise, none of the feminist presses were interested. But *Monthly Review* took it immediately.

In Nicaragua, I thought a great deal more about the issues raised in *Gathering Rage.* And I talked about my ideas with a number of women there, among them Sofía Montenegro, a brilliant feminist theoretician who is also the editorial page editor of *Barricada*, the Sandinista daily. I came home more than ever confirmed in my observations and thoughts. So, it was very gratifying to be able to go through those page proofs. With my mother I worked on the purely grammatical and typographical. And then I went through the book again, adding bits and pieces that my recent Nicaraguan experience made possible. The proofs go back to MR this morning. And the book should be out in October.

Barbara starts work the 12th of this month. She got a job teaching mainstreamed learning disabled fourth and fifth graders at the same school where she's been doing her student teaching. Adrienne Rich and Michelle Cliff will be visiting next week and we're taking a couple of nights off to drive up to Mesa Verde with them.[69] Ruth Hubbard and George Wald are also coming out for a few days at the end of September.[70] And in early September I'll be spending a few days in Mexico City, visiting my daughters there and my new grandchild: Sarah's son Ricardo Sergio who was born just before I left for Managua. I also have a new grandson in Paris, Daniel Pablo, born into Gregory and Laura's family the month before. In late October I'm taking a group of women to Cuba, the first time back for me in so long. So, there are exciting intervals in the offing, but most solidly work, I hope.

Dear Bob, please be in touch. I need to know how things are going in your life, what you are doing. Much love, Margaret.

---

69. Adrienne Rich (1929–2012) was an American poet, essayist, and feminist. She was a good friend, who volunteered to spend the week at my first immigration trial in El Paso, where she made herself indispensable. Michelle Cliff (1946–2016) was a Jamaican/American author and Rich's longtime partner. She and I taught together at Trinity College in Hartford for several years.

70. Ruth Hubbard (1924–2016) was a feminist biologist and the first woman to hold a tenured position in biology at Harvard University. She was a longtime friend. We wrote a book together, *The Shape of Red: Insider/Outsider Reflections*, published by Cleis Press in 1988 and in Japanese two years later. Ruth's husband, George Wald (1906–1997), was an American scientist and activist who studied pigments in the retina. He won a share of the 1967 Nobel Prize in Physiology or Medicine.

10 November 1992

Margaret and Barbara:

Your letters, your caring, your warmth, have meant a great deal to me. We share a most remarkable friendship, and yes in the silences we still know and can feel our closeness.

I can't really say that my future life choices are any clearer to me now than a month ago, but I am not as troubled by that fact as I was then—I trust that as I continue to be involved in what matters to me, I will remain open to meaningful possibilities and act on them.

Your excitement and joy, present in the developing of your next book on Nicaragua, is so good to hear. Your excitement was so clear to me as I sat on the corner of your bed looking over the photographs and listening to your impressions. I can still feel and see in your eyes and voice the power and resonance of the Nicaraguan women whose feminist identity and struggle have meant that they, with such clear conviction, have taken that struggle into their own hands and are shaping it by their vision. You mentioned that you might be able to share some of those interviews with me—if it is at all possible, I would certainly be most honored to read them.

Speaking of being honored by you, I had a call last week (which you are certainly aware of) from Phyllis at *New Directions for Women*. The thought of having a photograph which I took of Rigoberta Menchú appear with an article written by you is so incredibly wonderful and generous. I mentioned to Phyllis that the quality of the photograph may not be what they want for the publication and therefore I would understand if they did not choose to use it. I will be sending two photographs on to her to choose from, but since I was using a high-speed film at the time I took the pictures I feel that the images may be too grainy. Whatever the result,

I truly appreciate your suggestion to her—I am deeply honored.

I hope that as the school year moves along Barbara continues to find energy and satisfaction in the wonderful work—the clarity and insight, the heartfelt effort and commitment—she brings to the classroom. I'm with you, Barbara!

I'll close for now, as I look at your wonderful faces, smiles, and as I taste the aroma of sagebrush and juniper.

Love, Bob

Back to Robert's written responses to my recent online questions:

R.S./ In Scranton I joined up with a group of friends who were involved with the Fellowship of Reconciliation to form a core group of activists who would focus primarily on Nicaragua and El Salvador, and on the U.S. policy of covertly (and overtly) funding the Contras. We established information tables in the courthouse square in Scranton, where we would provide updates on what was taking place in those two Central American countries and inform the public of upcoming demonstrations, locally and nationally.

In 1986 one of the members of our local group went to Nicaragua as a member of a solidarity brigade, and I followed in February of 1987 to take part in the last stage of the coffee harvest. Our brigade numbered about 15, with members from across the U.S, and at the UPE[71] *we met up with other internationalists, especially a large group from Brazil, to harvest all the remaining coffee*

71. UPE, in Sandinista Nicaragua the state farms were called Unidades de Producción Estatal (State Production Units).

beans on the trees (green, ripe, and over-ripe, to clear the plants for the next season). The UPE was located in the mountains north of Matagalpa and, as if selected with me in mind, was known by the name "La Pintada" (an earlier brigade of Nicaraguan artists had painted murals on a number of the buildings there). There were nights when we could hear gunfire off in the distance. The Contras did everything they could to destroy all aspects of the country's coffee production and exportation.

Along with harvesting coffee, we had more than a week for a number of talks in Managua, meeting with government officials as well as local cultural workers. I had brought with me two of your books (before ever meeting you). And I was excited that during one of the talks we had a discussion with Vidaluz Meneses, who kindly signed the top of the page at the beginning of your chapter on her.[72] *At one of the other meetings a film was to be shown and our coordinator and translator, who knew that I had your books with me, said as we entered the house for the film that this was your home, where you'd lived in Managua. I remember it had a number of your photographs on the walls. Seeing those photographs did more than plant the seed that eventually led to working with you on the Everhart exhibition.*

Over the next five-plus years I made at least nine more trips to Nicaragua, and between 1988 and 1989 Amy I made a number of those trips together, helping to

---

72. Vidaluz Meneses (1944–2016) was a Nicaraguan poet whose father was a general in Somoza's army. She defied her family by joining the FSLN. The interview she signed for Robert is in *Risking a Somersault in the Air.* I also interviewed her for *Sandino's Daughters Revisited.* In both interviews she tells dramatic stories of her lifelong struggle for justice.

build a school in Condega in 1988, and then being involved in a number of projects in Estelí, mainly working with the organization of Mothers of Heroes and Martyrs. There were two groups in Estelí, one that managed to get the most funding from international solidarity groups (they also seemed to be the most educated and more middle-class), and another, made up of poorer women who had little say or access to those funds, and who tried to establish a small food stand, as well as making and selling plastic flowers for the home and cemetery, to raise money to help their families. Amy and I were more involved with this second group, and even though we were no longer living together, I would return on my own to bring funds and supplies. The first time we went back they asked if we could paint the interior of their stand, which of course we were more than glad to do. I remember the colors they chose for the paint, certainly not anything I would have considered, but we painted as they wished, and it turned out great!

I also remember when I brought over $400 in cash to the mothers in Estelí, certain friends in the States asked me how I would tell the women to use the money. I said: "However they feel it will best help them." It was one of those not-so-subtle paternalistic attitudes that continue to be expressed by so many well-intentioned people in the States. I said it was more important and respectful for them to make those decisions, and if what they chose worked out well, all the better. But no matter the result, it was their decision that they would either celebrate or learn from.

Prior to another trip I made to Nicaragua I was asked by another organization if I could bring much needed medical supplies for the hospital in Estelí. I had a good friend in Scranton who was the head of one of the city's hospitals, and he'd once told me with great pride that his father was an old Italian Socialist. So, I asked, in his father's name, if he might be able to put aside some operating room supplies. A few days later I picked up a huge plastic bag filled with items I didn't have a clue about and managed to pack them up and bring them down. Before I turned them over, another person, who was a nurse in the States, looked at the items in the bag and she said she couldn't believe what I had been able to bring. She said they were so expensive that in the States they would have cost many thousands of dollars! And of course, the Nicaraguan doctor and nurse who received this gift broke into tears as well as huge smiles!

During the time I was organizing protests in Scranton, and getting arrested at demonstrations against aid to the Contras in NYC, D.C. and Virginia, I was also active with CISPES, and took part in demonstrations against U.S. support for the government of José Duarte in El Salvador as well as against Proctor and Gamble, the US company that sold Folgers coffee and primarily used beans that were harvested in El Salvador, providing funds to the Duarte government and to the paramilitary gangs controlled by the landowners who grew the coffee.

It was at the October 17, 1988 "Blockade the Pentagon" demonstration where, after a very physical assault (I was clubbed between the legs by one police office), both Amy and I were thrown to the ground. Prior to that moment, Amy and I had only met once at the University of Scranton, where she was a student at the time. I had given a talk on Nicaragua, and then we both took part in the non-violent training session the day before the action at the Pentagon. Suddenly there we were, side by side on the ground.

I had been arrested a number of times by then but knew that this was her first time. Amy seemed very nervous, and I looked at her and said: "I had wondered what it would be like to lie in the grass next to you looking up at the clouds, but I didn't quite imagine it would be like this." She laughed and thanked me. We marked that as our anniversary from then on. And we both went on for the next two years getting arrested together on many more occasions, and even spent a week in jail after one arrest (we were the only two protesters out of hundreds who refused to pay the fine). I was arrested about two dozen times in all, from the first demonstration in D.C. until sometime in the early 90s.

Back in Scranton, I started two bookstores in the 80s that lasted a little over a year each, the first in 1987 and the second in 1989. Both were intended more to create an environment for sharing ideas than as viable businesses, and they did just that. They were meeting places where I hoped to find other people in the community who had similar interests. Neither would provide a source of income. I knew I would need to underwrite them with income from my position at the Everhart.

The first bookstore was named Voices. It was in a huge space on the first floor of an old department store that had very high almost floor to ceiling windows looking out onto one of the main streets in Scranton. I was as excited about the windows as I was about the interior space. The place hadn't been used in years, and the rent was low, so I was able to divide it up as I wanted. I still think of that as my favorite personal time. I was working at the Everhart, so the bookstore was open only at night. While I was working to divide up the space, I had a place in the back where I had a futon and often slept. Some nights we stayed open until well after midnight, and many old and new friends came to hang out, watch art films, listen to new jazz, discuss and read poetry, and share information on a wide range of political issues.

I was able to use the large windows as a billboard. My landlord was furious with me for that, but I said a bookstore is about free speech, and so are the windows. The books covered a wide range of subjects, from known and little-known poetry and literature to a large selection of artists' books (at that time only found at a few bookstores in Pennsylvania), to politics (including some of your books, again before I knew you) and Eastern Religions. There was a table to sit at and have a free cup of "illegal" Nicaraguan coffee and a large information table with folders on various issues. It was a wonderful place.

The store's second iteration, also called Voices, opened across the street from the University of Scranton on the ground level. This was the store that Amy and I opened together. It was much more political in the selection of books and videos offered, though also with free Nicaraguan coffee and a much more active bulletin board, this one against our local Congressperson. The landlord at this location never complained. He had a tailor shop in the space next to ours. This store was also primarily open at night, but a good friend who broke her leg offered to keep it open on certain days. She told me that one afternoon two men in suits came in and one of them bought a book by Eduardo Galeano. The two men in suits were what caught my attention. I thought that possibly they were from the local FBI office (a student who I knew, whose father worked for the FBI, told me that they were watching the bookstore—such a waste of tax dollars). It turned out that one was the editor of the major newspaper in town, and the other was the head of the printer's union at the paper, and a Socialist. We soon became great friends.

On the night I learned that we had invaded Panama to force Noriega out, I called the editor and said I wasn't sure what he was going to do, but we would be in the streets. The next morning, he had printed a condemnation of the invasion on the editorial page of the paper, one of the few papers in the country to do so. He got plenty of flak from other workers for months after that. And he is also the editor who, after I sent him material on your immigration case, wrote an editorial in your defense. Certainly, the best "two men in suits" story I will ever have.

In the early '80s I was on the board of our local chapter of the Sierra Club, and I remember at one meeting when the discussion of raising funds came up, someone suggested a bake sale. I said why a bake sale when we should be raising money doing something that truly mattered? Why not start a recycling campaign? I was often good for suggestions, but in this case some of the others immediately agreed and did all the legwork to find a monthly drop-off location where we could collect glass, paper, and aluminum. It turned out to be a success. At the drop-off location we could hand out information sheets on a range of issues and meet new people with similar concerns, as well as raise funds for the local chapter. The woman who became most involved with managing our project was eventually hired to direct the county recycling center, which was mandated by the State several years later. It was good that recycling became a priority at the state and national levels, but I felt the loss of person to person contact and exchange that was made possible at our monthly drop-off location.

In 1985 I was the regional coordinator and contact person for the International Shadow Project that was headed by the artist Alan Gussow. Alan and I had become friends when he was a visiting artist at Marywood in the early 80s and that's when he told me about a project he was organizing to take place on the very dark early morning hours of August 6, 1985, forty years after the U.S. dropped the first atomic bomb on Hiroshima. The bomb blast had caused many victims to vaporize in the intense heat, leaving what appeared to be shadows on the pavement where they had last taken breath. Many friends and I cut out black plastic full-bodied "silhouettes" of ourselves that provided the outline around which we rolled the washable white paint very early in the morning, on streets, benches, stairs, and sidewalks throughout the city. We also posted flyers nearby so those coming upon the shadows would understand what they represented. I spent time that day walking around the city, listening to the many interesting comments this provoked. Early on, a reporter for the local newspaper spotted me and said: "Hey Bob, you must be involved in this!" Then we went to both Marywood and the Museum where my friends and I demonstrated how we made the shadows, gave interviews, and I explained that we were part of the international project that Gussow created.

In 1991 I began to work on a project to develop a reader for teachers to counter the celebrations and misinformation that would be planned for the next year commemorating the 500th anniversary of Columbus's "discovery" of America. I attended a statewide teachers meeting in New York. And I traveled to Guatemala for the "Segundo Encuentro de los Indígenas" held in Xelajú (Quetzaltenango), at which Rigoberta Menchú spoke, her first trip back to Guatemala since she'd gone into hiding.[73] *Do you remember the photographs I sent you? They were from that time in Guatemala.*

In the States I applied for a grant from the Pennsylvania Humanities Council to publish a reader that would contain commentary by contemporary Native American activists along with a reading they recommended by another author. I received the grant, but when they reviewed it, they said it was too one-sided, not balanced enough. I was taken aback and explained that "the other side" would be in full evidence during the quincentenary, as it had been for generations, and that our publication would provide the balance for that imbalance. But they didn't accept my argument and refused to work with me to get copyrights for the suggested texts or help with the publishing in any way. In

73. Rigoberta Menchú Tum (1959) is a K'iche' Guatemalan human rights activist, feminist, and Nobel Peace Prize laureate. She has dedicated her life to publicizing the rights of Guatemala's Indigenous peoples during and after that country's Civil War, and to promoting Indigenous rights internationally. Her book, *I, Rigoberta Menchú,* has been translated into many languages.

the end I produced a photocopied volume I was able to use with local teachers, but it never progressed from there.

About my time in Guatemala, I have a very personal memory, one that has left a lasting impression on me for obvious reasons. I was traveling on a public bus one day and it was pulled over by the police. They wanted to see everyone's passport. I hadn't thought about it but, since each of my trips to Cuba were legal, my passport contained a number of Cuban stamps. That proved to be a red flag. The police searched my backpack, found my tape recorder, and in their effort to make it work, broke it. Then the officer told everyone except me to get back on the bus. Fortunately, the bus driver refused to leave, and soon many of the passengers got off the bus again and told the police they wouldn't leave until I was allowed to get back on. The police eventually and reluctantly let me go. I am not sure what would have happened to me if those brave passengers hadn't acted as they did. I tried to tell them how enormously grateful I was. I'm sure that wasn't the first or last time passengers on a bus in Guatemala felt the need to do this, given the political reality there. But I was deeply grateful for the gesture.

After the Sandinista loss in 1990, I continued returning to Nicaragua for a few more years. I also returned to Guatemala in the early 90s. I went at the very end of 1993, and a few days after arriving learned of the Zapatista uprising in Chiapas, so I cut short my time there and took the bus into Chiapas.

Entering Chiapas from the south in early 1994 was a bit surreal. Many were exiting, traveling south, and few internationals other than the press were making their way north. I passed many army tanks, officers checking cars and papers, but somehow managed to make it to San Cristóbal de las Casas where the town square was filled with people. The church was covered with newspaper articles, a huge satellite disc was aimed high to ensure TV coverage, and there was press everywhere. Right after my arrival, I applied for and received official press credentials (for the magazine I was writing for back in the States). If I remember correctly, I had the editor send me a letter of introduction by email when I was still in Guatemala, but I may have brought it with me for such an opportunity. When I was deported from Mexico four years later, that "official" document seemed to have no value.

It would take many pages to cover my time in Chiapas over the next four years (1994–1998), all the people I met who were working directly with the Zapatistas, as well as lasting friendships I made with so many Europeans who were also there in solidarity. On different occasions I was part of a rotating group of international solidarity activists who would go to Oventic as human buffers; and I also slept overnight in the office of COMPAZ that was trashed by thugs the day before, again as a deterrent to further destruction.

I brought a video editing machine from the States that the Zapatistas requested. I attended the "Special Talks" in the Fall of 1996, and was able to document the moment when Marcos made his first public "walk" through the streets of San Cristóbal. In 1997 I also journeyed (for a time hidden under bags on a truck, and then in the narrowest log canoe across a river) to Las Tazas where I had been asked to document the illegal deforestation in the surrounding mountains, which I did with both video and still photography. My video became a major part of a documentary called Lacandona: The Zapatistas and Rainforest of Chiapas, Mexico *produced by a group in Vermont. And I attended the Dialogues between the Zapatistas and the Mexican Government in October 1995, occurring under the watchful eye of Bishop Samuel Ruíz.*[74] *I was the second U.S. citizen deported by Zedillo from Chiapas. Being flown from Mexico to McAllen, Texas on 17 February 1998 (Maria Darlington, the first to be deported, was sent out on the 10th). Sadly, I have never returned. My deportation was for ten years, but I believe even that was eliminated after Zedillo lost his bid for reelection. I did travel to college campuses to talk about what was happening there, encouraging others not to be fearful of the deportations, and to go and help out.*

M.R./ Let me interrupt for a moment, Robert, because I have the letters you sent from Chiapas from 1994—the year of the Zapatista uprising—to 1998 when you were finally deported. The other day I came across two particularly chilling ones describing your deportation. I'd like to reproduce excerpts from them:

Friday, February 15, 1998

This week began with my need to obtain an extension of my visa normally a rather routine matter. I decided to ask for

74. Samuel Ruiz García (1924–2011) was a Mexican Catholic prelate who served as bishop of the Diocese of San Cristóbal de las Casas, Chiapas, from 1959 until 1999. He was progressive and supported the Zapatistas in their talks with the government.

additional days at the immigration office here in San Cristóbal where they give 15 days. They really don't want people to stay in Chiapas longer than that. Those who do wish to remain longer simply go to a city further north where you can often get 60 or 90 days.

What makes renewal more problematic here is that this is one of the few areas where they check "the black book" to see if you've had previous problems in Chiapas. I knew I had a record in their office but until now wasn't sure that I was in the book, especially with my new passport. I am sure now.

After filling out the form, which everyone must do, I waited only to be given a paper stating that I had to return the next day (Tuesday). This was the first sign that I may be in for trouble. Over the weekend several friends had their visas taken from them as they returned from Polho, and on Tuesday they were before me in the line to enter the immigration office. I knew what the questioning process would be like from my experience over a year ago when my visa was taken from me as I was returning from La Realidad. Since each person was about to go through nearly three hours of questioning, I knew they would never have time for me if I was fourth in line. They told me to sit and wait. I again complained (with humor) and about an hour later someone came out from the inner office and said that I should return the next day.

What I did not know at this point was that later that afternoon they had scheduled to meet with another U.S. resident, and she was going to be expelled. This I learned later that evening. When Maria Darlington was deported, she was taken directly from the Migra office to Tuxtla, from there flown to Mexico City and then on to Texas. She was not allowed to return to her house for her belongings or arrange to have her car taken back to the U.S.—she was only able to take what she had on her person. What she had been accused of doing was "participating" in political activities.

Maria is a 60-year-old Quaker originally from Pennsylvania. Like most of us she has been involved with various solidarity groups from the U.S., such as Pastors for Peace, that have distributed aid here. She has been in this area for a number of years, staying for a few months at a time, photographing and writing about the situation. The video clip they had on her (they film EVERYTHING) was made when she was photographing a march during which a Mexican friend asked her to hold one end of a banner while she went to the bathroom, only a few minutes. They could certainly tell from their video that what she was doing was filming, and this brief moment was not an act of "participation." Clearly, they wanted an excuse to expel her, possibly as an example.

Therefore, on Wednesday night I had to begin to consider what I would need to do next, such as get the numbers of a lawyer and the U.S. Embassy (which I did, though I realized that neither of these numbers would be of any real help). On the other hand, many people and organizations here are aware of my situation and they check in on me, or I report to them daily, so they know of my whereabouts and any possible change in my status—this is most comforting.

One additional thing I did Tuesday night was to prepare two bags which contained my cameras, some clothes and papers which I wanted to make sure I would be able to carry with me to the U.S. if I was to be made to leave suddenly as Maria had been. Being prepared, not paranoid.

Wednesday, I arrived at the Migra office early and within a half hour was told to go into the inner office. I was met by an immigration officer who was to interrogate me. As I sat down, he said: "You have been here before." And I replied "yes."

I could see my rather thick file on his desk, no surprise. After the initial name, address, etc. he began the three-hour series of questions which were very similar to the ones I had answered over a year ago. I said that he already had most of my answers, but I would be willing to go through the process again.

Questions followed such as: Who is paying for your trip? Why did you come to Chiapas? Where have you traveled while in Chiapas? (They know the answer to these questions, so I began each response with: "Well you already know that I have been to . . ."). What organizations do you belong to? Etc. They also ask certain trap questions such as: Do you believe that your human rights have been violated by the Mexican government? Have the military or other immigration officials molested you in any way? Then the key question: Have you "participated" in any political activities while in Mexico? They also ask what you feel you are entitled to do as a tourist. This question is what you respond to in order to protect yourself from the appearance of participation. Certainly, a tourist is allowed to gather information, photograph, observe, and experience the reality of the country. And this is in fact precisely what I do. Following this interrogation, I was given a paper stating I was to return tomorrow at noon for my visa.

When I arrived at the office Thursday just before noon, I was told that I would have to come back later because they had not yet received the authorization to give me additional days. I began to complain, and said I wanted to talk to the immigration officer. He came out and asked me to come into his office. There he said that there was nothing he could do without this authorization.

I asked him directly: "Could I be denied additional days and be made to leave immediately?" He asked me why I asked this question, and I replied that I knew that another U.S.

citizen had been expelled the day before and I was concerned. He said that he did not "feel" that this would happen to me since I had not participated in any political activity. I was not reassured by his comment. I knew that the delay was because they were looking through all the videos and photos they have in order to "find" something—apparently, they are having a difficult time.

Before leaving his office, I asked for a number I could call to speak with him. I wasn't going to make another trip to the office without knowing I was going to receive my visa. He gave me two numbers.

Later that day I called again and still no authorization—"call tomorrow."

On Friday I made three calls and the last message to me was to come in Monday morning. I said: "I'll call first."

Therefore, as I write this update I am still without a visa and waiting. I spoke with my parents last night and I was most encouraged to learn that there was an article in their local paper about Maria's expulsion.

My treatment and situation with Migra have become common knowledge here—many friends come up to me on the street to find out how I am doing, and I report to the office of the FZLN daily so that they are up to date on my status—this is comforting but unfortunately the paranoia is increasing. This is most tragic since it means that some of the individuals are now deciding not to go out to the communities and the peace camps where international observers are needed. If this is the result of this way of handling things, then the Zedillo government and the military (which is now for the first time displaying heavy tanks and amphibious vehicles in the area of La Realidad) will have managed to limit this fragile layer of security that the peace camps offer the communities.

To add to my case, *La Jornada* on Thursday stated that the Migra was investigating 10 to 15 foreigners for acts of participation in political activities.[75] And on Friday the PRD (the main opposition political party) protested the government's xenophobic policies which have forced 10 foreigners to be expelled, 200 to receive official orders to leave, 393 to be detained for questioning as to their activities, and at least 15 more under investigation.[76]

We read here of the interview Zedillo gave to the *NYTimes* last week—a monstrous omission of facts and distortion of reality to make his government appear better in the eyes of the international community—one more attempt to further his policy of "make believe."

I will follow up on this message early this week when I know more.

Friday, February 20, 1998

Monday morning, just after I called Migra, Scotty, the AP photographer from Guatemala passed me in the street. He was the AP photographer in Mexico two years ago and I knew him then and had seen him at the Migra office on Friday. He asked me what my immigration status was, and I said I was just told to come in at noon. (He was given a limited visa on Friday, so he was going to leave for Guatemala and come back

75. *La Jornada* is a progressive Mexican daily newspaper, accessible in a print edition and online.

76. The Partido de la Revolución Democrática (Democratic Revolution Party), more commonly referred to as the PRD, was the first left-wing party to unite the different leftist groups that existed in Mexico. Officially founded in 1989, the PRD, then known as the Frente Democrático Nacional (National Democratic Front), emerged following an internal split within the PRI around the PRI's decision not to incorporate democratic reforms into the party's 1988 presidential candidate selection process.

immediately). He asked me if I had already seen the morning paper and I said no, and he handed me his paper and said he had to run—seven bodies had been found in a mass grave outside of a town south of San Cristóbal—seven persons who had been "missing" for the past two months, killed by one of the right-wing paramilitary groups operating in that area of the state.

Taking a taxi to Migra at noon, we drove directly into a march involving over 1,000 Zapatista supporters who were demonstrating to mark the second anniversary of the signing of the still unfulfilled San Andres Accords. I had hoped that the march would have taken place later in the day so that I could photograph and listen to the speeches—but that was not to be. I was off to my eighth day of waiting for my visa at Migra.

After an hour of waiting in the outer office I was brought in to meet another Migra officer, one who had questioned me a year and a half ago—I remembered him and he remembered me. He said that I did not completely answer the questions asked the week before and I said that I did not repeat what I knew they already had in their files. He said that I needed to restate everything. After two hours of additional questioning everything seemed to be in order. During the questioning process he kept using the word "participating" which I corrected every time. I observed, witnessed, gathered information and photographed but did not "participate" in political events. After we finished, he said I would have to come back tomorrow and that this visit would be short—I would get my visa then. I asked if there was a chance I would be expelled, and he said: "No." I mentioned that I had been carrying many of my possessions with me when I came to the office, prepared to leave in a hurry if expelled. He laughed and said I would not need to do that tomorrow. I didn't believe him since he said that this day's interview had to be sent to Mexico City, and they would get back to him about my visa. This is never a good sign. An assistant then handed me a document (one similar to those I had received the previous week) which stated that my appointment for Tuesday was at 2:00 p.m.

While I was waiting to enter the office on Monday, another friend came in who had had her visa taken from her by the Migra soon after she'd arrived in Polho the previous Friday. Now she would have to begin the process I was completing. She is a student and has not been implicated in any prior activities in the area so I felt she wouldn't have a problem regaining her visa, though she was still quite nervous (and I am not aware of what has happened to her).

By the time I made it back into the center of San Cristóbal late Monday afternoon the march and demonstration were over, so I went to visit with some friends and check my e-mail. That night I went to bed early.

Tuesday began with an early morning visit from my friend who I had been with at the Migra office the morning before. She told me she had to go back on Wednesday to answer some questions, and I briefed her on what to expect. She also said that Migra officers had come to her house to check on who was living there, and the rest of the residents were very concerned. The home where she was staying (more like a private *posada* or hotel) has about eleven foreigners at any time, including some long-term visitors. This house check is an extension of the spot checks Migra officers are carrying out on the streets and in the Zócalo. They ask to see your visa and what you are doing in Chiapas. San Cristóbal is beginning to feel like a fascist police state and many foreigners are trying to keep a low profile or are going to the beach for a few weeks. Unfortunately, this is just what the government wants.

After saying goodbye to my friend and wishing her luck (we talked about dinner together on Thursday after she would have her new visa), I packed my bags once again in preparation for my visit to Migra and then went out to visit with a few additional friends. I had coffee that morning with a friend from Denmark who said he was considering writing an article on the problems at Migra and wanted to sit down and talk with me when I returned. We made plans to meet at 6:00 p.m. and go together to take photographs of an International Observer Delegation (over 130 members from Europe and the U.S.) which was arriving in San Cristóbal as we spoke. They would also be giving an open press conference that evening at 7:00. He wished me luck at Migra and we hugged and said goodbye. On my way back to my apartment to get my bags I saw another Mexican friend in the street who is close to the Zapatista struggle. He shook my hand as I passed and said: "Be very careful at Migra." I smiled and said I hoped to see him later.

My bags packed, I took another taxi to Migra for my two o'clock meeting. I waited in the office for about an hour before someone said it would be just another minute—actually about another half hour. Then the person who interviewed me the day before asked to see my passport and a few minutes later said that I needed to come into his office where without sitting down he informed me that the Mexican government decided I was to be expelled from the country immediately. I told him I was glad that I didn't believe him the day before when he said that I would not need to bring my things with me (though much of my clothing, stereo, etc. remains in San Cristóbal). I also told him I felt this was a huge mistake, and certainly not good for Mexico in the eyes of the international community.

Interestingly, one thing he mentioned was that the government had a problem with my writing for my homepage on the internet. I told him that up until now all I had was this homepage, and now they were giving me a voice, a voice I would use as best I could to let others know what was really happening there—just what the government doesn't want. I shook his hand and immediately left with a junior officer who would accompany me to Mexico City. We drove to Tuxtla (1 1/2 hours) and then took a flight to Mexico City (about 1 hour). Coming off the plane I was met by Mexican TV cameras and reporters, I didn't expect this and was not prepared to answer questions, though I did until the Migra officers there ushered me away just as I began to mention the government in my response (friends in Mexico have e-mailed me saying they saw me on TV that evening).

I was taken into a back office at the airport, met by a number of immigration officials and told I would have the chance to meet with a vice consul from the U.S. Embassy. I met with her for about 15 minutes, and she was helpful in a number of ways. She asked how I was and if I had been mistreated. I said I was fine and that my treatment was actually rather friendly and she said that before coming in to talk with me the officials outside said that I seemed calm (a doctor was actually sent in to take my blood pressure, a routine practice there, and he took it three times, asking what my normal pressure was: I said "120 over 80." With a look of surprise, he said that was my pressure at this time—apparently, I was more relaxed than they were, but then what was my choice?) The Embassy vice consul then offered to be in touch with anyone I wished. I said I wanted to be the one to call my parents when I arrived in the States, but she could give out my number to the press. Most importantly, she also mentioned that I might be asked by immigration to sign some papers but that I didn't have to do so. This turned out to be helpful later. She left and gave me her card and asked that I be in touch with her after I arrived home, which I have done.

A number of Migra officials then returned to the office with the papers. The first merely informed me that the laws of Mexico stated that with this expulsion I would not be allowed to return to Mexico without official permission from the head of State and that if I did come in without this permission and was caught, I could face up to 10 years in prison. Since this was essentially a copy of the law, I signed it. The next paper had my "charges" and since I did not agree with their characterization of my activities, I said I wouldn't sign that one. One person stayed with me trying to get me to sign (I would not be allowed to have a copy without signing, he said). I finally told him whether or not I signed it I was still being deported, and by not signing I would leave with my dignity and integrity, and I certainly intended to leave with those. He then left the room, and l began to write my thoughts on what was taking place. As the Migra officers looked in they appeared not to appreciate the fact that I was already writing. I was supposed to be nervous and unsettled.

Just under two hours later I was taken to my flight out of Mexico, destination McAllen, Texas. I said to the officer who accompanied me to the plane that it seemed he would be doing this on a regular basis for a while; he said he thought I was correct.

I arrived in McAllen at about midnight and took a taxi to a nearby Motel 6. I called my parents, and in the morning my travel agent in Scranton, and she managed to find me some rather cheap tickets, considering I was purchasing a one-way fare on the day I was to travel. I managed to get the last bus out of NYC, arriving home in Scranton at 1:40 a.m. on Thursday, where my parents met me at the bus station. I do have exceptional parents!

Earlier, before leaving McAllen, I had checked my answering machine and found two messages, one from the U.S. Embassy in Mexico checking on me and the other from the *NY Times* correspondent in Mexico. I ended up giving an interview to the Times between flights and the article appeared in Thursday's paper, unfortunately with the weakest of possible quotes but fair given the context of her article. Since then, the LA radio station affiliated with Pacifica Radio has called for an interview on Monday, the South American CBS affiliate has called for an interview, and a more regional public radio station wants to interview me next week. This is the voice they gave me. If they'd given me 11 more days, I would only have returned to my homepage.

What I learned when I called the U.S. Embassy in Mexico today was that the following day another U.S. citizen was expelled. I am not surprised. His crime is that he is a member of Pastors for Peace, seen by the Mexican authorities as a major source of their problems.

They claim we have no right to be there, that this is an internal Mexican problem in which acts of solidarity by foreigners with the people of that country, citizens who truly seek and appreciate our presence, is a dangerous precedent. To take this to the extreme, was Hitler's treatment of Jews, gays and gypsies merely a German problem which the international community was to ignore?

M.R./ Robert, your deportation from Mexico was frustrating because it prevented you from returning to that country for a long time and I know you have yet to go back. But it's a small price to pay for the experiences you had and for being able to contribute your solidarity to a very worthy struggle. And you certainly handled the deportation with integrity. I am particularly struck by your comparison of Mexico's treatment of foreigners in Chiapas in the 1990s with Hitler's treatment of Jews, gays, and gypsies—and I would include political dissidents—in the 1930s. Many might feel this is an exaggeration. But looking at it today, when we see a fascist encroachment on our freedoms in so many different areas, the comment was prophetic.

What sorts of political activities were you involved in after your return to the States?

R.S./ From 1988 through 1998 I attended the annual Bread and Puppet "Domestic Resurrection Circus" at their farm in Glover, Vermont. The trumpet player in the band, and his daughter, were among those who'd taken part in the coffee harvest with me in Nicaragua, and we became friends. And before I went to Vermont in 1989, I had been in touch with another friend I'd met in Nicaragua. He was working on translating the new Nicaraguan Constitution, and he sent us the English version. Amy and I took it to Bread and Puppet (1989 was the 200th anniversary of the U.S. Constitution and that was to be part of the Circus's that year). We found a spot in an open field and read it aloud, with many people stopping to listen and ask questions. And in the summer of 1998, after my deportation from Mexico, I organized discussions in that open field to talk about what was happening in Chiapas, something I *also did at a number of college campuses on the east coast.*

I should note that from late 2000 to 2010 much of my focus shifted to taking care of my parents and, full time after my father died, from 2005 to 2010 taking care of my mother who had Alzheimer's.

Those gatherings at the Circus were reenergizing experiences for activists like me, and also places where we would see each other again, share stories, and our plans for the following year.

For Robert, there would always be a following year and more plans for focused well-thought-out actions of civil opposition to government and corporate policies increasingly designed to maximize power and profit at the expense of human well-being. Particularly inspiring to me have been the innovative ways in which he has linked art, education, and political action. But when he retired from teaching and from shepherding the Maslow Collection, his small pension and lack of health care made it impossible for him to continue to live in the United States. His mother's Italian ancestry facilitated European Union citizenship, and he decided to move to a country where more compassionate laws apply.

He lived in Spoleto, Italy, for several years. I dreamed of visiting him there, but that dream never materialized. As Italy's cost of living rose and he struggled to learn Italian, he moved again—to the small, affable, beautiful, and richly cultural Isle of Møn, off the coast of Denmark. There he has been able to make a comfortable life for himself, integrating himself into a community peopled by those of all ages. When he has a medical appointment, the country's decentralized universal health-care system covers most expenses, including picking him up and taking him back home. The difficult Danish language eludes him, but most people speak English. He feels welcomed and at home.

These days, Robert's contact with the international community is largely through email and his Facebook postings, which include commentary on artists and exhibitions around the world as well as local events described through his ever-sharp cultural and political analysis.

III

ARTURO ARANGO: REVOLUTION FROM THE INSIDE

DURING THE MID- TO late 1970s, a group of young poets and writers gathered at our Havana apartment at least three or four evenings a week. They were half my age—in their late teens, as opposed to my late thirties—and came to look to me as an older sister or informal teacher as well as a friend. For me, they were a solid connection to Cuba's poetry world. Antonio Castro, the man I lived with at the time, was a poet and folksinger; he accompanied himself on a cuatro, a small stringed instrument typical of his native Colombia.[77] Occasionally other singers and songwriters would come, several of them among the innovative members of Cuba's Nueva Trova (New Song Movement: Silvio Rodríguez, Pablo Milanés, Noel Nicola, and Vicente and

77. Antonio Castro was born in Colombia, but his family migrated to Venezuela in the 1940s, compelled by poverty. A younger brother died of hunger on that arduous walk. Antonio was involved in one of Venezuela's revolutionary organizations, arrested, and imprisoned for five years. After his release, he went to Cuba to accompany and care for a combatant who was paralyzed from the waist down. We lived together during my last four years in that country. He died in Venezuela in 2022.

Santiago Feliú).[78] For several years, on Saturday mornings we'd all meet at a small plaza on the campus of the University of Havana to read to one another. Sometimes we were joined by one or more of the great Latin American poets of those times: Mario Benedetti from Uruguay, Juan Gelman from Argentina, Roque Dalton from El Salvador.[79] After Roque died fighting his country's dictatorship in 1975, we named the workshop for him.

Among the young Cuban writers, there was Alex Fleites, Víctor Rodríguez Núñez, Norberto Codina, Bladimir Zamora, Ramón Fernández-Larrea and his younger brother Gustavo, Reina María Rodríguez, and Arturo Arango. Alex now lives outside Cuba for periods but spends most of his time in the country. Víctor divides his year between Ohio, where he has just retired from teaching at Kenyon College, and Havana, where he spends summers and holidays. Norberto lives in Cuba. Bladimir remained there until his death. Ramón left Cuba many years ago, disgruntled with the revolution, and now lives in Barcelona, while Gustavo stayed on the island. Reina María lives in Cuba, where her rooftop atelier continues to provide a home for younger poets; her work has won many prizes. Most have published widely. Leonardo Padura also occasionally dropped by. His is one of Cuba's best-known novelists and his books have been translated into many languages. He is critical of the revolution but has developed a public discourse that allows him room to maneuver.

---

78. These singer/songwriters and a few others became well known throughout Latin America and the world. Noel Nicola and Vicente Feliú have since died. The others still perform internationally to huge crowds.

79. These three writers, all of them now long gone, are among Latin America's greatest.

Although he travels a great deal, Arturo continues to live and work in Cuba. In an article many years later, he would say that he received an important part of his literary education on those evenings at my house.

Today, these once intellectually hungry young people are now in their sixties and seventies. Each has made a life on one side or another of the great divide that separates those who remained in Cuba from those who emigrated. Arturo's friendship has been a constant for me. The most startling feature in his angular face is a pair of piercing blue eyes, the pivotal point in his warm smile. He has written several excellent novels, and travels to teach film-script writing, collaborate on films, attend conferences, and promote his books. But he has made his lifelong home in the fishing village of Cojímar, just to the east of Havana. He lives there with his wife, Omaida, and her mother, Nereida. Their daughter, Haydée, and her family live across the street. Their son, Alejandro, has also remained in the country.

When I asked Arturo if he had ever thought about leaving the island, his immediate response was "Never." And he added, "Aside from the country itself, there's my family and, just as important, the cultural community to which I belong. This is where I recognize myself, the place that feeds me spiritually."

Arturo comes from Manzanillo, Granma Province. A family of teachers: His father, grandfather, four uncles and their wives, mother, grandmother, and two sisters all exercised that profession. He also had two brothers. One recently died and the other is a geologist who lives and works in the eastern city of Santiago de Cuba. When we met, Arturo was studying literature at the University of Havana. He graduated in 1973.

I was curious to know if Arturo's whole family had remained in Cuba, as he has, or if some have emigrated.

A.A./ My family is divided in that respect. My mother's and father's families were very close, even before my parents married. My father's family owned a small private school that was closed by the revolution when private education was eliminated. My mother's family owned a modest furniture store which they gave to the revolutionary government in those first heady days after victory. My mother's relatives have all remained supportive of the revolution to one degree or another. They'd all collaborated prior to 1959, and I can remember two occasions when we hid combatants at the house. Among my paternal relatives, everyone but my father eventually turned against the revolution. Even my father became disenchanted, although he always said he hoped I wouldn't inherit his bitterness, and I haven't. After the nineties, many cousins, nieces and their offspring left. Most of them live in Miami.

Throughout our long friendship, Arturo and I have often discussed the ups and downs of the Cuban revolution. When we met, and for years afterward, we believed that, despite an arduous struggle, our dreams of a just society would materialize. I once asked Arturo if he could remember when he realized this wasn't going to happen.

A.A./ I don't think I can pinpoint the moment. But I gradually came to understand that those problems or conflicts we once saw as anomalies or momentary errors were, in fact, systemic. They belonged to the very essence of the system. For example, the failure to permit intellectuals a critical discourse. The Party and government's inability to allow diverse points of view, even from leftists. As the years passed, those systemic errors became more serious, especially in terms of the economy. And now we are paying a very high price.

Although I agree with Arturo's analysis, every time I've visited Cuba, I've come away with the sense that the vision espoused by Fidel and his comrades hasn't completely faded. Cubans are different since 1959. There is an innate sense of justice, even if it's mostly a justice deferred. One feels a sense of solidarity, of empathy for the impoverished of the world. I wondered if Arturo feels this way and, if so, how he would describe it.

A.A./ It's hard to say. On the downside, the most important thing working against that these days is the renewed importance money has. This has come to dominate our social relationships. Class differences have crept back in; there are people who live from hand to mouth, whose salaries or pensions are barely enough for survival. And there are others who have accumulated considerable wealth. But I know what you mean. In comparison with other countries where I've traveled, a real solidarity still exists here. And it shows itself every day. This is what remains of that society we dreamed of creating. Among young people, there is also a powerful resurgence of leftist thought: critical but hopeful. The problem is that the authorities, who are intellectually and politically lazy, treat these young people as if they were the enemy.

One of the revolution's greatest problems, and it's one in which we must all assume a measure of blame, is that we came to see the country as monolithic: the Party, Fidel, the government: all of a piece. And today, when we suffer from an administration that is absolutely broken, this is causing us enormous harm.

Arturo and I have been in constant contact through the years. He is the person I've depended on for accurate news about Cuba and help with various projects—the books I've written about Che Guevara and Haydée Santamaría, and my extensive anthology of Cuban poetry. In 2014, when the period of extreme censorship that Cubans refer to as "the Five Grey Years" was finally addressed publicly, I could count on Arturo to provide me with in-depth information.[80] On every visit to the island, we've gotten together at least once, and our correspondence is ongoing.

The following fragments from our letters touch on moments of particular interest. Because we communicated via email, many of our exchanges are dated on the same or successive days.

November 11, 2004

Dear Margaret:

Víctor passed on what you sent him about the election.[81] Before that, Gregory sent me what he wrote about the election

80. "The Five Grey Years" or "Grey Period" refers to a time in Cuban cultural life roughly from 1971 to 1976, although many would say it was much longer. A narrow-minded official named Luis Pavón had gained prominence, and censorship was rampant. Eventually he was removed from office and things got better. When Armando Hart became the Minister of Culture, he continued to rectify errors committed during the Grey Period. But in 2014, after a tribute to Luis Pavón appeared on Cuban TV, many of the country's writers and artists feared a return of that period. A series of public talks took place and articles were published. There was some important in-depth analysis. Arturo Arango, Reina María Rodríguez, Ambrosio Fornet, Desiderio Navarro, and others were among the writers who raised their voices, and they were joined by visual artists, architects, photographers, and musicians.

81. Víctor Rodríguez Núñez.

in Uruguay. I responded to Gregory, telling him I appreciated what I received from him and that my happiness would be complete if you sent me something similar on Wednesday. Here in Cuba, we were also very tense on the night of November 2nd. We read newsfeeds and shared the results that came in fits and starts. And, when the exit polls seemed to favor him, we briefly enjoyed the illusion of a Kerry win. Víctor kept me informed until around midnight. One of his messages was particularly encouraging and it continues to be so despite the outcome of the election. He described students where he teaches waiting to vote in long lines and in a freezing rain, apparently hoping to cast a vote against Bush. I don't want to repeat what Bladimir used to call "the dreamers' option," but here and there I do see interesting signs.[82] Yesterday a friend told me that Miami's Dade County voted Democrat. You can imagine what that could mean in the long run for US policy towards Cuba. And even now it tells us that those who are voting there aren't the dinosaurs who dominated the region's politics for decades. We are in for four tough years, filled with uncertainties, but perhaps the phrase you may have heard more than once when you lived here applies: "The good thing about this is how bad it's getting." Of course, it can always get so bad that a turnaround will no longer be possible. Kisses from one who loves you a lot, A

February 9, 2011

Dear Arturo:

I hope you are doing well. Silvia and others have asked me to send around the Spanish translation of my book, but I don't

82. Bladimir Zamora (1952–2016) was a critic, composer, and public intellectual, another of the old gang who died tragically of alcoholism much too young.

want to until you tell me what you suggest I do about that offensive phrase.[83] If you can, please suggest a substitution, even though I may not use it, so I can share the manuscript with others there. Thanks.

[undated]

Dear Meg:

Here's the Spanish version. I simply eliminated those three lines. The truth is, the way things stand here now, a more complex and detailed explanation would be superfluous.

Thanks for understanding. A big hug, A

December 25, 2013

Dear Arturo, my brother:

I hope you're well, the family too.

Today, reading news from Casa de las Américas (something I do frequently) I saw that they are planning a tribute to Haydée Santamaría on the 30th of this month for the 90th anniversary of her birth. How I would love to be there! I see that a Haydée Arango will be speaking. Is she your daughter?

I think of Haydée often. My book about Che, recently released, includes a chapter called "Che and Haydée." Despite their differences, and the idiosyncrasies that characterized

83. In 2009, Rutgers University Press published my book *To Change the World: My Years in Cuba*. A Spanish translation was made, and I very much wanted the book to come out in Cuba. An editor at Ediciones Unión expressed interest, then kept the manuscript for close to two years, neither going ahead with publication nor telling me why not. Clearly, there was a problem of some kind. Silvia Gil, the librarian at Casa de las Américas and an old friend, read and liked it, but she felt one comment I had made might be responsible for the holdup. I no longer remember the offending line. Eventually Ediciones Matanzas published the book, and it sold out in weeks.

each of them, they are connected in my mind for many reasons, among them an unusual and complex "purity."[84]

This prompted me to send this note, along with a hug and one for your daughter,

Margaret.

December 2013

Dear Margaret:

Yes, she's my daughter. Someone at Casa had the idea of inviting two young women named Haydée: Haydée Milanés, Pablo's daughter who will sing, and my daughter who will read a brief text (which she has yet to write).

[undated]

Dear Margaret:

I just returned from the film school where I've been installed for several weeks.[85] Tomorrow and Saturday I will be at the UNEAC[86] Congress out in Convention Palace, probably until late. I hope to see Zuleica Romay there and talk to her about my book.[87] And your book is something I also want to

84. I would finally decide to write a book about Haydée Santamaría. I did the fieldwork in 2014, and Duke University Press brought the book out in 2015. It is called *Haydeé Santamaría, Cuban Revolutionary: She Led by Transgression.* A wonderful Cuban writer, Aida Bahr, did an excellent Spanish translation. But, although Editorial Oriente contracted it for publication, it finally could not appear in Cuba. Ediciones Moneda in Viña del Mar, Chile, brought it out in 2021 as *Traspasar los límites: Haydée Santamaría.* In some of the following letters, Arturo suggests people who knew Haydée for me to interview and sent me other useful ideas.

85. Arturo teaches script writing at Cuba's film school in San Antonio de los Baños, a suburb of Havana. Because he lives quite far from there, when he has a heavy teaching schedule, he often spends the night at the school.

86. UNEAC, Cuban Union of Writers and Artists.

87. Zuleica Romay is an important person in the world of Cuban culture. At this time, she worked at Casa de las Américas. Arturo wanted to ask

speak with her about personally, rather than in an email. Can we see one another on Sunday? On Monday I've got to go back to the film school. Will you be going to Encrucijada?[88]

I think you should also talk to Rebeca Chávez, a filmmaker who is married to Senel Paz. She knows a lot about Haydée. It was Rebeca who gave us the material we published in *La Gaceta*.[89] She already knows about your book.[90]

I'm eager to sit down with you.

A big hug, Arturo

[undated]

Arturo, I got in last night after two days of travel. I'd like to design a special hell for bureaucrats. But I'm here, finally, and installed at Aimee Vega's house, close to Casa de las Américas. Aimee is a friend of my daughter Sarah. I think you know her.

I'm working well at Casa. They've given me a desk and lots of support. Especially Silvia Gil, but really everyone.

I want to see you as soon as it's convenient. And Omaida too. I called your house and spoke to your mother-in-law but I'm not sure she understood me, although she was very nice. She gave me a number where she said I could reach you, but it had 17 digits! One of the workers here called again and got the right number. I was able to speak with Omaida. I think you were teaching.

---

her why she thought Editorial Unión hadn't published my book about Cuba. When they finally spoke, Romay said she had read the book and liked it immensely.

88. Haydée's birthplace. I did go there.

89. *La Gaceta* is UNEAC's literary magazine. Norberto Codina and Arturo were its editors.

90. I did interview Chávez for my book. It was one of the best interviews I obtained.

I brought a CD with the manuscript of my book and all the photographs. I don't know if you were able to speak with anyone about it.

I love you a lot. Soon then, Margaret.

[undated]

Arturo, I fell asleep last night reading your book. I love it. Especially the interview titled "I Live in Cuba, and That's What Hurts the Most." It reads like pure truth. Thanks for this book which is very important to me.

It was great seeing you and Omaida yesterday.

Much love, Margaret.

April 22, 2014

Here is a copy of what Reina read when she received the National Literature Prize.[91]

It was wonderful having you here these days.

A big kiss, A

[undated]

Arturo, this visit has been beautiful for me as well. And I'm more grateful than I can say for having had so much time with both of you. Today was especially marvelous! Visiting Vigía,[92] having lunch with you in Matanzas, having so much

---

91. Reina María Rodríguez is a Cuban poet who has had a great influence among those of her generation and younger. She raised her voice firmly in protest against censorship during "the Five Grey Years." She received her country's National Literature Prize in 2013, and in 2014 Chile's Pablo Neruda Ibero-American Award for Poetry, among many other honors.

92. Vigía is a publishing house in Matanzas, Cuba, that produces handmade poetry books in editions of two hundred copies each. These books are in many special collections throughout the world, including MoMA. It's every poet's dream to have a book published by Vigía. Arturo took me to

time just to talk, and finally that visit to your home, brief as it was. I often think about when we first met so many years ago. Back then I couldn't have imagined these reencounters so many years later.

Thank you for Reina's words. I put the document on my laptop and will read it later when I get to the residence.

Don't forget the little anthology![93]

Thanks again for everything. Here's to seeing one another again very soon—maybe in Albuquerque?

All my love, Margaret.

April 27, 2014

Dear Margaret:

I knew you'd love Reina's speech. I don't know if you know that she's in the US, or at least she was when they announced the Neruda Prize. I'll look over your translation, even though my English really isn't good enough to catch any errors.

Needless to say, we loved the photos.

For us it was also beautiful to have that time with you. I am always deeply moved when, despite years, friendships remain so vital. I always think it's astonishing that people who are in a constant state of change and live in such different contexts can come together and find that their perceptions of the world are the same, that their ideals and loyalties haven't changed. It's always something to be celebrated.

A big kiss, A

Matanzas and introduced me to the people there, resulting in their publishing two of my books in the following years.

93. I had asked Arturo to help me produce a small anthology of contemporary Cuban poetry for *Malpais Review,* a literary journal in Albuquerque edited by Gary Brower.

[undated]

Arturo:

You'd told me that Reina was in the US. I imagine she went from there to Chile.

I know that Silvia Gil was quite upset at her declarations upon receiving the Neruda Prize. She didn't like it that Reina dedicated the prize to "those poets FORCED to leave Cuba." She felt that *forced* was too strong a word. Objectively, I agree that no one is forced to leave, but the problem is that life isn't objective. There are those who prefer to stay and others, because they have a different sensibility, can't. It's clear to me that those who have emigrated have affected her deeply. I imagine you are all affected to one degree or another. I don't know if Reina could have dedicated the prize to those poets without using that word. The speech I translated is impregnated with a deep sense of loss. And I found it to be very profound. I sent my translation to Reina and, when I'm satisfied that it doesn't have any errors, I will try to get it published here. Yesterday I finished three short articles on Cuba: one a general current assessment, one on Vigía, and one on Jaimanitas.[94] They'll be published in an online paper I write for called *The New Mexico Mercury*.

And now, I must organize myself to begin writing about Haydée . . .

April 28, 2014

Margaret:

Reina's dedication bothered me as well. Something like "to all Cuban poets wherever they may be" would have been better.

94. Jaimanitas is a fishing village on the outskirts of Havana where the Cuban artist José Rodríguez Fuster has adorned an entire neighborhood of houses with wild mosaics and whimsical sculptures.

Why exclude those, like herself, who live mostly on the island? On the other hand, there's an interesting nuance and I don't know quite what she meant by it. I think her exact words were "To all the Cuban poets who have had to leave Cuba." How should we read "have had to leave?" Víctor, for example, would be excluded. Did she only mean those who have been persecuted in one way or another? There are very few of those: Padilla, Díaz Martínez, Raúl Rivero, Ponte. I can't think of any others.

Many years ago, in Paris, I met a Mexican who worked for the European Literary Parliament. He asked me about a Cuban poet who was also a medical doctor, a friend of Ponte's, who had asked the Parliament for refugee status. She asked me if this poet, whose name was Pedro Marqués de Armas, had been politically persecuted. I assured her that he hadn't. The problem was, since he was a doctor they didn't just let him travel anytime he wished. That was the "repression" he suffered. She also asked me about Arturo Alape. "Well, if he returned to Colombia he could be killed," I said. The best part of it all was that immediately following that conversation, Pedro Marqués won that year's UNEAC poetry prize. He ended up leaving Cuba. Did he have to leave? Was he forced? Maybe Reina thinks he was. But at times positions that pretend to be inclusive turn out to be exclusive instead.

[undated]

Arturo:

I agree, Reina went too far. But it all depends on how one feels, and how Reina sees it. In short, the good thing is that we're in better times now, and among those who stay and those who leave there's that fluidity of the sea to which Reina refers.

The ease with which Cubans claim to have been persecuted—with a very few exceptions—has long seemed absurd to me, especially when one thinks of Colombians, Uruguayans, Argentineans, Chileans, Salvadorans, Guatemalans and others who really have been persecuted and, as you say, if they went back to their countries would be killed.

Exile is a complex issue. I remember eight or ten years ago here in New Mexico, the state chapter of PEN invited a Colombian writer, his wife and daughter here as political refugees. They were received with all sorts of special attentions. The guy rubbed me the wrong way. I did some research and discovered that he hadn't suffered repression of any kind in Colombia. And he lived like a king here, with an overblown stipend and no obligations whatsoever. I remember he even demanded expensive dental work for his dog! He finally left his wife for his secretary, the wife got ill and died, and then he too died, victim of an automobile accident. The poor daughter was left alone. A Greek tragedy. And all the while there are thousands of refugees who deserve the status but are kept out.

Enough for now. Much love, Margaret.

[undated]

Arturo:

I am in heaven! I've never enjoyed working on a book as much as I do this one. And at night Haydée comes to me in dreams, telling me how to approach this or that . . .

May 29, 2014

Dear Arturo:

Yesterday I was reading some in the book you gave me.[95] I've been trying to understand the Padilla case, not as I understood it at the time but as the Cuban writers of your

95. This may have been *El 71*, by Jorge Fornet, an astute cultural analysis of the world that year.

generation saw it back then. And how your assessment has changed since.[96] Working on my book about Haydée, I've been trying to imagine how she might have seen the Padilla affair. When I interviewed Retamar we talked about that, and he had some interesting things to say.[97] But I'm discovering that a great deal of what I am writing about Haydée depends on my ability to imagine what she experienced, thought, felt: not an easy task.

We're in Toronto right now, at the conference on women's history I told you about. Yesterday was the panel on Cuban women. It went well. And today there was a session with Gloria Rolando speaking about her films; I imagine you must know her.[98] Tomorrow, we head home.

I hope you are well. My love to you and Omaida, Margaret.

---

96. Heberto Padilla (1932–2000) was a Cuban poet who consistently bad-mouthed the revolution to foreign journalists and others. His book *Fuera del juego (Out of the Game)* won UNEAC's poetry prize in 1968 but was published with a disclaimer by the institution because of its critical nature. In 1971, he was arrested for "subversive activities" and held for a month, after which he made a public confession. His situation was loudly criticized by intellectuals around the world, dividing many who objected from others who remained loyal to the positions of the revolution. A year later, Padilla left for the United States, where he was widely feted. At the time, I accepted Cuba's official position. Since, I have come to see it as a mistake and ultimately counterproductive in that it was censorship and turned a mediocre poet into a hero for those who are against the Cuban Revolution.

97. Roberto Fernández Retamar (1930–2019), Cuban poet and essayist. He was close to Haydée and became director of Casa de las Américas after her death and following a period in which the institution was headed by visual artist Mariano Rodríguez.

98. Afro-Cuban filmmaker whose films document some of the history of Black women on the island.

[undated]

Dear Margaret:

I'm sure your research has given you more information than I have, but I want to give you my thoughts on Haydée and the "Gray Period." I never spoke directly with her about this, but I started working at Casa the year she committed suicide, and I spoke with many people who had worked with her during that time.

At that moment, I think most Cuban intellectuals and some outside the country who were revolutionaries or supported the revolution, believed that the Stalinization of culture was a mistake. A minor mistake, perhaps, and they preferred to keep quiet and wait for the assault to pass rather than create contradictions that could threaten the unity of the revolution or "give ammunition to the enemy." We believed that the development of the revolutionary process itself would eventually correct the situation. This is how we saw culture or the unfolding of ideas: as an accessory rather than as something essential to the construction of a new society. When I entered Cuban cultural life, we were obsessed with this. Why didn't we speak up at the time? Why didn't even those who had relative political power and enormous artistic prestige protest?

Haydée chose to defend Casa at all costs. Her decisions back then reveal the fact that she understood that they could shut the institution down. The situation was that serious.

And, you know, we always talk about art and literature. But the social sciences suffered even more, philosophy, sociology . . .

We must continue to talk about this because we are constantly going further in our analysis.

Tomorrow I'll begin to teach at the film school, and Omaida and I will be staying out there for two weeks. And on the 15th, I'll be going to El Salvador for eight days, also to teach a script-writing workshop.

A big hug, A

June 1, 2014

Dear Arturo:

I agree with everything you say. And I hadn't thought about how that period of severe censorship must have affected the social sciences.

But I was asking something else. I wanted to know if you have any idea how Haydée might have felt about how the revolution treated Padilla: imprisoning him, having him pronounce that farcical mea culpa, etc. There's no doubt as to who Padilla was, his positions, his attitudes, his self-aggrandizement and petulance. But in time I've come to believe that the way things were handled was counterproductive. It gave Padilla an importance he never really had as a poet, and divided intellectuals outside the country in a way that ended up hurting the revolution. I wonder if Haydée agreed with how the issue was handled. I don't think it was like her. My question was if you ever heard anything.

In any case this is marginal to what I am writing. The book is going very well, in fact I have a pretty advanced draft now. I'm trying to take care of myself because I've come down with one of those nasty colds and on June 8th, I begin my workshop at Naropa.[99] Have a great time in El Salvador. A hug, Margaret.

---

99. I was teaching a poetry workshop each summer at Naropa University's Summer Writing Program. Naropa is a Buddhist institution in Boulder, Colorado. Allen Ginsberg, Anne Waldman, and Diane di Prima started the writing program.

[undated]

I never really heard anyone talk about that at Casa. It was just something we all understood. I'm not sure how many, but my memory tells me quite a few years passed before anyone said publicly or even among ourselves that we thought Padilla's arrest had been a mistake. I remember one very important meeting at which Retamar attempted to theorize the Padilla case. According to him, and I'm repeating what he said almost textually, Padilla had tried to be indispensable like many petit bourgeois intellectuals who were with the revolution at the beginning. Later, when the revolution formed its own cadre, it no longer needed those intellectuals. Padilla didn't understand, Retamar said, that it was a different time, and he was no longer indispensable. He fancied himself a Cuban Solzhenitsyn, and the revolution didn't need a Solzhenitsyn. It was Retamar who told me that Padilla had an extraordinary memory, that he'd memorized the testimonies from the Stalin trials, and that in parodying them in his self-criticism he was sending a message to the world. For Retamar and company, it was clear there'd been a break between the political leadership and the artists and writers, and that the former bore all the blame. But back then I didn't know Antón [Arrufat], Pablo Armando [Fernández], or César López. I'm sure that they, who were all friends of Padilla's, had a different point of view.

Kisses, A

August 22, 2014

My book about Haydée is basically finished. The publisher tells me I can't keep on tinkering with it and has asked for my final revision. So, I'm struggling with "separation anxiety"! All that's left now is the index and reading page proofs. It should appear around August 2015 . . .

August 23, 2014

Dear Margaret:

I'm attaching the poetry anthology for *Malpais Review*. In choosing the poems, aside from their quality which was my first consideration, I considered how difficult they might be to translate. I also wanted to showcase each poet's main themes as well as different moments in their creative processes. In each case, they are arranged chronologically. I've been in touch with almost everyone, and they're delighted. I'm trying to contact the executors for the two poets who are no longer alive, and I hope they don't ask for money. The problem with executors here in Cuba is that they're often more interested in money than the poets themselves. I'm having a discussion with Soleida [Ríos] because she's been writing some interesting prose poems and I want to include one, but she insists I look at a different one. I'm hesitant about it because I think the references may elude a foreign reader. I'll send both so you can decide.

A kiss, A

August 23, 2014

Dear Arturo:

Can you tell me about Omar Pérez. Is it true that he's Che Guevara's unacknowledged son? Unacknowledged at least publicly . . . Did Che have other children aside from those from his two marriages?

[undated]

Dear Margaret:

As far as I know, only Omar Pérez. I'd be surprised if there were others. There wasn't that much time. In 1965 Che was already fighting in Congo. Of his biographers, I think the only one who speaks about this is Castañeda, the one with the most rightwing agenda. Castañeda writes that Hildita (whom I knew, she was a lovely person) called Omar and they began a sibling relationship.[100] I haven't seen Omar for years. I always liked him a lot. Little by little he seems to have moved away from intellectual circles. He is more connected to theater people these days, perhaps because of his yoga practice. He's also involved in Santería.[101] I once saw him playing the drums at a dance program that was semi-underground. He sustains radically left political views although it's been years since I've heard him make public declarations.

On December 17, 2014, Barack Obama announced he was reestablishing relations with Cuba, retreating from the decades-old policy that had brought so much pain to the Cuban people and never really succeeded in the U.S. government's goal of destroying the revolution. The news was met with optimism in both countries. I looked to Arturo for his take on how people were reacting in Cuba, and he responded the following day.

December 18, 2014

Dear Margaret:

O Globo, a Brazilian newspaper, interviewed me about what's going on here now. I'll send you my responses to their questions because they more or less cover the situation:

1) When you heard yesterday's news, what was your first reaction? What was the reaction of people around you, in the streets?

100. *Compañero: The Life and Death of Che Guevara,* by Jorge G. Castañeda (New York: Random House, 1998). Translation by Marina Castañeda.

101. Traditional African religion widely practiced in Cuba. At the beginning of the revolution, it was disparaged along with other religious expressions, although the culture surrounding it (dance, song, etc.) was exploited for tourists. In time, it has been treated with more respect.

I was at home. Around ten at night a friend called to tell me something was happening. He had heard that Alan Gross had been freed.[102] My wife and I immediately tuned in to Telesur. They were transmitting directly from the Mercosur Summit, and Cristina Fernández announced the liberation of the three Cubans who were serving monstrous prison sentences in the United States. I got emotional when I heard that Cuba and the United States had decided to reestablish diplomatic relations. Of my 59 years, I've lived 55 of them in that absurd situation that I assumed, perhaps unconsciously, would be forever.

2) Do you live in Cuba?

Yes. I live in Cojímar, a small coastal village outside Havana.

3) What are the first changes you're expecting? How do you think those changes will affect people's self-esteem?

I can't imagine. Yesterday's news was a shock. Everyone, including the best-informed analysts, were expecting a gradual process at best. The normalization of relations between the two countries is something to celebrate, but like everything in life it has it's positive and negative aspects. Obama's speech wasn't without the imperialist pretensions that brought about the rupture five decades back.

4) In terms of culture, do you think Cuba's cultural products will reach more people now? Do you think the cultural blockade might end along with the

102. Alan Phillip Gross was a United States government contractor employed by the United States Agency for International Development (USAID). In December 2009, he was arrested in Cuba while working on a program funded under the 1996 Helms–Burton Act, which explicitly called for the overthrow of Castro's government. He was held for five years.

diplomatic one? Do you anticipate more cultural exchange between the two countries?

I'm sure there'll be many more exchanges between artists from both countries, and I am confident that we'll see an end to the humiliating conditions endured by those Cubans who go to perform or work temporarily in the United States; because the laws that go along with the blockade don't allow us to earn money there; we've been forced to hide those payments in the most absurd ways. Great Cuban artists, especially musicians, have been very limited by the blockade. I'm hoping that the renewal of relations will facilitate a fluid exchange of the best of our respective cultures, free from colonial impositions.

5) Do Cubans really want the blockade to end?

Without doubt. Yesterday the streets were filled with people celebrating. They celebrated the return of the three freed prisoners and also the new prospects that will hopefully mean more material wellbeing for our country. All jumbled together, as is common in Cuba. And then, it was also the Day of San Lázaro or Babalú Aya, a very popular deity here.

6) How do you think yesterday will be explained to the children of the future? How will they hear about what happened? And about what's to come.

How will it be explained in the future? That depends on what that future brings. Perhaps in a few years it will be hard to imagine that Cuba and the United States, separated by a narrow arm of water, were living for so long in a mutually antagonistic state, always on the brink of a war which, fortunately, didn't come to pass.

[undated]

Thank you, Arturo. Things sometimes occur at just the right moment. This letter from you is one, because I've been working on a poem—that will probably take me a while—and learning that the reestablishment of relations happened on the Day of San Lázaro is interesting: a detail I didn't have.

One of your answers also made me think about the cultural blockade. Although I have spent the better part of a year writing about Haydée and her amazing ability to break through that barrier, I hadn't considered some of its aspects. For example, how it has affected the ways in which Cuban artists are paid in the US.

Much love, Margaret.

The opening created by Barack Obama and Fidel Castro brought positive changes in its wake. And a little over a year after this breakthrough, President Obama traveled to Cuba. On March 22, 2016, he made a speech there that reflected his understanding of the harm decades of bad U.S. policy had inflicted upon the Cuban people even as he urged Cuba to change its system of government in line with our country's long tradition of trying to get other nations to see that our political choices are the best. The following fragments of his speech are indicative:

> Havana is only 90 miles from Florida, but to get here we had to travel a great distance—over barriers of history and ideology; barriers of pain and separation. The blue waters beneath Air Force One once carried American battleships to this island—to liberate, but also to exert control over Cuba. Those waters also carried generations of Cuban revolutionaries to the United States, where they built support for their cause. And that short distance has been crossed by hundreds of thousands of Cuban exiles—on planes and makeshift rafts—who came to America in

pursuit of freedom and opportunity, sometimes leaving behind everything they owned and every person that they loved.

Like so many people in both of our countries, my lifetime has spanned a time of isolation between us. The Cuban Revolution took place the same year that my father came to the United States from Kenya. The Bay of Pigs took place the year that I was born. The next year, the entire world held its breath, watching our two countries, as humanity came as close as we ever have to the horror of nuclear war. As the decades rolled by, our governments settled into a seemingly endless confrontation, fighting battles through proxies. In a world that remade itself time and again, one constant was the conflict between the United States and Cuba.

I have come here to bury the last remnant of the Cold War in the Americas. [Applause.] I have come here to extend the hand of friendship to the Cuban people. . . .

For all of our differences, the Cuban and American people share common values in their own lives. A sense of patriotism and a sense of pride—a lot of pride. A profound love of family. A passion for our children, a commitment to their education. And that's why I believe our grandchildren will look back on this period of isolation as an aberration, as just one chapter in a longer story of family and of friendship.

But we cannot, and should not, ignore the very real differences that we have—about how we organize our governments, our economies, and our societies. Cuba has a one-party system; the United States is a multi-party democracy. Cuba has a socialist economic model; the United States is an open market. Cuba has emphasized the role and rights of the state; the United States is founded upon the rights of the individual.

Despite these differences, on December 17th, 2014, President Castro and I announced that the United States and Cuba

> would begin a process to normalize relations between our countries. [Applause.] Since then, we have established diplomatic relations and opened embassies. We've begun initiatives to cooperate on health and agriculture, education and law enforcement. We've reached agreements to restore direct flights and mail service. We've expanded commercial ties and increased the capacity of Americans to travel and do business in Cuba.
>
> And these changes have been welcomed, even though there are still opponents to these policies. But still, many people on both sides of this debate have asked: Why now? Why now?
>
> There is one simple answer: What the United States was doing was not working. We have to have the courage to acknowledge that truth.[103]

Unfortunately, that process that seemed so promising wouldn't last. When Donald Trump was elected two years later, most of the progress was erased. Confident hopes were dashed. And although many of us wished that Joe Biden had picked up where Obama left off, he never did. Gradually, the two countries returned to their current state of belligerent coexistence.

> April 2015
>
> Dear Arturo:
>
> I just got the dates for our visit. We'll be in Matanzas until the 30th. Then we'll be coming into Havana where we'll stay with our friend Christina until the morning of the 4th when we return to the States.[104] Unfortunately, I forgot about the 1st being a

103. To read the full speech, go to https://obamawhitehouse.archives.gov/the-press-office/2016/03/22/remarks-president-obama-people-Cuba.

104. Christina Mills, a Canadian doctor and old friend, lived in Cuba for more than five years as the editor of *MEDICC*, a trilingual magazine about the Cuban health system.

holiday there; I guess I've become too much of a gringa![105] I really hope we can see you, Norberto, and Silvia and Ambrosio (at the least). Tell me what you think. I've written to Silvia as well.

We'll bring you copies of *The Malpais Review* with the anthology you put together. Although the editor didn't use all the poems, I think it works well. As it is, the anthology takes up a large part of the issue. We'll bring copies for each of the living poets who reside in Cuba, the families of those who are no longer alive, one for you, and one for Casa's library. I already sent Víctor his copy.

A big hug, and hope to see you soon, Margaret.

May 10, 2015

Dear Arturo:

We've been home five days now. At times we feel as if we've gone through Alice's looking glass, that's how different the Cuban and US worlds are. For me, it was a shock this time when we arrived in Cuba and another shock when we got home. Strange circumstances of time and life.

I've read *En los margenes.* As with *Reincidencias,* it gave me a lot. The exercise of writing something someone asks for is an interesting one. I'm sure that, like me, you only do so when you have something to say. With this, as well as your earlier books of criticism, I'm impressed by the parallel journeys we've taken. You deal with the literary and sociopolitical world there

105. May 1, International Workers' Day, is celebrated throughout the world, and in Cuba it is a national holiday, featuring a big parade. Ironically, the events it references happened in the United States, one of the few nations that doesn't celebrate it. On May 4, 1886, the Haymarket Riot took place in Chicago. Eight years later, President Grover Cleveland, uneasy with the socialist origins of International Workers' Day, signed legislation creating Labor Day, to be celebrated on the first Monday in September.

and I with the one here. How I would love to have to be able to have a long conversation about so many issues, but I know your English isn't good enough for you to easily read my essay collections, just as my Spanish is no longer up to deciphering the hidden secrets of yours. In any case, I want you to know how much I appreciate this new book of yours and how often I know I will go back to it.

The same hug as always, Margaret.

May 16, 2015

Dear Margaret:

I've just gotten back to Havana as well. Switzerland was a lot of work, but I was able to disconnect from the problems of daily life here and that was relaxing. All's well here at home.

I believe what you say about parallel journeys being the basis for friendships that last. No matter how much time passes without seeing one another, when we come together everything has moved to a common point. And it's not about being in the same place we were five or twenty years ago, but that we've both moved in the same direction, because the world has changed, and we must learn to think about it differently.

My best to Barbara and a hug for you, A

As a counterpoint to how identified I am with several Cuban friends, the difficulty of communication—provoked by Cuba's antiquated email system as well as by the blockade—always made joint projects hard. We could no longer depend on a reliable flow of mail between the two countries. In Cuba, even email was limited. Servers frequently broke down. Intellectuals and artists who had access to outside servers had an advantage. And until a few years back, cell phones were rare. The following letters demonstrate the frustrations this caused and how we often ended up having to send things with friends who traveled.

May 16, 2015

Dear Arturo:

Our recent visit continues to be a vivid presence, especially our experience in Matanzas and the time we spent with friends in Havana, you and Omaida in particular.

I wanted to send some translations to Laura,[106] but Vigía's server has been down for a week; I think the whole city of Matanzas is offline. And I have several other problems. Alfredo Zaldívar told me to send him my Cuban memoir in Spanish as soon as I got home; he wants to include it on his 2016 list.[107] For me it would be a dream if this book could finally be published in Cuba. I sent him the book in 14 separate documents, one for each chapter, but they bounced back because of the inoperative server. And then I translated a book of poetry by Israel Domínguez and want to consult a few things with him (he himself is an excellent translator from English to Spanish and did a great job translating Barbara's opening remarks at her artist book show). But again, the problem with the server has made this impossible. Could you call Zaldívar and tell him I did send the book, but it bounced back? Maybe he can give you another address, perhaps in Havana, and I can try again.

It's true what you say that when friends have moved in similar directions, no matter where they are they continue to share points of view and ways of looking at the world.

---

106. Laura Ruiz Montes, a poet who is a senior editor at Vígia.

107. Alfredo Zaldívar, poet, founder of Vigía, and currently director of Ediciones Matanzas, the publishing house that eventually brought out this and other books of mine.

Lots of love to you and Omaida, and a kiss for your grandson, Margaret.

May 17, 2015

Dear Margaret:

I tried writing to Alfredo yesterday, but my mail also bounced. I don't have his home phone, only his work number, so I'll call him tomorrow morning without fail.

A hug, A

May 17, 2015

Dear Arturo:

I really appreciate you calling Zaldívar. It's possible that he received my first mail with the chapters attached, but that before he wrote acknowledging that, the server crashed. Or it's possible that he hasn't received anything. A friend of mine is leaving for Cuba in a week.[108] She's traveling with a group of artists. Matanzas isn't on her itinerary but she's thinking of renting a car and driver and going there for a day. I've sent her a letter for Zaldívar and another for Domínguez, each with a thumb drive containing what I want them to have. But I'm not entirely sure she will make it out of Havana. I could also send you the book for Zaldívar, but I don't know how easy it would be for you to get it to him. Then again, it's always possible that the Matanzas server will be up and running soon; in the land of magic realism anything can happen.

I'd love my friend to be able to visit Vigía, and not just to act as my messenger. She is a magnificent artist. We met in Cuba in 1972 when she was invited by OSPAAAL to study poster techniques with Rostgaard.[109] For decades, she has made posters for

108. This was Jane Norling, the protagonist of chapter one in this book.

109. Alfredo Rostgaard (1943–2004) was a Cuban graphic designer and artist. He was one of the leading designers of revolutionary film and political

some of the most important movements here. She is also a muralist and easel painter. I know Vigía would fascinate her.

Well, that's all for today from this cold and rainy North. Yesterday we got snow, a rare event in the month of May!

Much love, Margaret.

May 17, 2015

Dear Margaret:

I think you should send your memoir with Jane, and if she doesn't make it to Matanzas, she can leave it with me. There are always people traveling between the two cities, and I can make sure he gets it.

A kiss, A

May 17, 2015

Excellent idea. I'll send the memoir to her "overnight" and cross my fingers that it gets there before she leaves. And I'll give her your telephone number in case she doesn't make it to Matanzas. I think the group she's traveling with is staying at a hotel in Old Havana. In any case, if you can call Zaldívar and let him know what's happening, I'd be grateful.

A hug, Margaret.

June 1, 2015

Dear Arturo:

Good news. Yesterday I received two positive responses from magazines I'd queried about publishing Cuban poetry in translation. One is *World Literature Today*. By August 15th(!) they want a large selection, bilingual poems by four poets plus photos and bios of each, and a 2,000-word introductory note by

---

posters through his work at the Cuban Institute of Film Art and Industry (ICAIC), the Organization of Solidarity with the Peoples of Africa, Asia and Latin America (OSPAAAL), and other Cuban agencies.

me. *World Literature Today* is a very fine journal. The other magazine, also excellent, is *Prairie Schooner*. They want to publish poems, but only in English and without photos or an introduction. They're giving me a two-month deadline. I have enough poems that I won't have to duplicate.

I hope to be able to comply with both magazines. I'm depending on your help. I'll have to stop working on anything else for a couple of weeks, but I'm glad to do that. An interesting detail about the editor at *World Literature Today*: he answered my query the same day I made it although a tornado had just blown the roof of his home! *World Literature Today* is in Oklahoma where they've had some dramatic weather lately.

Well, I just wanted to give you this news. It seems Cuba is in demand here these days.

A hug, Margaret.

[undated]

Dear Arturo:

After sending off the two selections of Cuban poetry, I started thinking about all the Cuban poets I've translated over the years, from that little anthology I did for *Colorado State University Review* in 1978 and *Breaking the Silences* (1982) to my most recent efforts. I'd like to do a really comprehensive anthology: work from the past half century.[110]

Looking at what's appeared in the US, so many of the translations are mediocre or frankly bad. So, I went to work. I think this is the moment for such a volume. To date I've got more than 500 pages! But I want to send you my provisional list

110. This project materialized. It was published as *Only the Road/Solo el camino: Eight Decades of Cuban Poetry* (Duke University Press, 2016).

of poets for your opinion. I'm attaching it here. When you have time, let me know what you think.

Much love, Margaret.

June 7, 2015

Dear Margaret:

I have your list and, as is only natural, have some discrepancies. Almost as a curiosity, I'm attaching a statistical analysis I made a few years ago of 20th century Cuban poets included in several good anthologies. Every selection has its personal component and therein lies its value. Which is why the recommendations I'm suggesting go beyond those inclusions or omissions at the margins of the Cuban canon.

There are some important omissions on your list: Emilio Ballagas and Virgilio Piñera, among those who were publishing before 1959. Ballagas is one of Cuba's most respected and studied poets; he has some truly anthological poems. Piñera has been reevaluated in the past several decades. His was the dissonant voice in the Orígenes group, the "dirty conversationalist" among his peers.[111]

I'd also include two poets from my generation: Luis Lorente and José Pérez Olivares. They are very different from one another. Luis has always been more lyrical, more metaphorical. Olivares's work links poetry with history and the visual arts. He deals in the human condition beyond the merely circumstantial.

I realize that most of the poets I crossed out on your list are women. This isn't a desire on my part to exclude women, but more a comment on your intention to include them. I think that if you include them based on gender rather than the quality of their poetry, you're doing a disservice to the anthology as well as

111. *Orígenes* was a Cuban literary magazine founded by José Lezama Lima and José Rodríguez Feo. Between 1944 and 1956, it published forty-four issues, usually three times a year.

to them. There are some women living in the United States whose work is better, I think. Particularly Magaly Alabau. I'm sending you an E-book collection of her poems with this letter. Also, Lilliam Moro and perhaps Carlota Caulfield.

A kiss, A

[undated]

Dear Arturo:

This is really helpful. I'll take out Magaly Sánchez, Yolanda Ulloa, and Digdora Alonso as well as Víctor Cassaus. And of course, Ballegas and Piñera have to be included. I'll read Lorente and Pérez Olivares. Thanks for sending me Magaly Alabau's book; I'll read it too. Laura Ruiz also suggests I take some poets out and include a young poet named Luis Yussef. Do you know his work? I agree with you about not including women just because of their gender. Still, I am always striving for parity. I also sent my list to Silvia and Ambrosio. I think Ambrosio, in particular, may have some interesting suggestions.

Barbara and I are worried and sad at the moment. Gregory's youngest son, Daniel, suffered a bad accident last Tuesday while playing soccer. Another player inadvertently hit him hard in the lower back. He has internal bleeding, and the doctors still aren't sure where it's coming from. And his liver was damaged. The bleeding is serious, causing severe anemia and a lot of pain. He's been in the hospital since the accident, in intensive care, and they're monitoring him around the clock. The whole family is there, but they can only see him for brief periods and one at a time. My first thought was to fly down, but I realized that would only complicate the situation. Still, it's hard to be so far away.

Yesterday I gave a poetry reading in Santa Fe, an hour north. I read some of the poems I wrote after my recent visit to the Island. They were very well received. When it comes to Cuba, everything here is very black or white: the right with its usual dismissive rhetoric and the left speaking of a tropical paradise with no contradictions at all. In these poems, I've tried to go deeper. It's very different to do this in poetry than in an essay.

Thanks again for all your help. A kiss, Margaret.

[undated]

Alfredo Zaldívar wrote me a beautiful letter. He finished reading my Cuban memoir and likes it very much. At the same time, he feels there are a few things that would be anathema to the powers that be there. He listed them. He thinks that softening them a little they are salvageable. I'm not opposed as long as someone like Alfredo suggests it, because I know he will try to change them as little as possible. He says he's going to consult with you. As always, I value your help.

Much love, Margaret.

June 12, 2015

Dear Arturo:

Great news. I got a letter from Alfredo Zaldívar saying that Ediciones Matanzas will publish my memoir in 2016! He says he spoke with Zuleica Romay at an event where they coincided and asked her if she had read the book. She said yes, you had given it to her, that she liked it and had told Ediciones Unión they should go ahead and do it. Alfredo said he thought it needed a few small changes and she said that was entirely up to him and to me. As you know, Ediciones Unión asked me for the book and then had it for two years without getting in touch with me. At this point, I wouldn't even want them to do it. The book is for Ediciones Matanzas. I'm happy, and once again I want to thank you for all you've done to help me realize my dream of making this text available in Cuba. I'm celebrating!

June 18, 2015

Dear Arturo:

Duke University Press wants to publish my anthology of Cuban poetry. My editor there—the same person with whom I worked on the books about Che and Haydée—is very excited. I think this will be a good home for the book. So now I must obtain written permissions from 56 poets or their executors—a big task, but I have 20 of them, mostly thanks to you and Norberto . . .

July 9, 2015

Dear Arturo:

I hope you're well and that you were able to return from Dominicana as scheduled despite the storm.

Things are good here. My editor at Duke just approved the contract for the anthology. It includes a complimentary copy for each of the 56 poets, something I fought hard for. Of course I'll make sure you get one as well. I must send them the final manuscript by the 23rd of this month, so I'm going full blast right now.

In other news, my book about Haydée is out. It sold 450 copies in the first hour! This past Saturday I launched it here in Albuquerque. It was a full house and great event. I'm still looking for someone willing to take copies to Cuba. I asked Norberto, but he says he's already overloaded.

Gregory was here for five days, a beautiful visit. We took him to Mesa Verde, spectacular ruins in southern Colorado. We had a great time. Gregory is a totally delighted grandpa!

Arturo and I exchanged at least two dozen letters around the issue of the written permissions Duke's legal department required for the poetry anthology. He and other Cuban friends went out of their way to help, in one case going so far as to visit a poet in his hospital room; he had just had a kidney transplant.

Above: Cuban writers Alex Fleites, Víctor Rodríguez Núñez, and Arturo Arango in the 1970s. Photo by Ramón Martínez Grandal. Below: Arturo Arango and Omaida Milián. Photo by Margaret Randall.

All the living poets were enthusiastic. None asked for money. A couple of executors for those no longer alive were more demanding. I ended up spending eight hundred dollars of my own money for permissions to use the work of two long-deceased poets I felt had to be included.

Duke did a beautiful job, and the anthology was named one of the seventy-five best works of translation in the country the year of its publication. My greatest joy was traveling to Cuba with a suitcase filled with copies, one for each poet or executor and several to donate to libraries. Casa de las Américas hosted a gala reading and some of the poets in the Havana area read their poems. The event also turned out to be a gathering of old friends. I was only sorry that the book couldn't be sold in Cuban bookstores; even if Duke had been able to make a special price, it would have been out of range for those on the island who are accustomed to their government's subsidization of books.

August 9, 2015

Dear Arturo:

I started crying when I got to page 291 in your *Terceras reincidencias*. The thing is, I'd read a lot of the book but not all. Today I wanted to read the rest—which, by the way, I found fascinating—and then I got to "Final Conversation." Suddenly, there I was in your telling of those times. I was very moved by what you wrote, and of course it brought back so many memories: that era, those profound friendships that constitute real family, family that comes together around shared experiences, art, convictions, hope. And then the marginalization of which I was a victim, the endless questions, and the loyalty and support you gave me. Of course I'm quite proud of the fact that I spoke out against sexism and homophobia. Love, Margaret.

[undated]

Dear Arturo:

I had no idea that in 1974 those who befriended homosexuals were barred from joining the Young Communists! How ignorant and arrogant the power structure was back then! Of course we have long known about the excesses of that era, but personal stories are always more shocking than statistics.

Aside from all this, the book is wonderful. And it's especially important to me in terms of defining artistic expression at the margins, or in the context of, political policy.

How I would love to be able to sit down with you and go over the introduction I've just finished writing for the poetry anthology. I've been working on it for months, adding and subtracting, trying to do justice to Cuban culture in the periods covered, attempting to avoid that gringo rhetoric that almost always reduces things to neoliberalism versus communism. . . . I hope I've been able to achieve what I set out to do.

A big hug, Margaret.

September 2015

Dear Arturo:

Between tears and laughter, I read your magnificent tribute.[112] Many thanks for sharing it. His riff on that famous Ginsberg line, "I've seen the best minds of my generation destroyed by madness . . .", moved me especially. I wish I had known Alberto. But I'm proud to have included him in the anthology. This morning, minutes before your text arrived, I

112. To Cuban writer Alberto Rodríguez Tosca, the news of whose death arrived just as my anthology of Cuban poetry was going to press. He'd actually died the previous September of complications from a kidney transplant. He was the poet I included in my anthology, who a Cuban friend had visited in his hospital room to get him to sign the written permission I needed for Duke's legal department.

received news from Duke that they'd been able to make the pertinent change to his bio. If I'd had your words then, I might have been able to include a few lines, but it's too late for that. When I come to Cuba, I'll bring a copy of the anthology for his brother; Norberto says he can deliver it. I hope the Cuban press has noted the loss of such a fine poet (the loss of his novels because of a technical mishap hit me hard—a fear we all share in this digital age). "I always carry memory in my pants pocket!" Thanks again, and all my love, Margaret.

October 2, 2015

Dear Arturo:

I want to ask you a question. How do you think Cuban literature (poetry, novel, short story, essay) has influenced the literature of Latin America?

A hug, Margaret.

[undated]

Dear Margaret:

I'll try to answer your question. In 1971, at the time of the Congress on Education and Culture, Ángel Rama published an essay in *Marcha* called "Cuba: Towards a New Cultural Policy."[113] Among many other ideas, he said that in Cuba a Stalinist cultural policy couldn't take hold because Stalinism negates the artistic vanguards, and Cuba had supported its vanguards who by then enjoyed an irreversible tradition.

This is true, but I would take his argument further. If we understand Stalinism not only to be a dogmatic and repressive

113. Ángel Rama (1926–1983) was a Uruguayan writer, academic, and literary critic known for his work on modernism and for his theorization of the concept of transculturation. He was influential, especially among progressive Latin American intellectuals. *Marcha* was an important left publication in Uruguay.

way of dealing with ideological processes but above all as defining Socialism as a construction centralized in the State (the economy, ideology, etc.), Cuba did install a Stalinist system, the remnants of which are still with us. The essential issue is centralism, and everything emanates from that. It is state centralism that, in one way or another, removes every possibility of creating a new type of participatory democracy. At the same time, Cuba's political and revolutionary policies differ a great deal from those in Russia and in the Soviet Socialist Republics as a whole, just as Fidel's personality was entirely different from Stalin's.

If I'm right, then culture was the principal site of Cuba's resistance to Stalinism. And this was for one main reason: the revolutionary, liberating and emancipating work that existed in Cuban culture from the 19th century on. This is why, after 1959 important anti-Stalinist nucleuses appeared. Fidel's role back then was largely that of mediating and balancing the diverse currents that existed among the revolutionary organizations. This was particularly true of the 26th of July Movement (at first representing a strong bourgeois tendency that was later purged as the process was radicalized), the old Communists (all of whom were Stalinists), and others such as the Student Directory that was basically petit bourgeois.

During those early years, while the economy and political system were being centralized as per the Stalinist model, there were also some very strong differences with Soviet ideology. It's important to note that Cuba is part of Latin America and had strong ties to the Non-allied Nations and other Third World countries.[114] This was something that separated us from Soviet

114. Established in 1961 in the context of Cold War pressures, the Non-Aligned Movement (NAM) was founded in 1961 to support developing

orthodoxy, and it not only had Fidel's sympathy; he was its leader. This provoked quite a few contradictions with the Soviets and with other Communist parties on the continent. This is a story you know better than me.

And so, in Cuba there are intellectual currents that considered Stalinism to be a dogmatic concept, yet they adhered to a Stalinization of the economy. *Pensamiento Critico Magazine* espoused this position, as did Casa de las Américas on and off.

All of this is to say that in Cuba we were consolidating relations with the Third World and with the anti-colonialist or antiimperialist liberation movements, and this produced a critical revolutionary line of thought in opposition to the Stalinist influence.

So much for the first part of your question. As for the second, in terms of literature I don't believe there has been a generalized trend, but rather different writers exerted different levels of influence. At the time, Cuban poets mostly wrote in a colloquial or conversational style, but this was also a style that in other Latin American countries had paradigmatic examples (Cardenal, Roque, Parra). Retamar, who is undoubtedly a great poet, wasn't part of this current. It wasn't a common trend among our prose writers either: Carpentier, Lezama, Piñera. In Argentina, for example, Piñera had a strong influence, and later Lezama's work received great attention. I think currents that had to do with affinities also had an influence, for example Cintio and Eliseo in their closeness to the Catholics and to Cardenal. And then there were the magazines. *El*

---

countries in their efforts for decolonization, independence, and formation of democratic systems as well as in protecting the sovereignty of political, economic, and cultural order of these states from outside interference and aggression.

Caimán Barbudo here was part of a process that also included *El Corno Emplumado, El Techo de la Ballena, Los Tzántzicos, Cormorán y Delfín*, but they didn't necessarily influence each other.

During the 1970s I remember that many Latin American writers who visited Cuba expressed disappointment because our literature seemed minor to them, self-contained, not overly courageous. I'm talking about those who came after the great names I mentioned above.

I hope this is useful.

A kiss, A

October 3, 2015

Dear Arturo:

Many thanks for devoting so much time to my question. It's a great help. In any case, when we go down in February, I hope to be able to speak with a few people about these issues.

I hope you are well. On Wednesday we are going to New York, then Hartford and after that Los Angeles. We'll be back in Albuquerque on the 20th. One more question, of a practical nature. In February we want to stay a couple of weeks. I don't know if the Feria is putting us up for a few nights (I still haven't received an official invitation). I know that lodging is getting more difficult with the number of people traveling now. Do you know of a place in Havana that is centrally located where we could rent a room and bath? Preferably somewhere with a telephone and not too many stairs. If you know of something, let me know. My daughter already sold her apartment, and our friend Christina no longer lives in Cuba. Love, Margaret.

November 28, 2015

Dear Arturo:

I am deeply sad today. A dear friend of mine, the South African novelist Mark Behr, died yesterday at the age of 52.[115] He was teaching in Johannesburg and death came very suddenly. He seemed one of the most physically healthy people I've known.

His death came as a particular shock because I'd been thinking a lot about him lately. He was an Afrikaner, from a poor and very conservative family. As a young man, he fought on the wrong side in Angola. That earned him the money to attend university. At the university he was recruited to spy on the ANC. And it was while doing so that he realized he was on the wrong side of history. He went to the ANC and confessed. The ANC told him to continue as he had been, but working for them, and he became a double agent until victory in 1994. A testament to his courage and commitment is the fact that when he revealed what he'd done to the students on whom he'd been spying, every one of them remained a close friend until his death.

His novels are spectacular, but I don't think they exist in Spanish. I'd been thinking about him because I've been writing about the war in Angola and thought it could be interesting to have some testimony from someone on the other side who came to realize he'd been in the wrong. Too late now.

Much love, Margaret.

January 2016

Dear Margaret:

Oma and I just came back from spending time in Cienfuegos, isolated from the world. We stayed at Pasacaballos, a hotel at the entrance to the bay, an hour's drive from the city or

115. Mark Behr (1963–2015).

fifty minutes by boat. We disconnected from the news and had a wonderful time except for the fact that both of us, in different ways but almost simultaneously, hurt the soles of our right feet. The wounds aren't serious, but they are painful and are taking their time to heal.

Meanwhile, I just received the dates of my February teaching schedule in Guadalajara. I'll be there from the 7th to the 14th, which means we won't be able to see one another this time. I'm disappointed.

I also realize I know few internationalists.[116] But I have found someone who is willing to give you an interview. He is the writer Emilio Comas Paret. I don't know if you know him. A book of his just came out, about his experiences in Angola, and he has a copy for you. He also knows many other internationalists. I've asked him to help you and he's happy to do that. Emilio is a really wonderful person, with great integrity; he's also a good friend of Norberto's. I'll send you his email so you can write to him and set something up. He lives in Vedado and often hangs out at the UNEAC, where he's worked for many years. Norberto also has other friends who might be useful. One of them is a maxi facial surgeon whose experiences would be different from those of someone who went to Angola to fight. This month, before I leave for Mexico, I'll try to find you a few more possibilities, so you'll have as plural a vision as possible.

Big kisses, A

116. In early 2016, I was doing the fieldwork for *Exporting Revolution: Cuba's Global Solidarity,* which Duke would publish in 2017. The book documents Cuban internationalism in the fields of medicine, education, sports, and other areas. Arturo is referring to my having asked him if he knew internationalists I might interview while in Cuba.

[undated]

Dear Arturo:

I'm so grateful you were able to make time for us despite having just come back from Mexico the night before. As always, it was wonderful spending time with you both. Each time we see one another, it's as if nothing at all has happened since our last encounter. I hope it will always be that way.

Much love. A huge hug to Omaida. Margaret.

March 2016

Arturo, how are you doing?

Barbara and I listened to Obama's speech in Cuba. Without apologizing for all these years of US aggression (which would have been my preference of course), he did say some interesting things within the neoliberal framework. Did you listen? What did you think?

I read *OnCuba* regularly, always looking for a new text by you. The other day I read an article by Marilyn Bobes about a recently released novel by Chely Lima.[117] I don't know if you remember, but Chely was the youngest poet I included in *Breaking the Silences* way back in the eighties.[118] I hadn't heard about her in almost 40 years. When I began to read poems to make my selection for *Only the Road/Solo el camino*, I remembered her work and asked about her. No one was able to tell me anything. After reading Marilyn's review, I wrote asking if she could put me in touch with Chely. And within an hour I received an email from Chely herself—or I should say himself!

117. *OnCuba* is an online newsfeed from Havana. Marilyn Bobes is a Cuban poet and friend. Chely Lima was a Cuban poet who eventually emigrated to the United States and died in Miami from chronic heart problems.

118. *Breaking the Silences: 20th Century Poetry by Cuban Women* (Vancouver: Pulp Press, 1982).

He now identifies as male and lives in Florida. He left Cuba in 1990, lived in Quito for a decade, and then went to the US. I asked if he was still writing poetry, and he sent me a digital collection. Many of the poems are about having lived for so long as a man in a woman's body. They moved me tremendously. No time now to include him in the anthology, unfortunately; it's already in production, but I want to translate him for an English-speaking readership.[119]

[undated]

Dear Arturo:

I like your latest column, "Who eats the eggs and who the chicken." It's particularly profound, important. Because of its recent history, I imagine Cuba often thinks of itself as an exception. I don't think it is. Sadly, I believe that its future, maybe even its near future, will give in to the forces now so evident here and in Europe. With its own idiosyncrasies, of course. I love the way you always situate your opinions in a historic context.

We are in Boulder right now. We were in New York at the marvelous "Beat & Beyond" gathering (Beat poets and some who were influenced by them, all of us elderly now, getting together to reminisce and recreate some of our most memorable moments). Then we were home for a week, and now I'm about to begin my yearly stint at Naropa University's Summer Writing Program. I have a great group this time around. I'm tired but also happy to be in this place that is always so stimulating.

I miss our correspondence. Much love, Margaret.

---

119. I did translate Chely's book, *What the Werewolf Told Them / Lo que les dijo el licántropo* (New York: Operating System, 2017).

[undated]

Dear Margaret:

Your comments on my column are always encouraging. It's been interesting keeping it going and thinking of how it's evolved. I've just been invited to write for *El Universal* in Mexico. They asked me first when Obama's visit was taking place, but since then they want more. I've decided to send them texts that are more literary in nature and save my political commentary for *OnCuba*. I wrote a piece for *El Universal* on *Paradiso*[120]—it just celebrated 40 years since it was written and no one paid any attention—and another on Pasternak, the CIA and his Nobel.

I've been doing all this despite my limited free time. I've decided to resign as head of the department at the Film School. I'll continue to oversee the master's program and impart classes in script writing. And although this will represent an important reduction in salary, I'll have more time to write.

A big kiss, A

[undated]

Dear Arturo:

I'm so glad you are giving up the administrative work while continuing to teach. Our lives sometimes seem like a constant battle to do everything without giving enough thought to what's most important. I imagine you can make up some of the lost salary with what you earn outside the country. Or writing what you need to write. As I get older, I find I must prioritize more; I just can't do everything.

120. *Paradiso* is a novel by José Lezama Lima. Its homosexual theme created quite an uproar when it was first published, and although first published in Cuba, copies were removed from bookstores there. Later the revolution realized its great worth and it was reprinted and applauded on the island as well as beyond its borders.

> We're still at Naropa. The Jack Kerouac School of Disembodied Poetics is without doubt one of the most creative places I know. Each time I come, it's a valuable experience. This year my students are better than ever and also more diverse; I have one from Beijing, one from Mumbai, one from Sweden, and the rest are from the US. Three men (I usually get all women). All are excellent writers and quite different from one another. Last night was my poetry reading. The twelve teachers invited each week generally give a reading and a lecture. At the reading we were Bobbie Louise Hawkins: undoubtedly one of the best short story writers in the language, now elderly and physically fragile but terrific as ever, Tisa Bryant, Corinne Fitzpatrick and me. The audience is always deeply attentive: usually around 500 between those at the school and from the surrounding community. Today will be our last workshop and tomorrow is the end of this session. Barbara and I head home on Sunday.
>
> I imagine your grandson must be growing fast. Is he walking yet? Our Guille is beginning to walk but still a bit uncertainly. He'll be one in a week and a half. Hugs, Margaret.

It's hard to pinpoint when the Cuban Revolution stopped progressing toward its original goals of a truly just and inclusive society without class differences, without racism, with gender equality, and universal health care and education for all. For years, we believed things were moving in that direction, that errors could be corrected, perhaps even that the United States would lift the blockade. In our enthusiasm, we didn't understand the distortions that had been built into the revolution from the beginning or the persistence of a succession of U.S. administrations in punishing Cuba for daring to defy its control.

In 1970, I was among a huge crowd listening to Fidel Castro admit that year's push for a giant harvest yielding ten million tons of sugar had been a mistake. Agricultural advisers had warned that attempting such a harvest—which necessarily meant abandoning other areas of the economy—was counterproductive, and they'd been ignored, in some cases even demoted from their jobs. Now Fidel was telling a shocked nation that those discredited advisers had been right. As head of state, he assumed responsibility for the setback.

How many political leaders are capable of this sort of honesty? I can think of only two or three during my life. Today's Cuban government lacks that transparency, has been inept in its handling of a precarious situation, and is clearly unable to turn a stagnant economy around. The honest communication that was the norm when Fidel was alive no longer exists. It's easier to repeat the stale arguments that Cuba's troubles are entirely due to the blockade or triggered by the collapse of the Socialist Bloc, while repeating the stagnant rhetoric that insists current efforts will be successful.

While Fidel's honesty and self-criticism were unusual, he was also responsible for concepts that eventually contributed to some unresolvable contradictions. From the beginning of the revolution, a series of slogans, such as "Men die, but the Party is immortal," promoted the idea that the Marxist journey toward a socialist and eventually Communist state had an end point, beyond which history would stop evolving. Presumably, the revolution would reach that state and that would be that. The Soviet interpretation of Marxist-Leninist thought predominated, to the exclusion of all others. This was reinforced by the important amount of aid the Soviets provided, which necessarily carried with it social and cultural influences.

In Cuba, during the years I was there, only a Stalinist interpretation of revolutionary change was taught in the schools. Other thinkers, such as Trotsky, were ignored; reading and discussing them discouraged. Trotsky's idea of permanent revolution is fluid. It postulates that no revolution can survive in a single country and that until revolution exists worldwide, such efforts will be doomed to failure.

At its core, the interpretation consolidated during the Stalin era was antidialectical. Surely Fidel, brilliant as he was, must have understood this. Perhaps he was afraid to go there because it would have sewn doubt in people's minds at a time when confidence in the classic model, unity in the face of a powerful enemy, and sacrificing individual aspirations to the common good were necessary to keeping up morale. Some analysts emphasized the ways in which Cuba's strategies for change did differ from those in the Soviet Union; they referred to the Cuban model as "sunny," "Caribbean," or "Marxism in Spanish." And it's true there were differences. But they were superficial, not systemic.

As I've often said, even though so much of the original revolution no longer exists, when one visits Cuba today one comes away with the almost inexplicable impression that people there are different: more internationalist and equality-minded, more compassionate and generous even in circumstances of great scarcity, more willing to sacrifice so that everyone receives their fair share. Universal health care and education have managed to survive, although greatly diminished in terms of availability and services. Clearly, there is some element at play that transcends the materialistic and verges on the spiritual. Some among those who made the revolution always understood this: Che Guevara, Haydée Santamaría, and Alfredo Guevara, to name three.[121] When we think of those leaders, it's these qualities we admire most.

My son, Gregory, who was educated in Cuba during those years of strict adherence to Soviet-style dogma, began reading Trotsky and others when he was in his mid-teens. Gradually, he came to understand the limitations as well as the beauty of the Cuban path to change. He often tells me that he doesn't believe the Cuban Revolution failed, but, rather, that it is one of many such efforts throughout history and across the world that push humankind toward a goal of eventual equality. He points out that we have lived on Earth for millennia and it's only been about 150 years since the Paris Commune. Each experience, short-lived as it may be, takes the process further.

In my perennial optimism, I believe humanity will eventually achieve a more justice-oriented social organization, precisely because we need it so desperately. Either we achieve it or we disappear. In our letters, Arturo and I often discussed these contradictions as they pertain to Cuba.

August 2016

Dear Arturo:

I loved your column today. It also made me deeply sad. What can we expect to happen? It's frustrating, after so many years, to see that things continue basically the same.

Here, too, we've been living with a feeling of desperation. Watching the Republican convention on TV was like witnessing scenes from 1930s Germany. Now it's the Democrats' turn: their convention is perfectly organized, with moments of real brilliance, but it's been incapable of convincing the supporters of Bernie Sanders that Hillary has changed. We can't forget her

121. These three leaders defied periods of official censorship and narrow-minded thinking, providing homes for cultural imagination and risk.

involvement in multiple wars, her unconditional support of free trade, her macabre actions in Honduras and elsewhere. It's significant that a woman has broken through the "glass ceiling," but it would have been so much better if it had been a woman with better political positions. It's a depressing time. I fear that Trump will be our next president.

Meanwhile, I continue to translate books of Cuban poetry, most recently one by Reynaldo Garcia Blanco and another by Yanira Marimón. I'll be sending these to the publisher after the release of those by Laura Ruiz, Alfredo Zaldívar, and Israel Domínguez (the latter in production now). If you know other poets there you feel should be in English, let me know.

And the anthology, which will come out in October, continues to spark a lot of interest. I have a very full fall and spring calendar for presenting the book in different parts of the country: Albuquerque, San Francisco, Berkeley, Oakland, Chicago, New York, Miami, etc.

That's all for now. Much love, Margaret.

May 2, 2017

Dear Arturo:

I hope things there are going well. I've been reading your columns, and always find them excellent. The most recent one is very important. I didn't leave a comment because I didn't feel, that being an outsider, it would be appropriate. But I imagine it's provoked a good deal of discussion.

We're well but tired. Since January we've been twice to New York, I made that quick trip to Cuba, and then both of us traveled to Chicago, San Francisco, Miami, and Ohio. In Ohio we stayed with Víctor and Kate and met Miah—a lovely visit.

Exporting Revolution: Cuba's Global Solidarity just came out. Although it's in English, I'm sending you a copy because you were such a help, and I quote you. I'm sending it with a friend in New York, Marithelma Costa, who will be traveling at the end of the month. She's going to give a lecture at Casa de las Américas on Puerto Rican literature in the United States, and I've asked her to leave the book with Silvia Gil or Ana. One of them will call you when it comes.

This has been a very unusual spring. Two days ago, there were twelve inches of snow in Santa Fe. And it's been super cold.

In other news, we continue under the shadow of the sociopath. Much love, Margaret.

May 2, 2017

Dear Margaret:

I'll watch for the arrival of your book. On the 9th I leave for Switzerland until the 19th.

I don't know if you know that Antonio Castro has been here in Havana since early March, being treated for Parkinson's and epilepsy. Norberto and I went to visit him at the hospital in Siboney. On that first visit we found him very deteriorated. We made plans to pick him up and take him around. This past Saturday we did that and spent some time in Vedado, went by your old building, stopped at Norberto's for a while and then had dinner at the house. He seemed a lot better. Kisses, Arturo.

May 27, 2017

Dear Margaret:

I have your book. Silvia sent it to me. I've barely skimmed it because Omaida and I spent all week out at the film school and only came home last night. I'm heading into my last three weeks of classes and often stay out there to avoid those tiring trips back and forth. Today Omaida and I are celebrating our fortieth anniversary. Kisses, Arturo.

May 27, 2017

Dear Arturo:

How wonderful that you're celebrating forty years of marriage! Congratulations!

Barbara and I have been together for thirty now, or four if one only counts those since we were able to marry legally. Each day is a gift.

Silvia told me she'd sent you my book. Although it's in English and I doubt you'll read it, I wanted you to have a copy. You've always been such a huge help, aiding me in my research, discussing ideas, acting as a valuable sounding board. I am forever grateful.

I don't think this book will do as well as the anthology. But it's one I felt compelled to write. I'm trying to promote it now, one of the aspects of being a writer that least appeals to me. Arranging events is tedious, although I love the events themselves.

In three weeks, we'll be going to Boulder for my habitual workshop at Naropa. That's always a good experience, the opportunity to work with excellent students and hear poets from different places.

Meanwhile, I'm busy as always writing. Mostly poetry right now. And I have a new little project that's giving me a great deal of satisfaction. As you know, this coming October will be the fiftieth anniversary of Che's death in Bolivia. One aspect that has always bothered me about the way in which Che has been presented in the official histories is that those women who fought alongside him have generally been ignored.

Except for Tania, the token.[122] Last month in Chicago I met a young Venezuelan poet, and he mentioned the name of Rita Valdivia. Rita was Bolivian, a promising young poet and a member of the ELN who died fighting with what remained of Che's forces in Cochabamba in July of 1969. She was 23 years old. The poetry she left behind is surprisingly powerful. And it's not your typical poetry of struggle but filled with innovative imagery, almost surrealistic. I started looking for information about her and got quite a bit from sources as diverse as Edmundo Aray and Elizabeth Burgos.[123] I've written a brief essay on her life and translated the only five poems of hers that seem to have survived. I want to publish this as a different sort of tribute at the beginning of October.

Much love to you and Omaida, Margaret.

February 1, 2018

Dear Arturo and Omaida, Silvia and Ambrosio, Jorge and Zaida:[124]

I'm writing from Uruguay, where Barbara and I are visiting Gregory and his family. We've been here since January 24th. At the moment, we're out at Punta del Este with Goyo, Laura, Lía, Guzmán and their children, including newborn Emma. Martín, Daniel and Mari join us on weekends. The adults as

122. Tamara Bunke, a young woman of German origin, was recruited by Che and took part in his final campaign in Bolivia. Her life and death have been glorified in many texts, as if she was the only woman to have taken part in that effort.

123. Edmuno Aray (1936–2019) was a Venezuelan poet, short story writer, and editor. Elizabeth Burgos is a Venezuelan anthropologist, former wife of the French philosopher Régis Debray, and editor of Rigoberta Menchú's biography.

124. Jorge Fornet is Silvia and Ambrosio's younger son; Zaida Capote is his wife. I had known Jorge as a child, and he and Zaida became good friends, with whom we always enjoy reconnecting on our visits to Cuba.

well as the children spend our time sleeping, eating, playing, going to the beach, and talking—that is to say, pure relaxation and joy.

Goyo asked me to write to you all to begin to plan our visits in March. As you know, we will be in Havana from the 11th to the 15th, which doesn't give us a lot of time. Goyo and Laura also want to see some of their old friends, but we want to make sure to get together with the six of you. At the very least, we'd love to spend an afternoon with Silvia and Ambrosio, an evening with our old gang (Arturo, Omaida, Alex, Norberto, etc.), and have dinner one night with Zaida and Jorge. How does this sound to you?

We'll be here until February 22nd. Then less than two weeks at home before heading for Cuba (where we'll spend the first part of our visit in Matanzas). In Havana we'll be staying at that bed & breakfast in Vedado, where Barbara and I stayed before.

We're all so happy to be seeing you soon. Hugs, Margaret.

February 2, 2018

Dear Arturo:

Wonderful that you and Omaida will be in Matanzas. Goyo and Laura are going out on a bus that leaves from UNEAC on the 5th because the inauguration of the Book Fair has been pushed up a day and is now scheduled for the 6th. Apparently, this is because of the municipal elections on the 11th. Barbara and I won't arrive in Cuba until the 6th, so we're being met at the Havana airport and driven directly to Matanzas. Zaldívar tells me that Goyo, Laura, Barbara and I will be staying at the same guest house in Matanzas. By the way, I've written several times to Zaldívar lately without a response. I don't know whether he's in Cuba at the moment or in Nicaragua for the poetry festival in Granada. I'm waiting for him to send Barbara and me a schedule of our activities in Matanzas. I guess he'll write when he can.

It would be great if you and Omaida could get together with us in Matanzas. I know I have a poetry reading at Editorial Matanzas on the 7th (part of its series called Poetry on Wednesdays). On the 8th I have a public conversation with Aida Behr, who translated my book about Haydée. On the 9th they tell me I have something with you, Arturo. And the opening of Barbara's exhibition at the Matanzas Museum is sometime on the 10th. I also want to attend Goyo's book launch. So, there's a lot planned for those days. Maybe we can find a moment to have lunch or dinner together. In any case, Barbara and I still want to invite you and Omaida to dinner somewhere in Havana on the 14th or 15th, because I think it will be more private. But if that's not possible, we understand. I know how many cultural activities are planned for this time of year in Cuba.

I knew about the problem between Víctor and Norberto. Víctor told me in detail when we were together last year in Ohio. And he mentioned it again when we saw each other in Ciudad Juárez. I know they haven't spoken in a while. I'm so glad you've been able to convince them it's time to bury the hatchet. I wish we could host our gathering, but Albuquerque is much too far away! We can help with money for food and/or drink. Your house would be a lovely venue, but I must tell you that wherever you decide to hold the party, someone will have to pick Barbara and me up and bring us back to where we'll be staying. Neither of us are any longer in condition to use public transportation. Anyway, you decide . . .

I hope Alex will be in Cuba when we're there. I don't know if I told you, but on our way to Uruguay we had a long layover in Miami and saw Gilda and Kelly (Ramón Martínez Grandal's widow and daughter). They told us that Alex visited Grandal in the hospital a few days before he died, a visit that did him a lot of good.

Silvia Gil, who was there, told me that Goyo's book launch at the Cuban Pavilion during the Havana Book Fair was very nice. Quite a few people came, and they ran out of copies for sale.

I'm grateful to Norberto for getting me a copy of Guillermo's book. From Laidi Fernández de Juan's review on Silvio's blog, it seems very interesting.

Okay. I leave all decisions about our upcoming visit to you. As you make them, let me know.

I love you a lot, Omaida too. So eager to see you both. Kisses, Margaret.

February 10, 2018

Dear Arturo and Omaida:

The get-together on the night of the 11th sounds excellent. At the same time, Barbara and I would love to see the two of you separately. Would dinner on either the 12th or 14th work? We'd like to invite you to a restaurant of your choice and have a couple of hours to talk. Let me know what you think.

Here in Uruguay, we're enjoying the southern hemisphere and the distance from the criminal state of politics in our country. And every day we marvel at how our newest great grandchild was able to survive her birth and is flourishing. Every day she is stronger and more active.

We get back to Albuquerque on the 21st and leave for Cuba on the 5th.

Arturo, do you think it would be possible for you to get me a copy of Guillermo Rodríguez Rivera's posthumous book recently published by Ojalá? It would mean a lot to me.

I love you both, Margaret.

March 16, 2018

Dear Arturo and Omaida:

What a lovely evening at your house! The food was great and the company more so. I'm sorry that Barbara and I got tired so early. It seems as if my habit of falling asleep on the couch surrounded by conversation and music back in the old days at the apartment at Línea 53, has returned with a vengeance. And, since her recent health problems, Barbara has trouble staying awake long into the night. Gregory and Laura told us that the gathering continued to be wonderful. And we had a great time. Thank you for everything.

And thanks for Alfredo Guevara's book of essays. It promises to be a fascinating read.

I also like Guillermo Rodríguez Rivera's book, *To Say it All,* even though he writes about an incident with Robert Cohen and me that I don't remember at all.[125]

Have a good trip to Barcelona. We'll be in touch. I love you both, Margaret.

March 17, 2018

Dear Margaret:

It was a beautiful evening for us as well. We love having folks to the house and we'd been wanting to have you for years. And I was so happy that Norberto and Víctor reconciled. They had breakfast together the following morning and both told me things went well.

By the end of that night, Víctor's energy still seemed limitless. I tend to tire when events go late (I've gotten into the habit of retiring early and getting up at dawn). Goyo was also

125. Robert Cohen is a U.S. poet and journalist, the man I lived with my final year in Mexico and after I got to Cuba, until 1975. He is the father of my daughter Ana.

> nodding toward the end of the evening. This return for him and Laura, after twenty years, must have been beautiful and challenging at the same time. I imagine they're still processing this new reality.
>
> Big kisses, A

As I've said, this chapter was made possible by the fact that Arturo had saved all our letters. His difficulty was in finding the time to copy and send them to me. Through the years, he had changed email servers and computers, so the letters from different periods were stored in several different systems, some easier to access than others.

On October 2, 2024, he wrote:

> Dear Margaret: I'm sorry for the delay in sending you this latest batch. I wanted to do that this week but haven't had the time. Because I was out of the house for four weeks, you can't imagine the problems I've had to deal with—between those that had piled up and those I must resolve before Omaida and I leave for Dominicana where we'll be from the 6th to the 20th. Nereida [Omaida's mother] is 93 and she'll be alone during the day. And daily life has gotten very hard here. We use cannisters of gas for cooking, and since September 6th none have come into the distribution point. On Saturday they sold 200 but after waiting in line for six hours we came away empty-handed. Now we've got to be on the alert for when more will be available. Add to all this the blackouts; in Havana they're fewer but they exist. Today we'll be without electricity from 10 a.m. to 2 p.m. I don't want to overwhelm you with these details, but just to give you an idea . . .

Cuba's Federation of Cuban Women (FMC) held a much-anticipated congress in March 2019. Arturo knew I would be interested in what transpired. Sadly, the results were disappointing. Arturo sent me an article by Alina B. López Hernández that appeared in *La Joven Cuba*, an online publication. She listed a long list of complaints, among which were: the urgent need to improve the quality of locally produced sanitary napkins, raising women's salaries, residual discrimination against Black women, barriers to single women adopting children, economic protection for single mothers and women raising children alone, and the low level of discussion in the Congress itself. In her article, López Hernández wrote that "According to the intellectual and militant feminist Margaret Randall in her book *To Change the World: My Years in Cuba* (Editorial Matanzas, 2016), in the 90s there existed an interesting and little-known effort to create an independent women's organization here."[126] I found it sadly telling that that effort would be news in Cuba.

Arturo also sent me a published text by Cuban poet Víctor Fowler, who wrote about watching the FMC congress on television: "As the camera panned the plenary hall, I observed 200 women clapping enthusiastically. We learned, once again, of the organization's positions regarding an independent, anti-imperialist, Third World, Latin American, internationalist and Socialist nation. But I have no idea what its positions are on marriage equality, homosexuals (female and male) in the public sphere, transgender identity, femicide, laws against violence against women, and euthanasia (among others)."

126. The author is referring to MAGIN, organized by a group of feminist journalists who had made a gender analysis of Cuban society and found that after four decades of revolution the country still permitted denigrating images of women to appear in the press and in commercial advertising. They found the revolution's handling of women's issues in general to be seriously wanting. When the group tried to obtain judicial status, the FMC intervened. "As usual," López Hernández wrote, "the Cuban Communist Party used the permanent threat from the north and the need for unity as its excuse in denying MAGIN legitimacy."

It was clear that many Cubans were raising such concerns, publicly or privately. But the revolution's official institutions didn't have the courage to address them.

May 18, 2019

Dear Margaret:

I'm sure you saw that your Haydée Santamaría medal has been given ample coverage in the Cuban press, in *Granma* as well as on the evening news.

I'm sending you my proposal for the excerpt from your book about Haydée that we want to publish in La Gaceta. Aida sent me the whole chapter and Norberto and I selected the passages in which Casa's essential voices appear. Also, those in which you quote from letters that haven't previously been published. The whole chapter is very good, and if you approve our selection, it will be a magnificent tribute to Casa and to Haydée.

Kisses, A

[undated]

Dear Arturo:

I've been thinking of you. I was about to write when your letter appeared in my inbox. The excerpts you chose from my book on Haydée to use in *La Gaceta* seem excellent to me. And I love the fact that they constitute a tribute to Casa as well as to Haydée, especially at this moment when Casa has awarded me such a great honor.

I hope that Omaida has finished her treatments. How is she doing?[127]

---

127. Omaida had been receiving chemo and radiation treatments for breast cancer. Happily, they were successful and, as of this writing, she remains in remission.

I've recently received several honors. Probably because of my age. After the "Poet of Two Hemispheres" prize in Quito, I heard I was finally going to get an Honorary Doctor of Letters from my hometown university. This had been in the works since 2017 but two of the regents, both Republicans, said "over their dead bodies." In fact, the university didn't give any honorary doctorates in 2018 to avoid having to give one to me. But then last year's elections installed a Democratic governor—a terrific woman who has already done a lot of good for the state. As soon as she was inaugurated, she removed those regents and replaced them with others. The ceremony was last week, maybe you saw the photos on Facebook.

And on Friday Barbara and I will be going to Boston for the Haydée Santamaría medal.[128] It seems that several members of the Cuban delegation were denied visas, among them Jorge Fornet. But Zuleica and Suilan are coming, and one of them will bestow the honor. I'm immensely moved, and even more since I've read the list of the seventy or so people who have gotten this medal in the past: Gelman, Benedetti, Galeano, Frei Betto, Cardenal, Guayasamín, Silvio, Alfredo Guevara, Hart, Arnaldo Orfila, Viglietti, etc. etc. So many of them good friends. And you know what Haydée meant to me.

Despite this honor, my book about Haydée is still being held up—for reasons no one has been willing to tell me. Nancy Morejón, who I saw in Quito, said she'd try to speak with Juanito at the Book Institute, but since then she's written to say that each time she's been given an appointment it gets canceled and all she's been able to find out is that "the matter is in the hands of the Ministry of Culture." I've heard from friends and can

128. The medal was presented to me at the Latin American Studies Association (LASA) meeting, held that year in Boston.

glean from the press that there's a lot of bureaucracy there now. The cancellation of the Gay Pride parade was embarrassing. I also know there are many scarcities these days and difficulties in daily life. Trump is doing his dirty work everywhere. Here in the US many states have limited access to abortion. It feels like we're going back to medieval times. All my love, Margaret.

[undated]

Dear Arturo,

I see that the pandemic has unleashed itself in Cuba, as it has in so many other countries. Do you have sufficient vaccinations? Goyo tells me it's also bad in Uruguay, where there was no vaccine available for a while. I can't imagine the confusion there around the currency change: so many years with only Cuban pesos!

I've been working a lot. I'm still promoting my memoir that was released in March. Another book, *My Life in 100 Objects*, came out in September and I've been reading from it as well. My new poetry collection, *Out of Violence into Poetry*, will appear in May, with a Spanish translation to be published in Chile in October. Raúl Zurrita just wrote to tell me he will send a few lines for the back cover, which made me very happy. In September a book of my essays will be out here and in Mexico, so I've been working with several translators, going over various texts.

My current project is a book I'm calling *Artists in My Life*. It's about some of the visual artists whose work has impacted mine, among them Elaine de Kooning, Shinkichi Tajiri, Georgia O'Keeffe, Frida Kahlo, Leandro Katz, Gay Block, and Sabra Moore. The last chapter will be about Barbara. This has been a lovely project in terms of research and writing, and a lot more tedious in terms of obtaining permission to reproduce paintings. You know how that is, the same problem I had with the anthology of Cuban poetry in 2015. But the book should be beautiful. It will be published by New Village Press, a house that does good color reproductions.

All my love, Margaret.

April 6, 2020

Dear Arturo:

I don't know where you are right now. I hope in Cuba, where it is safer and where you'll have better medical attention in case you need it. These are extraordinary times everywhere, and not only in terms of public health. The economy and society in general are also affected. We're fine so far. Fortunately, New Mexico doesn't yet have many cases of the virus and our state government is good. This isn't true nationally. Trump has made the crisis worse in every way possible.

I've been working on a series of poems out of this situation and have more than twenty of them now.[129] They'll be released in book form in January from Wings Press. And they're being translated in Buenos Aires for publication there.

Write when you have time. Much love, Margaret.

April 6, 2020

Dear Margaret:

We were in Guadalajara until March 14th. On the 16th I started teaching at the film school. On the 20th we came home (Oma and I stayed out at the school those five days, taking all the necessary precautions because we'd been in three different airports). Last Sunday, the 29th, I learned that one of my students had

129. *Starfish on a Beach: The Pandemic Poems* (San Antonio: Wings Press, 2020). *Starfish on a Beach: The Pandemic Poems / Estrellas de mar sobre una playa: los poemas de la pandemia,* coedition (Buenos Aires: Editorial Abisinia; Bogotá: Escarabajo Editores, 2020).

fallen ill. I was considered one of his direct contacts and obliged to isolate immediately. I could either go to a community center set up for that purpose or stay at the school. I chose the latter. I wasn't too worried because I hadn't seen that student for nine days and hadn't been back to the school either. On the 30th they sent a car for me and another professor. On Wednesday they tested us, and I was negative, but the other professor tested positive. He has no symptoms but is now hospitalized. I'm alone in an apartment here; the whole school has been quarantined. They take my temperature four times a day, bring me my meals and anything else I need. Needless to say, I'm trying to keep my mind active: finishing up some work, reading, watching movies. At home all is well. Omaida has only been going out for necessities, and the kids—who are with us these days—are fine with the routine.

Take care of yourselves.

A huge hug, A

p.s. Have you heard from Víctor?

October 13, 2020

Dear Arturo:

It's been a while since I've heard from you. I hope you're well. I know the situation there is difficult. I want to know how you personally are doing.

We're doing all right. Here in the state the number of cases has gone up of late. We take the necessary precautions and live our lives. I've been doing on average five to seven virtual events a week, some with a lot of people, others with less. I've been promoting three new books and have participated in poetry festivals in Colombia and Argentina. There's one event that I'd love you to be able to attend, although I know this may be impossible from Cuba. On October 28th the University of New Mexico will celebrate the publication of my memoir and the fact that its library houses my archives, photographic as well as literary. At 2 p.m. that day there'll be a panel of "experts" who have used the archive. And at 4, a public conversation between Gioconda Belli and me. I think this latter is especially interesting (we taped it a couple of months back). She starts out interviewing me about my memoir, but then we begin to speak about what it was like for each of us, two strong women, to work in revolutionary movements led by misogynist men. I don't know if you'll be able to tune in, but I hope so.

It's been sad not to be able to visit you as we've been doing. I love you and Omaida a lot. Let me know how you are, Margaret.

October 14, 2020

Dear Margaret:

We're well. In Cuba, and especially in Havana, the number of cases has gone down. The government has changed its strategy due to lessons learned so far and in line with the demands of the economy. Havana is now in phase III of recovery, and except for two provinces, the rest of the country has entered what they're calling "the new normal," which is to say an abnormal state in which there's a certain freedom of movement with people returning to work and to school. And starting tomorrow commercial flights will return, except here in Havana.

I'll try to tune in to the program. Because of the blockade, some of those platforms are blocked, as you know. And we're all on pins and needles waiting for the election. Víctor tells me they're in the midst of a cold war that could turn hot at any moment. Frankly, I think the sociopath will be reelected.

A big kiss, A

November 7, 2020

Dear Arturo:

The news, so long awaited, that Joe Biden and Kamala Harris will be installed in the White House in January, is a huge relief. No one expects miracles. Neither Biden nor Harris is truly progressive in the ways we'd like, and they must deal with all Trump's crimes, plus half the population that still considers him its leader. Nonetheless, his reelection would have meant a descent into fascism that would have affected the entire world.

I know that Cuba has been a particular target of Trump's vile policies. I hope Biden will bring some relief in that respect, perhaps even the end of the blockade. There's a lot of work ahead, but this is a moment for joy and hope. Big hugs, Margaret.

[undated]

Dear Arturo:

Here, the transition from Trump to Biden has been like a breath of fresh air. We know elements of fascism remain and the threat is still present. And we know that Biden is far from a progressive leader. Still, last Wednesday so many of us here experienced a feeling of relief, of hope. I don't think I realized what living with Trump on a daily basis had been like, the constant weight of that, until I was on the plane going to Florida. I don't know if you saw any of the inauguration. There were some truly memorable moments, such as 22-year-old Amanda Gorman reading her poem, Sonia Sotomayor administrating the oath to Kamala Harris, and Lady Gaga singing the national anthem dressed like a figure from *The Hunger Games*! Symbols all, but meaningful. Perhaps the most important moment was when Biden mentioned white supremacy by name in his speech. I think of Cuba, of all of you. I so hope things can improve soon.

Love, Margaret.

[undated]

Dear Arturo:

Here too practically everything is virtual these days. I had an event next month in New York, but it was suspended and then we agreed we'd do it via Zoom. It's a shame but there are some advantages. People from all over the world can attend.

I'm having some fun lately rewriting some of the world's myths—Greek, Mesoamerican, and others—in the form of poetry. It's great to be able to reimagine them, if only in poems.

How I miss the trips to Cuba that Barbara and I had been able to make these past few years. I hope the pandemic allows us to go again before I'm too old to travel! All my love, Margaret.

November 26, 2020

Dear Arturo:

I want to ask you about the San Isidro Movement. I've been reading about it. I haven't wanted to sign anything because I don't know if it's another rightwing attempt to attack the revolution over minor problems or if it's legitimate. I know that the censorship is real, and I condemn that. What can you tell me about the hunger strike. When I heard there were people who had sewn their mouths shut it made me shudder; I remembered when the Uruguayan dictatorship did that to political prisoners, some of whom came to Cuba after their release to receive corrective medical attention. . . .

November 26, 2020

Dear Margaret:

About San Isidro, I'm sending you some documents. No one has sewn their mouth shut; that's false. Yesterday two of them stopped the hunger strike and another who wasn't drinking took a glass of water. It's all been distorted for political gain.

Arturo attached several articles to this email, helpful because news of dissent in Cuba is so often exaggerated or distorted in the mainstream international news media. Because it is typical of what he sent, I will quote excerpts from one of them, written by Eduardo del Llano and posted on his Facebook "Página Official":

> The resurgence of acts of repudiation and legitimized violence against those with different opinions who express them peacefully is unacceptable. This form of repression never completely disappeared, but it's had a resurgence now and it's as humiliating as it is anachronistic.
>
> It's clear the government doesn't want to deal with the opposition, and it must. And the sooner, the better. . . . But the San Isidro Movement doesn't convince me either. Rather than put forth a coherent list of demands, it launches absurd provocations. Taking up the banner of Denis Solís is a mistake, indefensible really, since he repeatedly attacked a policeman. . . . We all know that in any other country he would have had a knee on his neck or several bullets in his back. . . . To get the world's attention, the SIM calls the government a dictatorship. Calling the International Red Cross was symptomatic; why not simply accept the help from Cuban doctors, which was readily forthcoming?
>
> For the nation to have a luminous future, or any future, both sides must be willing to listen, negotiate, compromise. It would be unacceptable if someone should die. These are young Cubans whose ideas I may not agree with, but I defend their right to have and express them.
>
> Although the international press doesn't acknowledge it, Cuba has been able to control the Covid pandemic more efficiently than countries ten times richer and send help to other

nations as well. How much harder could it be to learn to listen to those who dissent, report on the issues as they happen, and do so with transparency? We urgently need to create a vaccination here called CIVICS.

January 24, 2021

Dear Margaret:

We're all well, the family and our friends, although the county is in terrible shape. The pandemic is out of control. As of today, there are 691 cases. Yesterday they reported 200 in Havana alone, a shocking number. And throughout January we've had to deal with both Covid and the changes in the economy, the latter requiring a reevaluation of everything from salaries and savings to expenditures. Personally, we're not in bad shape, but we're being very frugal. All this makes for a good deal of stress. In Havana they suspended classes a few days ago but not public transportation except between 9 p.m. and 5 a.m. We went shopping on Friday and Saturday and the lines are interminable. All in all, a very difficult situation. The one bright spot is the encouraging success in producing a Cuban vaccine. Have you and Barbara been able to get vaccinated?

A big kiss, A

March 5, 2021

Dear Arturo:

Norberto sent me what he wrote on the occasion of Ferlinghetti's death, very powerful.

I wrote to Zaldívar to ask about my anthology of Beat poetry. It would be wonderful if it could really be published there, especially for Edelmis Anoceto who worked so hard and did such magnificent translations. I confess that I'll believe it when/if it happens.

I hope you had a great birthday. Much love, Margaret.

May 1, 2021

Dear Arturo:

Yesterday I read what you wrote about Bladi.[130] I was on the highway so only saw it on my phone. Now I've just finished reading it more carefully. I so appreciate that you mentioned the homophobia he suffered. I can hear him now, with that way he had of using "*usted*" even when speaking to friends (from his peasant upbringing, no?). I miss him a lot. I'll always be grateful to Duke University Press that it was willing to insert my dedication to him in the poetry anthology at the very last minute. I'm glad to know there are doctoral dissertations on Bladi's work, that young people are paying attention to his great contributions. We must continue to celebrate his brilliance!

Much love, a hug for Omaida, Margaret.

July 17, 2021

Dear Arturo:

Every day I look to see if the pandemic has loosened its hold in Cuba. I know it will. Uruguay was one of the countries with most cases per capita in the world and now they have very few. I know that in Cuba the organization of healthcare and people's discipline are good. And I think it's incredible that the country has been able to develop two efficient vaccines, but because of the lack of hypodermic needles hasn't yet been able to vaccinate everyone. It seems that vaccinating the entire population is the only way of controlling the infection. Here in the US the numbers are on the rise again.

On another subject, a very good magazine called *The Café Review* has asked me to prepare a brief anthology of Latin American poetry in English. I'll only have 90 pages, so I'll be

130. Bladimir Zamora, our dear friend, who died in 2016.

quite limited. But I've already selected some wonderful unpublished poems by Rául Zurrita, Alfredo Zaldívar, Carlos María Gutiérrez, Juan Gelman, Jorg Enrique Adoum, Reina María Rodríguez, Roque Dalton, and Magda Portal, among others. I also have several texts by indigenous poets writing in their original languages. I want to include Nancy Morejón, but she hasn't responded to my mails. She almost always answers right away, so I don't know if she's having trouble with her email. Would you call her? What I need are a couple of unpublished poems—either already in English or I can do the translations. And a brief bio. I'm counting on you. Thanks. Much love, Margaret.

August 17, 2021

Dear Margaret:

I've delayed in answering you because I've had a lot of work but also because I myself am having difficulty understanding, and taking a position, in the context of the current Cuban reality. The texts I've sent you have been useful to me as well, even when I have some differences of opinion with some. I don't need to tell you that the situation is extremely complicated: the pandemic that's still not under control, the incessant effects of the blockade, the right's hostility that basically floods the mediums of communication and social media, thirty years of continuous crisis, and a government that lacks Fidel's political astuteness and that in time has inherited a country that is authoritarian, with a vertical power structure, and whose way of running things hasn't changed.

I've been reading some books about Cuban culture in the 1960s, and every day I'm more convinced that the Soviet Union is responsible. Without her, the Cuban revolution wouldn't have survived, but in following the Soviet model, in injecting it into the genes of the Cuban power structure, these distortions were inevitable in the long run. The centralism, the intolerance of different ideas, the lack of channels for an authentic participatory democracy, the mediocrity of the press, the consolidation of a rhetoric in which no one any longer believes (least of all the young): all these are the legacy of that model.

The great mistake of the 90s was not having made an authentic and profound critique of the entire Cuban model and, even worse, of that other revolution so damaged by Stalinism and its residual problems. An important part of our population is under 40. It was ten when the Socialist bloc disappeared, and we entered the "special period."[131] It doesn't feel that it's part of the solution, nor does it see a prosperous future for itself. It's that simple, that terrible.

As you can tell, I'm very down. A big kiss, A

August 17, 2021

Dear Arturo:

I can't imagine how you must be feeling, how so many dear friends must be feeling there. To think of the situation in Cuba from here in New Mexico is very different from experiencing it as a Cuban living it every day.

I agree with you. The Soviet (or Stalinist) model saved the revolution even as it hurt it terribly.

I appreciate everything you send, and I share it with Gregory and others who are interested. Like you, I agree with some texts more than others, but what impresses me is that there seems to be a public discussion composed of many voices.

131. Following the implosion of the Soviet Bloc in 1989–1990, Cuba suffered severe scarcities of everything from food to medicines. The early 1990s were particularly difficult years. Fidel dubbed them "a special period in a time of peace."

Although I don't know how many of those texts are published in Cuba, or if the political leadership reads them.

I hope you can find a way to lift your spirits. I think it's important to be able to have the emotional energy to keep on thinking, living, writing.

I too am feeling down. For various reasons, among them the situation in Afghanistan. I think especially of the women and young girls and how they will suffer under the Taliban. I resist by continuing to think, imagine, write. Much love, to Omaida too, Margaret.

September 16, 2021

Dear Arturo:

Although I've read the articles on the new Family Code that have appeared in *Granma*, I can't figure out if it covers families composed of two women or two men, or if it even contemplates marriage equality. The language seems so vague that I don't understand what it all means. Can you explain? Much love, Margaret.

September 16, 2021

Dear Margaret:

I'll try to explain by going back a bit. When we debated the new Constitution, one of the articles referred to marriage equality. The churches launched a tremendous campaign against it. The State considered the opposition and what finally appeared in the Constitution is vaguely worded. Textually: "Marriage is the voluntary union between two people with a legal right to it and with the goal of making a life together." They settled on the word "people" rather than "man and woman." And they postponed a definition of marriage itself for the Family Code, which will be submitted to a referendum.

Many of us consider this to have been a mistake, because submitting it to a referendum means it will be voted on by everyone and rights should be inalienable.

The churches and other conservative groups will do all they possibly can to stop marriage equality, and I fear they will also go after abortion.

I've noticed that in the mass media there's been a new emphasis on presenting gay reality, whether through fictional figures, interviews with activists, or by including them in public debates. I've heard Teresa Fernández (Pablo Armando's daughter) speak twice, and she's been excellent.

I'm especially troubled by the caution with which the government feels obliged to act with the churches. It doesn't want another fight with the Catholics like the one in the 60s, and it's a very powerful international lobby. And a few evangelical congregations in Europe have come out against the blockade, so that's another lobby it can't afford to lose. In short, I believe the government wants to approve marriage equality but without taking on the fight with these conservative sectors.

I hope I've made the whole situation clearer for you.

Kisses, A

December 14, 2021

Dear Margaret:

Finally, I can write a decent letter. I've had a lot of work these past weeks, first at the home of a friend where we've been working on a film for a Dominican director, and then as part of the jury at the Film Festival. I had to view a huge number of films of varying quality. Fortunately, the members of the jury worked well together and there weren't many disagreements. Add to all this, the chores of everyday life.

The family is well, and the pandemic seems to be ceding. Everything points to the Cuban vaccine's effectiveness. Just last week we all got our fourth dose.

As for the country, it's a complex situation as you know. On the one hand, the economic difficulties (resulting from the combination of the blockade and our own inefficiencies and bureaucracy). Many young people see no future for themselves, and the enemy has built on this. The government's political and ideological ineptness is also to blame. The same old empty rhetorical discourse is repeated again and again. Nonetheless, there are some bright spots: there's been some good work in some of Havana's poorest neighborhoods as well as in other cities, a positive outcome of the demonstrations on July 11th. And people have been able to freely raise their voices and express their dissatisfaction.

There's a lot more to say, of course. At the moment our most urgent tasks are to continue to fight the pandemic and recover as much as possible economically. The economy has become less centralized with more space being given over to the private sector. Are we bringing capitalism back? Which leads us to the more important question: is it really possible to construct a Socialist society in a single country, one that is isolated and blockaded and without a rearguard? Our recent history would seem to say no.

Once again, thank you for your friendship and company, A

April 6, 2022

Dear Arturo:

Ambrosio's death is such a loss. I just found out from Ximena. When you have a moment, let me know what happened. Of course, I knew he had become quite fragile. But oh, I will miss him. Much love, Margaret.

[undated]

Dear Arturo:

It's in situations such as those you describe, in which ordinary people are so willing to help however they can, that one feels what's left of the revolution. It's the evidence that our dreams haven't all gone up in smoke. Goyo and Laura are in Paris this year (he's on sabbatical) and a few weeks ago friends lent them a house on the Adriatic coast. Goyo told me a similar story. He said that passing through Rome they were looking for a place to have dinner. They finally found a restaurant called Malatesta (after the great Italian anarchist). They went in and found it filled with local people. They ate a lot and well—main dishes, wine, dessert and so forth—and when they asked for the check, their waiter didn't bring an itemized bill but simply said: "Twenty-five euros, please." Great food and incredibly inexpensive, so they returned the following night. This time they ate even more, and it cost less, only 20 euros. Goyo said he thought they'd make a mistake, and the waiter replied: "Well, okay, give me 25 if you want!" Goyo finally figured out that if the guy liked you, he charged you less and if he didn't, more. He also said that at all the restaurants in Italy you have to pay for water but on the menu at this one it said: "We don't charge for water here; it's everyone's right."

What a different world it would be if that sort of attitude predominated!

Much love, Margaret.

August 14, 2022

Dear Margaret:

A long time without communication. Personally, we are doing well. Alejandro and his daughter had dengue and then Covid, but both were mild. They're fine now. Beyond health issues and the daily grind, we have been overwhelmed by the recent fire[132] and other symptoms of the deterioration of our reality, here and elsewhere. Omaida was especially affected by the fire since she still has relatives there, although as far as we know everyone is okay. I wrote immediately to Alfredo and Norge and they're both fine. The fire was to the east of the city and the smoke traveled in the opposite direction. In Cojímar and Havana in general we had two mornings with gray skies, almost black.

At the same time, people's responses have been beautiful, those who had to fight the fire directly and also the inhabitants of Matanzas; they were incredibly generous with one another. Taxi drivers wouldn't charge people to ride. Others gave free lodging to the national journalists who came to cover the incident. Restaurants and cafes provided free food and water. Mexico and Venezuela also responded immediately. We are very good friends with the Mexican ambassador (he was cultural attaché for six years before assuming his current position) and he went to Matanzas several times to coordinate anything his country could do to help put out the flames. Now it remains to be seen what the consequences of the accident will be. In the short term, a lack of gas due to the amount that was burned and the fact that the tanks where it was stored were severely damaged. And then the damage to the environment which we can't yet know.

Through it all, I keep writing. I've accumulated short stories and a couple of novels that don't yet have publishers. I've

---

132. An explosion at a petroleum depot caused a massive chemical fire outside the city of Matanzas, resulting in deaths, a great deal of destruction, and economic loss.

also been working on the script for a film that's now being produced in the Dominican Republic.

Wonderful that you'll be going to Mexico and can spend some time with Sarah and Ximena. Give them both my love.

A big hug, dear friend, A

May 4, 2023

Dear Arturo:

I dreamed of you and Omaida last night and realized I must write. I get stronger each day, but the situation was critical. Somehow, I got an E. coli infection that traveled to my only kidney and then into my bloodstream and I became septic. I was in the hospital for a few days, at risk of dying, and dealing with a health system that is basically broken. In the end, my will won out and I made it through. I'm still recuperating, and it's been harder than I expected. But every day I feel a little better. Such that we're going to make a road trip for Barbara's birthday that we'd been planning before I got sick. We're going to Marfa, a small town in Texas that is famous for its art installations. We'll be traveling with two friends who know the place well, so they will help with the driving.

I know that the situation there is super difficult. I almost couldn't believe that the country wouldn't be celebrating May 1st as it has every year. The gasoline shortage must present daily challenges. I ask myself how this whole mix of problems caused by the blockade and by a lack of internal competence will end. I know that many young people are leaving, which must make for an important deficit in the labor force. I remember the promising years of the Cuba we once knew and feel such pain. Know that I think of you daily. Write when you can. Much love to you both, Margaret.

May 4, 2023

Dear Margaret:

How frightening that infection must have been, and what a relief to know you are better. Your spiritual and physical strength amaze me.

The situation here, as you say, is agonizing. The worst part is that we don't see a solution. Without doubt, it's a combination of the blockade and the incapacity of the government. They are incapable of looking ahead, proposing solutions, even of paying attention to people's alternative suggestions. There's no real participation. And the exodus is terrible. When I walk around Cojímar, most of the people I see are elderly, bent over, with canes, out to fill their basic needs because there's no one to do it for them.

In general, we're okay. Haydee and her family are in Norway for three months on a university exchange. They were there last year around this time and for the children it was an incredible experience. Since they live across the street from us and we are used to seeing them every day, you can imagine how much we miss them.

The most difficult thing these days is the shortage of gasoline. I keep a couple of liters in my car for emergencies, or to be able to make it to a nearby service station when I hear some has come in. To go to Havana for work, I take the bus or a taxi. The hardest part is tracking down groceries because the nearby markets where we can go on foot don't have much in stock. But we are okay, as I say. We usually have enough to get by. And my trips help a lot. At the beginning of June, I'll be going to Switzerland for a few days and the last two weeks of that month we'll both be in Guadalajara.

Take care of yourself and enjoy that trip.

A big kiss, A

June 17, 2023

Dear Arturo:

Speaking with Gregory today, he told me about a film by Juan Pin[133] that was censored after it was shown at the film festival and he said that you and others signed a letter of protest. I imagine there's a back story; if you have time write and tell me. I'm very interested in knowing what happened. Love, Margaret.

June 18, 2023

Dear Margaret:

I'm writing from Guadalajara, where I arrived last night with Omaida. I'll be teaching this week and then we'll stay the following week on vacation.

Yes, Goyo is right. In synthesis, a few weeks ago they were going to show three films at a small theater called El Ciervo Encantado. One of them was *Havana* by Fito (an Argentinean filmmaker) and Juan Pin. Someone at the Ministry of Culture prohibited the showing. News of this spread from person to person and Fito complained to the Argentinean Ministry of Culture. They got in touch with Juan Pin and proposed it be shown on TV. He tried to hold out for the Chaplin Theater but those from the Ministry of Culture insisted on TV. Juan Pin said he'd have to consult with the agency to which they had sold the international distribution rights. That agency said the film couldn't be shown on Cuban TV. Juan Pin said he was satisfied that the Ministry had backed down but that the film couldn't be shown in that venue. The Ministry said they were showing it there anyway. All these details are confusing, but

133. Juan Pin is a Cuban filmmaker who is a family friend, the brother of one of my daughter Ximena's boyfriends in high school.

the important thing is that the original act of censorship snowballed, threatening to violate the filmmaker's rights. The print that was finally exhibited turned out not even to be the final cut.

Immediate protest, involving figures such as Silvio, José María Vitier, and Marcia Leseica,[134] developed into two different groups. The first consisted of nine people (including myself); for several years we've been generating a movement to renovate the Cuban film industry. The second was a group of younger people. We wrote a declaration; they called for an assembly at which our declaration was read and approved. We asked for signatures from all those connected to the world of film, and the response has been extraordinary.

I helped write the document but couldn't attend the assembly because I'd just returned from Switzerland on the night of the 12th and had to leave yesterday morning to come here. I needed to deal with all sorts of issues at the house. The Ministry of Culture proposed a meeting for this coming Tuesday which I also won't be able to attend. It's clear they don't know what to do with such an immediate response to their irresponsible act.

A kiss, A

Censorship has been a topic of discussion throughout my correspondence with Arturo. Censorship exists everywhere, although it manifests itself differently depending on the country. In the United States, most people don't call it by that name, but power, money, and access determine what gets published and how many people it reaches; alternative voices are censored

134. The singer/songwriter Silvio Rodríguez, the composer José María Vitier, and Marcia Leseica, who was vice president of Casa de las Américas at the time.

by virtue of their lack of access to the major media or because they are drowned out by the "official story." Additionally, in recent years hundreds of books have been banned from school libraries and curricula, and this has gotten worse as Trump's brand of neofascism prospers. In Cuba, since the government and Party have so much more of a direct relationship with people's day-to-day lives, censorship has targeted individual writers and artists who dare to challenge the system's narrow vision. Throughout its six decades of revolution, periods of extreme censorship have generally accompanied moments in which the nation has felt most threatened by outside pressure. At those rare times when it's felt less so, freedom of expression has flourished. In both countries, over the past two decades the proliferation of social media has made absolute control more difficult and protest easier.

Of course, one hopes that a revolution that promised freedom wouldn't censor any voice. I am disappointed that the Cuban Revolution still engages in the practice, but always encouraged to see people fighting back, particularly respected writers and artists with long traditions of important work. And I'm encouraged that the country's cultural leadership generally listens to those voices. A distinguishing feature of the Cuban Revolution has been the fact that various currents have always existed simultaneously, providing space for discussion.

September 27, 2023

Dear Arturo:

I just heard that you've been initiated into the Academy of Letters with the letter that Arrufat vacated when he died. Such a well-deserved honor! I'm celebrating with you! Much love, Margaret.

September 28, 2023

Dear Margaret:

Thanks for your message. This has been a beautiful time, especially because of the love of my friends, although I confess that academic honors aren't that important to me.

A kiss, A

Arturo and I continue to correspond. I believe we will do so until one of us is gone. I hope his letters may one day reflect a better reality in Cuba, a country we both love: he because it belongs to him and me because it has contributed so much to who I am.

IV

KATHY BOUDIN: AN EXAMINED LIFE

KATHY BOUDIN WAS BORN in 1943 into a Jewish family with a rich left-wing history. Her father was Leonard Boudin, a constitutional lawyer who had defended the great baritone Paul Robeson, among others; her mother was a poet; her great-uncle was the Marxist theorist Louis B. Boudin; and her uncle was the progressive investigative journalist I. F. Stone. Before his retirement, her only sibling, Michael, was a federal court judge, although of a conservative bent.

In 1965, Kathy graduated from Bryn Mawr College as that year's valedictorian. She did a senior year abroad in Russia and applied to and was accepted at Case Western Reserve University School of Law but attended for only a short time. The war in Vietnam was raging and racial oppression was rampant. To Kathy and her friends, it seemed a time for organizing. In 1969, she and other members of Students for a Democratic Society (SDS) left that campus-based group to launch the Weather Underground (later called the Weather Underground Organization, WUO). Crackdowns on anyone who protested were increasing in frequency and intensity. For the next decade, she would be involved in a series of actions, including bombings, only one of which resulted in human casualties.[135]

In 1980, Kathy, David Gilbert, and Judy Clark, along with members of the May 19th Communist Organization and the Black Liberation Army, robbed a Brinks armored car in Nanuet, New York. Kathy was in the front seat of a U-Haul truck used as a switch-car getaway vehicle. When the police stopped them, she was terrified. The officers saw that she was unarmed and put their guns away so as to be able to open the back. Her accomplices then leaped out and shot them both. In all, the operation took the lives of three law-enforcement officers: those two policemen and a guard.

That morning, before embarking on the fatal operation, Kathy and David had dropped their fourteen-month-old son, Chesa, off with a babysitter. What did they imagine their chances were of picking him up that afternoon? I believe many educated upper-class revolutionaries at the time suffered from white guilt, and perhaps Kathy's collaboration with the Black Revolutionary Army was an effort to be part of its struggle for racial justice. Over her years in prison, Kathy reflected long and hard on having been involved in an operation that caused the loss of human life.

Kathy was arrested while attempting to flee on foot. As part of a negotiated plea agreement to avoid triple murder

---

135. The one exception was the Greenwich Village town house explosion that took place at 18 West Eleventh Street on March 6, 1970. Several members of the Weather Underground were hiding out and making bombs when one of them exploded and a succession of subsequent blasts destroyed the building and killed three of them: Theodore Gold, Diana Oughton, and Terry Robbins. Kathy and Cathy Wilkerson escaped with minor injuries. But these were the tragic deaths of militants, not civilians.

convictions, she eventually pled guilty to felony murder and robbery for an agreed-upon sentence of twenty years to life. She would serve almost twenty-three. Her time on the inside was spent getting a master's degree in adult literacy, creating model programs for incarcerated mothers and their children, developing an exemplary AIDS education and treatment project, writing several books, helping to raise her son while separated from him by prison walls, and reflecting on the choices that led to her involvement in the Brinks robbery.

In 1986, while I was teaching at Trinity College in Hartford, Connecticut, my close friend Ruth Hubbard suggested I might like to meet Kathy at the Bedford Hills Correctional Facility in Bedford, New York. Bedford was only an hour-and-a-half drive from Hartford, and one day Ruth, who lived in Boston, picked me up and we made the trip together. Thus began a deep friendship that continued until Kathy's death, in 2022. Whenever I was on the East Coast, a priority for me was visiting her.

I don't think I will ever forget the images and emotions around that first visit. The small town of Bedford is typically upscale suburban New York, but as we approached the prison, we began to experience that sense of foreboding such bleak fortresses project. The entrance process is made to instill fear. We didn't have to endure the body searches often associated with such places, but even being patted down and ushered from one confined area to the next, with the accompanying sound of metal locking against metal behind one, are designed to make one uncomfortable. By the time we arrived in the visitors' room and were seated at one of the steel tables bolted to the floor, I was suitably chastised by a feeling of powerlessness. From her elevated perch, a guard observed everyone and everything. A few inmates in loose-fitting dark green cotton shirts and pants sat around the room, conversing with their respective guests, some of them children.

Then and later, I tried to imagine what it feels like to be denied one's freedom, not only of movement but of relationships, communication, agency, and so much else that we take for granted. To be confined to a small cell and arbitrary rules and regulations regarding bathing, telephone calls, how one chooses to dress. Being denied the ability to have a relationship, raise one's child, visit a friend, take a walk. And to be subject to random searches of one's cell or one's body meant to keep one in a state of constant stress. I also knew being denied these aspects of life probably wasn't the worst thing about incarceration. Not knowing if or when one might be released—if one would have a future after prison—would be a constant weight.

When Kathy entered the visiting room accompanied by a guard that first day, there was a subtle shift. She walked toward us, a warm and welcoming smile on her face. I felt immediately at ease, as if she were an old friend. I spent several hours there, and gradually those surroundings, calculated to intimidate, disappeared due to Kathy's ability to make me feel at ease. Oh, there were the absurd rules I would come to know so well over the many years of our visits—having to purchase stale fast-food products from clunky dispensers the prisoners themselves weren't allowed to touch, being reprimanded for too much personal contact, the requirement that all gifts go through the prison's system for receiving any item sent to a prisoner—but these became irrelevant as our friendship grew.

Over the next decades, I accumulated a trove of letters from Kathy and sent as many to her. Sadly, I didn't keep copies of mine until near the end of our correspondence. Although her letters to me are housed in my archive at the Center for Southwest Research at the University of New Mexico, Albuquerque, I closed them to public view during Kathy's life. Too many books and articles of a mean-spirited or vindictive nature had been written about her, and I didn't want to risk someone taking something from our correspondence and using it for another such publication. When Kathy died, I released the hold.

Many of Kathy's letters were handwritten on yellow legal paper or whatever she had access to at the time. Some words are difficult to decipher, and I have had to use the context and my imagination in making decisions. When the prison authorities allowed her to have a typewriter and then a computer, I was able to transcribe them more easily. However they arrived, they always moved me deeply, as did our visits.

I have arranged the following letters and excerpts in chronological order so as to give a sense of how our friendship developed. Although what follows are mostly Kathy's letters to me, the fact that she always commented—sometimes at length—on what I had written will enable the reader to sense something of the rhythm of our dialogue.

June 6, 1986

Dear Margaret,

Although we had never met, I feel as if we have been connected through many years—through mutual friends, through your wonderful books, and perhaps most of all by sharing a set of historical conditions which led each of us to make decisions about how to live our lives, decisions which although different also had a lot in common.

I want to thank you very much for the book of poems which you sent me at the time of my sentencing. It meant a lot to me partly because of the poems and partly coming from you as someone whose life choices and books had always given me strength.

Also, at that time Brooke and Debbie and Ruth[136] gave me *Women Brave in the Face of Danger.*[137] That is a book which I loved and which I have been able to share with women here.

I read *Sandino's Daughters* shortly after my arrest in 1981. It is a book that stands out in my mind because I was reading about other women, like me, who had chosen a particular means of participating in the struggle. At that point, the distortions of the press as to any reasonable motive, the freakout of friends and relatives as to how I could have wasted my life and hurt my son, and the criticism of us and desire to disassociate by the left relegated me to a pretty demoralized state. While I had come to terms with my own questions, my own feelings, *Sandino's Daughters* helped by providing a context from which to look at myself. (I'm not comparing Nicaragua to the US so much as saying that the book, by dealing personally with life choices made by young women committed to the struggle for change, did help me feel better and stronger in a difficult situation.)

I read *Cuban Women Now*[138] in the 70s when I was underground. The book was very important in struggles we have engaged in within the women's movement. It provided a lot of important information that was helpful when debating or struggling over issues such as "what does women's liberation mean," to whom, where, etc.

---

136. The feminist biologist Ruth Hubbard was the person who took me to Bedford Hills Correctional Facility and introduced me to Kathy. Debbie is Ruth's daughter, Brooke her daughter's partner.

137. *Women Brave in the Face of Danger* (Freedom, CA: Crossing Press, 1985). Photographs by Margaret Randall accompanied by brief texts by Latin and North American women).

138. *Cuban Women Now* (Toronto: Women's Press, 1974).

I always had a certain identification with you in those years because of Cuba. I had gone there in December 1960–January 1961. I returned to the US on the day they (the US) broke relations. The three week trip was one of the formative events of my life. The idealism, the sense of human beings being able to stretch towards their full potential, the collective spirit—on the one hand—in such contrast with the cynicism in the US, the lies of the "free press" *New York Times* which suddenly I really experienced, then the Bay of Pigs invasion in the spring of 1961 confirming everything I had heard there.

Both sides of my experience set me on a direction of wanting to be part of revolutionary change in the US, and Cuba has remained a country which I admire, try to study and learn from.

Naturally a lot has happened in the world since then, and the struggle of countries to develop socialism, to pull out of the conditions created by colonialism, to survive in a world dominated by imperialism: these are all factors which have taught our generation that transformation is harder, slower, than we understood back then, almost 30 years ago.

After I was arrested and was able to comprehend what the event meant in terms of just how long a time in jail I might face and the separation from my son who I had waited so long to have (37 years), I had to assess my life—partly I had to figure out a way to literally mentally and politically survive the pressures.

I was looking at a situation of 11½ years underground and then a minimum of 20 years in jail. What's more, I felt that David and I had made a terrible mistake for both of us to be in a situation to get arrested and leave our 14-month-old son. Finally, I felt there were serious strategic errors in our work.

At the time, I read a book by Janet Shenk and Robert Armstrong about El Salvador.[139] There was a passage in it in which what it is to be a revolutionary was described. I can't remember it precisely, something about how they are people who dedicate their lives to transforming society, who try to be scientists. Then there was a passage about how sometimes they make terrible mistakes (they were, in fact, referring to something on the level of the murder of Roque Dalton).

I remember reading that and a sense of peace (accompanied by tears) swept over me. I was able to feel myself very strongly in a worldwide tradition of people whose life choices were determined by historical conditions and by the desire to create a society of equality and justice. In this period, socialism and anti-imperialism were intrinsic to the struggle and I had an identity with others whose lives had also entailed tremendous sacrifice and hardships, including of course death and torture. And including serious mistakes of both a personal and political nature.

During the almost five years that I have been in jail I meet people every day whose lives have been ruined by drugs, by the violence directed against them as women, by racism, and I realize how incredibly fortunate I am to have led a life of meaning, a meaning I chose to give it, and that I was privileged enough to be able to lead according to my own choices.

Sometimes the choice to be a revolutionary is accompanied by a deep loneliness, especially when everyone else's life has assumed a kind of normalcy. And for me, I have had to really think deeply about what it was that affected me in my life and why I made those choices.

---

139. This must have been *El Salvador: The Face of Revolution*, by Janet Shenk and Robert Armstrong (Boston: South End Press, 1982).

The period of "waiting" that you are in now must be difficult.[140] I know in terms of dealing with prison that the pretrial period is very rough because everything is up in the air, on the one hand temporary, and also the future is unknown, such that it's very hard to focus. I remember, in moving from jail to jail, Judy[141] and I always struggled within ourselves about how much to really set up our cells versus how much to live out of bags and not decorate them. But we always opted for setting them up to be all that they could be. It was, in a way, a struggle for life as opposed to death in a psychological and political sense.

I had the privilege and honor of doing a little legal work on the issues that are in your brief, reading the cases on economic and emotional duress. Undoubtedly my work simply repeated what others were doing simultaneously but I was glad to be able to do even a little. And I am anxiously awaiting the decision.

I am going to end here but I hope in future correspondence I can describe some of the work I am doing inside. My life is very full in terms of work. And thanks to people like you, who have traveled a similar road as I, I feel the strength of the international revolutionary community.

Of course, if there is anything I can do, please tell me.

I am writing you through Ruth and I want to enclose a poem by Assata Shakur,[142] and to send you, sister/comrade, a hug from afar. Love, Kathy Boudin.

---

140. Kathy is undoubtedly referring to the fact that the deportation order put me in a state of uncertainty. Would I win the case and be able to stay in the United States, or lose and be forced to relocate somewhere else?

141. Judy Clark was arrested with Kathy and was with her at Bedford Hills. She was paroled in 2019, after serving thirty-seven years.

142. Assata Shakur (1947) was a member of the Black Liberation Army. In 1977, she was convicted in the first-degree murder of a state trooper during a shoot-out on the New Jersey Turnpike that took place in 1973. She

AFFIRMATION

I believe in living
I believe in the spectrum
Of Beta days and Gamma people
I believe in sunshine
In windmills and waterfalls
Tricycles and rocking chairs
And I believe that seeds grow into sprouts
And sprouts grow into trees
I believe in the magic of hands
And in the wisdom of the eyes
I believe in rain and tears
And in the blood of infinity.

I believe in life
And I have seen the death parade
March through the torso of the earth
Sculpting mud bodies in its path
I have seen the destruction of the daylight
And seen the blood-thirsty maggots
prayed to and saluted.

I have seen the kind become the blind
and the blind become the kind
in one easy lesson
I have walked on cut glass
I have eaten crow and blunder bread
and breathed the stench of indifference.

---

escaped from prison in 1979 and resurfaced in Cuba in 1984, where she was granted political asylum. I taught her autobiography, *Assata,* to university students throughout the 1990s.

I have been locked by the lawless
handcuffed by the haters
gagged by the greedy
and, if I know a thing at all
it's that a wall is just a wall
and nothing more at all
It can be broken down.

I believe in living
I believe in birth
I believe in the sweat of love
and in the fire of truth.

And I believe that a lost ship
steered by tired seasick sailors
can still be guided home
to port.
—*Assata Shakur*

September 27, 1986

Dear Margaret,

By now you have gotten your decision. From what I was told by Brooke and Debbie and Ruth, it was negative but was as good a decision as one might have hoped for in terms of how it was written. I don't know if that is how you view it exactly, and I know that however it was rendered the continued uncertainty that you are living with has to be very very difficult.

When I was trying to figure out whether to take a plea bargain, which more or less eliminated my right to appeal, versus going to trial which would mean the right to appeal, one of the considerations that more seasoned political prisoners raised with me was the emotional instability that clearly absorbed that roller coaster way of living, if I felt it was worth it. There definitely is a toll taken in the constant ups and downs and waiting that I see people go through here. Learning to live very much in the present is something I do more of now. Perhaps it also has something to do with age, but some of it has to do with recognizing that the future is uncertain enough that I must appreciate what is around me now.

It comes down a lot around my son. For example, if I were to be mainly waiting until I got out to have the relationship with him that I would dream of, I would miss his childhood. I must try to make as rich and full as I can my relationship to him under these conditions. Similarly, if I were to constantly be aware of what I am missing, I would be taking away from what in fact I have. I find myself trying to squeeze from each moment of beauty as much as I can, whether a beautiful sunset, a lovely flower, a flock of birds, or a good jazz tape. It sounds from your letter that you are living more fully than there are hours in a day in spite of how you must feel in terms of being suspended.

I had a very long tormented experience before getting arrested of trying to decide whether to go above ground. For me, being above ground, even in this situation, has been quite liberating in certain ways. Freedom is a strange thing and, as is obvious, people live in a lot of different kinds of prisons. Now, living in the "real prison," I can say from experience that there are worse kinds, or at least different kinds.

Since I have been here, I have been working on a number of levels. I made a decision after all these years of mainly being an organizer, political worker, etc., that I wanted to develop some other skills. It is something I have always wanted, but at the height of the 60s when it was time for me to go to graduate school the needs of the time made me want to do nothing but organize. And by the time I began to study Vietnamese history and the struggle, the notion of being a professional revolutionary, a cadre, replaced any other professional goals. In a sense I still have a lot of that identity, but I also wanted to supplement it with some skills. I decided to get into adult literacy since it seemed a useful skill and one with political possibilities. I have been pursuing an independent master's degree course of study (this has given me some structure for learning), and I have been doing a bunch of tutoring. For the past five months I have been a teacher's aide in the elementary or basic reading program where people from 0 to 6th grade level are. I work there about three hours a day.

I also work in a foster care/parents' rights program in which we try to inform women of their rights and responsibilities around visitation with their children, custody issues, etc. And I've worked on trying to improve the situation here around sports. We formed a sports committee. And last year, when a lot of people came down with AIDS, we formed an AIDS committee to try to deal with some of the hysteria.

In terms of the kinds of work I do here, I really feel it has a variety which feels very good. The hardest thing is that a lot of it feels lonely. But I have a long view. Many women here are doing long sentences. Perhaps I am too idealistic, but I think if I work over and over again with some of the same women perhaps over the years some sort of community of women who experience themselves as sisters/comrades might develop.

The hardest thing for me has been trying to have some inner life, as you put it. In a way, I move from project to project without feeling I am able to deal deeply with things. It's strange to say that life in here can be experienced as a whirlwind in which there isn't time to do everything, but it is. I actually love poetry and there have been a few times in my life when I wrote.

But it has always depended on having a certain intimacy with a friend, usually women, which allowed for a certain opening inside and resulted in poetry about many different things. I wish I could push myself to write without waiting for a certain type of friendship to create the context for doing it, since that could be years in coming.

It's strange, but in here people have had to experience such hard knocks that they deal with the most difficult things by saying: "Well, I'll survive, I have to, I can take it, don't worry about it," and the feelings end up being dealt with by "moving right along" instead of dealing with them deeply. "Moving right along" is a way that people feel stronger, less vulnerable, and even I have adopted such an approach to some degree. I liked your poems—going back to experiences, taking them seriously. They made me try to think back, but it also relates to the present. How to think about things even as they are happening, so as to take them seriously, to absorb them deeply.

One other thing before I end . . .

I think I'll end here. I just got the news that a Puerto Rican who is doing 20 to life, her 14-year-old daughter was stabbed to death in Harlem last night. It's hard for me to think about much else. So many people's lives are blown apart by violence in here.

I hope to hear from you soon. Love, Kathy.

March 1988

Dear Friends,

I want to write a mid-winter letter. I've been terrible about correspondence, but I want to be able to write so I'm going to write a collective letter.

For me personally two major things have happened. One was that Judy got moved from here to the federal prison system, to a detention center in Tucson, Arizona. This is an unprecedented move because she is a state prisoner and, like all state prisoners, should be kept in a New York state prison. There are some states, such as Massachusetts, New Jersey, and numerous others, in which they can "board" state prisoners with a federal prison. This gives states the "flexibility" to ship out prisoners they don't want, like organizers. For example, Sundiata Acoli[143] was put in the federal system and has been held at Marion. But New York State has no such contract. So, this is unusual.

When Judy first arrived at Bedford Hills in the fall of 1983, they kept her isolated in SHU (the special housing unit, as they call it, which is where people are kept in their cells 23 hours a day when they are punished; this is where she spent the past two years). They kept her in isolation for two and a half months until she finally had a hearing, and she won. There was another strange twist to it, namely she and I were about to begin a project on AIDS just before Judy was taken to SHU. We had begun to build a support committee for people with AIDS. It was a small step which had some public impact. Then David began his work at Auburn with the concept of an ongoing peer counseling group, in which the men would be trained. This model made a lot of sense to us and the crisis around AIDS had deepened so we embarked on developing something similar here. We had developed a proposal, and the day Judy was taken she and I were having a meeting about the project with the superintendent. We had a very productive meeting, really hammering out what concrete implementation would be like. We met for over two hours. Towards the end of those two hours a phone

143. Clark Squire, who was arrested with Assata Shakur in New Jersey in 1973.

call came, and the superintendent left the room and came back and said she had to end the meeting. Judy and I went back to our respective living units with a lot of excitement about the work. And when she got to her unit, she was told to go back to the administration building where she was put into federal custody and taken to Arizona. She is alright but it is a very isolated scene. She describes it as between being in the SHU isolation and a Holiday Inn—good food, salads, a little patio with an exercise bicycle and sunshine, videos all day, and yet living in a complete void: ten or so other women isolated in a tiny unit in a men's prison, visits only on weekends and only three visitors permitted aside from immediate family.

The second major thing that happened is that David was moved from one New York state prison to another. This is actually very common practice. There are many men's maximum-security prisons, and it is fairly unusual that David wasn't moved for four years. But two things about it are not usual. First, David was in the middle of building the first state prison program of prisoner-led ongoing work around AIDS based on the idea of peer counseling. David's analysis of why he was moved at that time is directly linked to the administration wanting to block the development of this program. Secondly, David was moved in the middle of a two-day visit with Chesa. When Chesa went back the second day, he was told that his father wasn't there, and they didn't know where he was. Even as I write it takes my breath away.

These places can be incredibly consciously cruel. They function like big impersonal machines. Here, when people's relatives die, the families can call the prison and leave a message with the watch commander so that the woman can be notified immediately. Yesterday a friend of mine told me that two days ago her mother died. Her family had called the prison to notify her. And the prison officials never did. Three days later, when she hadn't called home, someone came up to visit and tell her.

In September, the teacher of the adult basic education reading class resigned for personal reasons. I had been the teacher's aide in that class, mainly spending a year and a half correcting workbooks and learning about an approach to teaching reading which I thought was horrible. In an unusual move, I was allowed to have the class myself as the teacher in the interim until they hire someone. This has never happened before. This gave me an opportunity to teach reading in which content is primary and skills are derived from content.

I worked on two separate projects which ultimately merged. The first related to AIDS. We had the video of the ABC National AIDS test that had been a two-hour TV show in September. We watched it in the classroom and the women were riveted to the show. They had a lot of questions about the issues, about the concepts of many words (i.e., immune system), about spelling everything from patient and disease to pneumonia, hemophiliac, etc.

Following the show, we did a period of time working on AIDS. We had vocabulary, writing, reading, a lot of discussion of issues such as should you take the test or shouldn't you, who should you tell if you test positive, what would be a good program for AIDS here at Bedford Hills for those women who have AIDS and for those who don't. The experience in working with the issues of AIDS was a striking example of how the emotional importance of words and subject matter can transform the reading and learning process. Women are writing on their own and bringing in what they wrote. They learned words way beyond what anyone would think they could learn. The classroom was transformed from individuals reading short paragraphs in workbooks to a group of women together involved in dealing with a problem we all face. And my relationship as a teacher was transformed from being someone who was really apart from the women and who corrected workbooks to someone who was part of the process of working on a common problem and who could teach reading and writing skills in a meaningful context.

The second process which began at the same time was that of the women writing a play. Two times a week, for an hour each, we decided would be set aside to write our own play. We began by looking at what is a play. Then we read some short plays written and performed by an adult literacy program from the community. Their plays were perfect because the women completely related to them, and it provided a model for what we could do. One was called "The Problem of Drugs in the Family." Another was about tenants having a rent strike because of housing conditions. The women were so excited about them that they put these plays on in their living units, involved other women and even some of the guards. Then we talked about the elements of a play, looked at how plays are built around conflicts and resolutions. We analyzed these plays for those elements, evaluated the endings, and talked about how we could do a different ending. And then we moved on to writing our own play. Our play was about issues of AIDS that women here face: should they take the test or not, should they tell their parents to whom they are going to be paroled that they have tested positive and/or have AIDS, should they tell their lover here that they just found out they have the virus. We developed the issues. Characters emerged. People developed dialogue and worked on writing it down.

When we put the play on for the women, it took this whole experience into another dimension: the role of theater in a community working on common issues. We put the play on four times for students in the school, about 150 women saw it. Then we put it on for one of the living units, another 70 women watched it. Finally, we put it on for some counselors and others and did a video.

The reaction of the audience was as if they were living through the play. They laughed, they cried, they identified with all the characters and their reactions of fear, of compassion. When I look back at some of the work I've done here, theater work stands out as some of the best. Women here are so incredibly talented in acting, and acting just makes so many issues come alive. I've learned a lot about dealing with issues in ways other than a serious presentation, discussion, analysis. People often say to me: "Kathy, you need to lighten up." And I don't know if I have "lightened up" but I have learned about different types of learning and talking about issues.

We recently have had a project which was very positive in terms of AIDS work. Probably everyone knows about the Names Project, the national project whereby friends of people who have died from AIDS made quilt squares 3 feet by 6 feet in memory of their friend who has died. And all these squares are joined to the national quilt. The first I knew of this was during the June Gay Rights March in Washington when the entire quilt was laid out in front of the National Monument.

We decided to make quilt squares for the women who have died from AIDS here. About 12 or 13 or 14, maybe 15 women have died from AIDS here, although a number of them were released shortly before they died. But we hope that we can begin a tradition here. We will be sending the squares we made to be part of the national quilt. This idea, this quilt, is a very powerful force because it helps people to feel a sense of community, it helps people grieve, and it helps overcome the isolation that AIDS has surrounded people with.

We worked as a group of 10 to 15 women over a period of a week and the feeling was very positive. People's artwork was beautiful. A friend of many people, a woman who had been here nine years, just died last Friday of AIDS. She had been paroled a few months ago. Monday we are all going to get together and make a quilt square for her.

There is more that could be written but this is long enough to ask you to read. I know I haven't been very good about a lot of correspondence, but I hope letters like this can help.

Much love and solidarity, Kathy.

May 1, 1991

Dear Margaret,

This is just a brief note to tell you I am looking forward to seeing you in the morning on Thursday May 9 and that I received your letter. After I saw you, I think I had a sense that more problems were to follow, that the axe had still to fall a few more times, which it did. Judy and I were both kicked out of the college classes we were auditing. Her mentor for her master's degree who was also teaching one of the psychology classes we were both auditing was fired based on them saying that she was too close to Judy. And she is not allowed in at this time to work with Judy on her degree. I am no longer allowed to use the computer, and the college director erased/deleted my article from the disc, the literacy article I was still in the middle of working on. The repercussions among friends who get scared when the powers that be decide they are in a phase of dumping on us have still been emerging. It is just a sad situation about

> human nature to watch people become afraid and want to dis-associate. So, I guess there will be lots to talk about when you come. On the other hand, one benefit of being kicked out of class at the beginning of spring is that I am playing softball three nights a week, slowly enjoying the spring weather, still working on my article I had a hard copy of, and back working around the AIDS issues, thinking still about what is next for me in terms of focus, enjoying my friendship and a telephone relationship with my son. And surrounded by *New York Times* and various and sundry unread magazines piled by my bed and hoping that I will come to read them. And enjoying reading your book of essays and looking forward to our visit. All my love, Kathy.

This note shows the constant tensions of prison life, the sudden cruel decisions that are part of a prison system based on retribution rather than rehabilitation. It also evidences the ways in which Kathy's natural optimism and resiliency allowed her to try to make the best of such treatment and find ways to endure it. At times it depressed or momentarily immobilized her. But she never really let it get in the way of her work with her sister inmates, the programs she designed and carried out on their behalf, and the writing she was able to do—although the latter was the most difficult.

Kathy was writing a lot during these years, sometimes alone and sometimes in collaboration with others. Her long, well-researched article on teaching and AIDS work behind bars appeared in the *Harvard Educational Review* (Summer 1993). She and Judy published a long article about the AIDS work they had done with the Bedford Hills women. The poor quality of the Xerox copy in my file prevents me from deciphering the name of the publication, but I am able to read the article, and it is brilliant. Kathy sent me a typescript of a short story called "The Same Moon," by a prisoner named Precious Bedell and herself. It is a beautiful story about a woman who is an inmate telling her young son on the outside that when he looks at the moon, they will be having the same experience, and it will bring them closer despite their painful separation. There is a letter from me to Morning Glory Press in Buena Park, California, that apparently accompanied my submission of that story to them. There is also a brief rejection note from that press.

Kathy's father, the great constitutional lawyer Leonard Boudin, also died around this time. Because I was on the East Coast then, I was able to go to his memorial in New York City. In one of the many acts of cruelty to which she was submitted during her years in prison, Kathy was denied permission to attend. I could only try to imagine what it was like for Kathy to lose her father and not to be able to be at this celebration of his life. For me, the event was the only time I saw Chesa, then around twelve, as I remember. He was being raised by Bernardine Dohrn and Bill Ayers, comrades of Kathy's in the Weather Underground. Despite growing up with both parents in prison, he would become a Rhodes scholar, attend Yale Law School, and serve as district attorney of San Francisco until he was recalled by a conservative campaign.

July 13, 1991

Dear Margaret,

This letter is long overdue. I have been very glad to get your letters, and I feel badly that it has taken me so long to answer. The same holds true of my delay in answering Barbara's letter.

Of course, I am ecstatic that you will be nearby next spring, although I'm really sorry that it didn't work out for you to not be able to come. In other words, the bad situation at least had one positive outcome. The issue of you realizing that you were "being blacklisted" is something I can relate to. Much of the time, I live with the fantasy that I am a normal person leading a normal life, trying to pursue normal work. I try not to think about being in prison. I try to engage my mind and my heart, my energy, saying to myself that this is my life to be lived fully at this time. Then, when things happen that remind me that I'm in prison, that I'm seen as a terrorist or a criminal, that I'm spending twenty years here, I feel a mixture of freakout and peace. Freakout because it is so awful. Peace because it is a better appreciation of reality.

Your description of your mother and father recalled to me a little of "Tell Me a Riddle"[144] and also of one other thing. A close friend of mine who works here just this past ten days had an experience reminiscent of what you are describing. Her mother was visiting her last week from Puerto Rico. She was diagnosed as having a mild stroke and my friend is dealing with her mother's loss of control over her arms, speech being slurred, and I've been living this with her so I can really appreciate the agony of a slow deterioration. My friend's mother is 53. I know your father is 85. I know this will be occupying a great deal of your emotional energy in the coming period because, as you said in your letter, it is about your father but also about your mother and father's relationship and all of this is about your life as well. I imagine you and Barbara will appreciate your closeness through all of this, and also that it will be

144. A short story by Tillie Olsen.

hard. I am glad, I must say, that it all happened fast with my father.

Biking, yes, I have always loved it. But for me it was whizzing among buses and cars or, on a Sunday morning appreciating the quietness of the city. My bike took me from an Italian neighborhood to a Puerto Rican neighborhood to a Jewish area to a Russian area to Chinatown to Wall Street to the rich white Upper East Side to the outskirts of Harlem. My bike has let me experience New York City and all the peoples who live there. I've never been on a country bike trip. Chesa went on a 4-day bike trip in the Mohave Desert this March, and I saw beautiful pictures of it. Someday I can see myself going biking in the country.

Thanks for the pictures of your children. It meant a lot for me to put faces on names and histories and, what's more, they are beautiful. By now you must have many stories to tell from your family reunion.

I am not sure what to say about my life. My work is spread between ACE (counseling, educational, and organizational work) and two afternoons a week I do work around mother/child separation, a lot with women who have already or are losing their children because they were on drugs and didn't see them and their parental rights have been terminated. I'm also doing a second simpler article on my literacy work, and I hope, by the time I write next, I'll have some good news about my big writing project. Through it all, for me, things are not really how I want them. But I can't put my finger on what it is. One thing for sure is that ACE as an organization takes up much too much time. By the way, the conference was good, not huge, definitely smaller than it should have been, but as a conference it was very good. Perhaps in a year and a half ACE will sponsor a national one; it needs to be done.

Today I spent the day in the office with women making quilt squares for loved ones who have died. Ten women came for the afternoon, and we have ten for next week, ten for the following one, and so on.

The whole set of decisions by the Supreme Court plus Marshall's resignation and Thomas's nomination has all been terrible. It has made me think a lot about my father and how painful these developments would be for him.

Margaret, I have read both your revised version of your poem and your piece on censorship. I would rather talk about them in another letter because I want to do justice to them, and it is late. I liked them both, but that isn't adequate feedback. Forgive me for not writing about them in this letter but I will.

I think this letter is a little melancholy. I'm sorry, it is my mood. I hope you are well. Much love, Kathy.

October 29, 1991

Dear Margaret,

What a long time since I have written. This has been a difficult time. I have thought of you and Barbara a lot and of course I am looking forward to seeing you. I wonder how your work is going. I have been so self-absorbed that a lot of the rest of the world has faded. The situation that led to all this paranoia around me was one of those unpredictable events and mainly it was very sad and unnecessary. I felt for much of it as if I were in a Kafka novel being accused, tried, judged, and punished for something or things that I knew nothing about.

Then, all of this coincided with the tenth anniversary of the event that led to my arrest, which made everything even more intense. Honestly, there were days when I felt if I pointed to the beautiful sunset, they would think I was carrying out some plan. It is as if I have been endowed with these incredible powers. Anyway, not only has it been destructive in the present, but it all brought back the past and also gave me a lot to think about the future and what I am up against. Much of the time I try to live my life productively in the here and now, but this period has required a different approach.

As for the here and now, I do foresee improvement. I have tried to deeply enjoy autumn. In the summer I took a two-week vacation, something I haven't done for years. I am in a writing workshop which, although my writing is not good at this time, does provide a context for me to feel real and also to do some minimal amount of writing. But as minimal as it is, I really look forward to the workshop each week.

I finally was able to get started on writing the book, and I found working on my first tiny section of it quite rewarding in terms of new insights, and also a challenge in terms of writing. So, I am looking forward to continuing. Not much new has happened with me in terms of work, a lot the same. I think the developments in USSR and Eastern Europe have absorbed a lot of my thinking, especially during the summer. And more recently both the Thomas hearings and the events in the Mid East—actually they have helped me to feel absorbed by events and history outside of here, however insane those situations are.

I wonder how you are, what you are writing and reading. Are you healthy? It's late. I am going to say goodnight and add a bit more in the early morning before mailing this off.

Now it is morning. The birds are singing, and the sun is already up. Yesterday I collected the last of the red leaves and I will have a little of the autumn with me all winter. I know you have already gone or will go to the conference soon. What a time in the Middle East: there is so much to talk about. I will call within days. Much love, Kathy.

[undated]

Dear Margaret,

Now it is the third day of lockup, and I have to start this letter again because today they came and took every single paper, book, picture from my cell. I only have left plain white typing paper. They took about twelve boxes of files, correspondence, books, papers, legal materials. They said I would get them back later today. So now I must write you again.

I was sorry we missed our visit, but I really was glad that you were able to take control of your life and set limits that worked for you. And I'm looking forward to our next visit. Also, what you and Barb have written about your parents—your father and your mother—it has to be very very difficult. We lose our parents in different ways, at different speeds, each has its own quality of loss. I used to wonder if I was glad my father died fast or whether I would rather have had it take a long time, stroke, Alzheimer's. And obviously there isn't really a best way because the main thing is the loss, which I know you are feeling already. Did you ever read a book by Jane Rule called, I think, *Memory* or *Memory Board*? About two women, one of whom had lost her memory. They were lovers and it is the story of them relating to each other as they are older.

As I think I told you in the letter I began last night, I absolutely loved reading *Bridges*. I think a lot of the writing in it was superb. Isn't it interesting how I got so much of out of reading it now, how much a mood or a way of living can shift perspective towards what one is reading. But I wanted to thank you very much for sharing *Bridges* with me.[145]

145. I have no memory of this book. It may have been *This Bridge Called my Back*, edited by Cherríe Moraga and Gloria Anzaldúa, originally published in 1981.

> I have been putting time into writing my book about teaching. I've been struggling with the conception of it—how much analytical, how much narrative, how much theoretical, how to make it have heart and feeling and poetry. And then the issue isn't literally how much of each but rather what is my conception of it as a whole. I've tried to think of other books I've read that might be a kind of model for me, sometimes that's helpful. They seem to see it as a concrete example of Freirean or critical thinking teaching, so they want the narrative, the concrete examples of teaching and teaching projects so that it is reproducible and has a theoretical framework and a sense of the prison environment and who the women are, but saying all that still requires something that I haven't arrived at yet which is a conception of what it should be like. I'm working on it as I write the narrative.
>
> I would be eager to read your next draft of socialism and women. I wonder how that is going for you.
>
> I know that with spring here you must be glad to be feeling that soon you will be returning home. I am happy for you.
>
> I look forward to our visit. Much love, Kathy.

This would not be the last time Kathy wrote to me about her frustration at not being able to decide on a conceptual framework for her book on parenting from prison. She repeats the dilemma in several subsequent letters. I knew that the many projects she took on—her own master's degree, AIDS work, adult literacy, and parenting from prison—made her feel useful in the here and now. But they also helped her avoid the deep reflection necessary to settling on the conception necessary to thinking through and writing such a book. Prison life has many difficulties. It is not simply a matter of being locked up, but how a punitive system shapes one's thought processes and emotional life. I decided to leave the repetitions in because I feel they evoke a tangible sense of what she went through.

Sunday, April 26, 1992

Dear Margaret,

Yesterday the book by Galeano arrived, and the day before your manuscript. So, I am filled with both reading and a sense of you.

I was very glad to see you and I only wish we had been able to take more advantage of your proximity while you were here.

They have once again changed the phone system and now I am really cut off. So, it won't be until you get back to Albuquerque that we can talk. But I will call you then for sure as well as rely on correspondence.

On Friday the *NY Times* published a long article about my brother and my family, perhaps you saw it. The occasion was the nomination by Bush of Michael for Court of Appeals judge in the Boston region. The article was built around the extremes that Michael and I represented, so it has me as a bomb maker, revolutionary killer, and Michael as defender of corporate interests. Needless to say, there was no sense of any of the work I do here since that would have ruined the point of the article. It gave me a taste of what it will be like when I try to build support for parole, the types of publicity I can expect. But that I knew. More immediate for me is the fact that I learned the *Harvard Educational Review* was going to be reading my piece the last week in April or first week in May, so I felt like the timing of the publicity around me was pretty terrible. And I got very depressed. But I know I am simply in the tradition of so many wonderful people, yourself included, whose very name carries with it a lot of power and it just scares people to associate. And I have to understand and deal with it.

This week here there was a kind of parallel situation with me related to my trying to get the AIDS work published. I was told not to do any direct corresponding/negotiating on that issue because they don't want my name linked with it and they basically just don't trust my independent relationships with outside people. So, I have felt a bit creamed from both directions. I'm not really writing to complain but more to share. The one project in which I feel the greatest ability to do independent work is my book on teaching and I am hoping that our correspondence around that will be of help.

I am having a problem with the outline of the book. I am sending you the preliminary one along with the prospectus that I submitted last September. The outline isn't adequate because it takes too long to get to the story. The editor has urged me to write in a "feminist" tradition, using my own voice, the story, the personal experience, as the central part of it. Theory has to be there, but it should come out of the story. I think the problem for me is my conception of the book. But I am trying to write something that is moving, moving because it is about women in the process of growth, of struggle to be as much as they can be, and an approach to education that I feel does that. I don't know how to discuss the overall concept with you in this brief letter.

The publisher wants a sense of the women here and a sense of the prison. As I mentioned to you, one idea is to not do one chapter that tries to summarize that but rather to have a series of profiles throughout it. Also, I've been thinking about the book being organized around the units of study: AIDS/ the play, mothers and daughters, money, survivors in prison/the handbook. And then for aspects of people's lives to emerge in the context of those units, through profiles, interviews, excerpts, the teaching/learning.

> I am sending you two things in addition to the outline and prospectus. The first discussion that I had with one of the women here. I wasn't really organized when I did it, as you will see, but it will give you an idea. And then my present approach to interview questions as outlined in the pages of my questions. However, I really want to have discussions with the people, not just about education but about broader aspects of their lives—mothers, daughters, drugs, dreams, coming from another country etc. and I haven't formulated questions in those areas. And then it also seems so broad that I wonder if it is too broad and unfocussed. In other words, the book is about education and learning/teaching, yet the content of the education is determined by who the people are, so I want to show that, yet then it is exploring every aspect of people. Anyway, these are the issues I'm struggling with.
>
> I just received your letter today (Tuesday). Since I had written this, I'm going to mail it to you and send another letter with the promised interview in that one. It was great to hear from you. I'll be writing again in the next day.
>
> I look forward to reading your manuscript and I hope that I can be of help to you. Life has been very very intense this past week on a personal level, and I think a lot of good things are happening. I won't be able to speak with you until you get back to Albuquerque. I hope that your last weeks here are productive. It was wonderful seeing you. All my love, Kathy.

Kathy finally received a letter from the *Harvard Educational Review* dated December 2, 1992, accepting her article "Participatory Literacy Education Behind Bars: AIDS Opens the Door." As a writer myself, I know what waiting for acceptances and rejections is like, the eagerness to know what others think of one's work. What I cannot imagine is how being in prison intensifies that experience, adding an extra layer of frustration and sense of helplessness. I knew the work that Kathy had put into this article, and I was happy that she shared the acceptance letter with me.

Arranging our visits was always complicated. I had to find out if she would be available on the day I could go. Sometimes we were able to arrange this by phone. More often, I checked in with someone in her group of local supporters, someone who was able to contact and consult with her. I remember once when Barbara and I were visiting with my youngest daughter, Ana, who lived in Brooklyn. We wanted to include a visit with Kathy on that trip and had gone to great lengths to make sure the day we chose would work. Ana lent us her car and we set out. But on the way, I suddenly became very ill. Instead of continuing on to the prison, Barbara, who was driving, had to turn around and get me to a hospital. I had pneumonia and was hospitalized for close to a week. We had no direct way of notifying Kathy of our change in plans, and she waited for us for hours, with no idea of why we failed to appear.

It wasn't until a day or two later that the person in her local support group was able to explain to her what had happened. Although I knew that Kathy has been forced to get used to such situations, I felt bad that I caused one of them. The following note is an example of how long we often had to plan to get together.

April 13, 1996

Dear Margaret:

The 13th of June is fine, and I am so looking forward to a reunion/visit with all three of us. This is a quick note just to get it off to you. Your book arrived and I am excited to read it. Much love, Kathy.

p.s. Your description of the hike was painful but when you said that you were glad to have done it, I guess I felt some relief.

(By the way, I wrote a note to Adrienne Rich at the address you gave me.)

March 16, 1997

Dearest Margaret:

It is hard to believe that we have not exchanged a full letter since your visit. I have, of course, your collective end of year letter, which I have read over and over again because there is so much in it to absorb. It is as if the thought of not knowing when we would see one another again and the inability to call, to speak, just led me to shut down. But, as I sit here today, as winter is giving us a major final burst of its presence, and I reread your letter of March 1995—before your visit and Barbara's post-visit letter and your collective letter, I feel as if I have let something very precious to me disappear from my mind's eye. And I want to try to reconnect.

Some years ago—it is hard for me to remember just how many—you offered me your friendship and it was very important to me, feeling the different life experiences that we had shared, if from different geographic areas and different personal histories, there was so much that created in some way a braid of experiences which allowed our friendship to develop in the visiting room context, by mail and phone, in a way that helped me expand beyond the confines of not just being here but more abstract barriers. I think our first talk that helped me was that experience of each of us having come back—the return, the struggle to return, the terms of return, new terrain inside ourselves, inside the new country. Then sharing relationships, the ways in which they work, and then go on, or don't go on, depending. Then the inner journey, one which you had taken and were continuing to take, one which I ventured into and am still on, writing and writing, family, mothers and fathers and children, and aging and caring for our parents, and death and change and choices. As I look back there has been a richness and a deep importance to me in our friendship, and I don't want to lose that.

It's too long. I can't believe that I missed your 60th birthday, didn't get to celebrate it with you.

It sounds as if your ability to totally work on your relationship to your body—your weight, your sense of confidence in it, ability to take on physical challenges: what a wonderful triumph for you during these past years. Your international life and traveling still seem overwhelming to me, even to read. I don't know whether it is because of my being so limited in space that it seems so overwhelming. In the past 13 years I have lived in two cells on the same living unit, and just seeing the part of the sky from a new angle was something that I found thrilling (it will be visible only until they construct the new building). But I love to hear about the things you do since it does really expand my world.

It is hard to know where to begin in terms of myself. My most important intimate emotional relationship is with my son, Chesa. In a way it is scary since at the age of 16 ½ he not only wants his own space emotionally, but he will soon no longer be home and who knows where college and travel will land him. But I am thoroughly enjoying my relationship with him, and he is in fine shape. He is a very nice person, very hard working both physically and intellectually. He loves construction work, cleaning, sports, reading history and novels. And I love him. It is basic and is a source of life for me.

My mother's closest friends, four of them, have continued a friendship with me, and I talk periodically with my brother and cousin and that helps to a degree to keep my connection to family. But it is hard to not feel the family energy as I did when my father and mother were alive.

Work here continues. I still do work in the area of AIDS and women's health. I am about to begin my six sessions of Parenting from a Distance, a three-month journey with a group of women which, as you know from our previous discussions, is so rich and absorbing. I start on Monday. I am training five other women from here on teaching literacy, so in a sense I am able to share my experience and knowledge from the literacy work without having to do the literacy instruction myself which I have not wanted to get back into.

I have continued on my own internal search about myself, and I have learned a lot. It isn't that I've reached a point of peace and clarity, as much as worlds and details, experiences that I had been unaware of, or part of my vision, my landscape, as I continue trying to understand the course that my life took and to somehow integrate what I feel good about with what I feel bad about. My greatest frustration is with myself around writing. I have been unable to write poetry for the most part, just a kind of frozenness, and after writing a great deal last fall (none of it published yet in academic journals), I didn't do any writing during the winter. I still, believe it or not, have been waiting for this book about AIDS work to come out. Who knows, maybe there is something good about the fact that it has taken so long. We were at least able to get an introduction from Whoopi Goldberg and another from the superintendent here, and perhaps if it had come out sooner, we would not have gotten either of them. Overlook Press says that they want to release it in September because it is the best time for publicity. So that still hasn't happened.

Honestly, Margaret, I want to try to write two books that are on my mind. One is about the experience of being a mother before and during imprisonment. The texts that you read in the Parenting from a Distance material, your encouragement in your March letter which I reread today, were helpful. We are having it published in the form of a kind of self-help manual, soft cover, printed by friends, distribution by us for other prisons. But my wish is to now turn it into a book.

My second project is to look at the kinds of programs I have been involved in here, such as our AIDS program, the literacy work I did, the parenting center, and try to passionately illustrate that people who are society's rejects, when able to tackle significant issues in their lives, can make enormous contributions to society and dialectically through their own growth. I don't have a clear thesis to the book on mothering. It will have to emerge as I write and work. And it is something that comes from my own journey, filled with the conflicts, ambivalences, sense of frustrations and failures, the thorny path that women must walk on. The other book is perhaps more the recurrent theme of the movements which we have all been part of and is reflected in the best of the work I have been able to create in here, and also that others in here have done. I know I have a tendency too often to have two options (smile, eg. Ruthie and David)[146] and as I hear myself writing about two books, I know I have to try not to let this happen. Probably I would move forward first with the one about mothering. But

146. Ruthie Rodríguez was another prisoner with whom Kathy had a relationship for several years. David was her husband and the father of her son, who was serving a life sentence in another prison.

I keep saying, well maybe I can work on both. The greatest problem is that thus far I have not been doing either. The day to day flesh and blood issues of life, and death, and children, and visits, and teaching that make up my work in the AIDS and Parenting Center jobs keep pulling me, and I relive each day choices that somehow happened to me from early on: to delay those periods of taking personal space, to connect to myself, which is the only way to write and read. And yet, whenever I have been able to discipline myself to such a process, the sense of personal power that I experience precisely because it does come from the energy that comes from helping others—there is a depth in such a process that then lends to the work. So, for a month now I have been articulating this to myself and to some visitors, in the hope that my voice will lead me to cut back, to create the space for the writing and will help me figure out how to structure a vision. I don't want to lose sight of these two books that I want to write, yet don't want to become paralyzed by not being able to move forward on one. Poetry, it is like a bird inside oneself that seems to hibernate at times and its song just does not seem to emerge when I whistle.

I assume that I am struggling with judging the product which is in some Platonian version of perfection in my mind, rather than throwing myself into the process for itself, out of which will emerge a product. Much of which may be far less than perfect and occasionally some of it will be even better than what I can imagine. But until I swim in the process, nothing will happen.

I guess I struggle against depression (not clinical, just a weighty pessimism) around getting out of prison and throwing myself into work and helping others really helps because I feel my life is worthwhile regardless. Anyway, it is hard to believe but I go to the parole board in four years. Unfortunately, they do not have to let me out and it will be quite a struggle. So, I am also gearing up psychologically for an unwelcome but necessary public process.

Meanwhile, the world has taken all of us by surprise and the best we can do is keep on. I don't believe, as Anne Frank said, that people are really good at heart. But I do believe that when people are able to live in a safe and positive context, to be respected and loved and able to work and love, the best will emerge. And to the degree that we can do that in our small areas, while continuing to push for a society that does that on a macro level, the best will come out of people's hearts.

Whenever you have time, of course, I would love to hear from you. And even better, are you on any tours that will bring you east and allow us to visit?

Be well, my friend, and I give you a big hug. Much love, Kathy.

August 14, 1997

Dear Margaret,

It is strange, but when I saw the envelope to me with your name on the return address, I had a premonition; somehow, I felt that it had bad news. Why? Perhaps because I had not yet written to you after receiving your wonderful spring letter and one from Barbara and I just felt that probably I wouldn't get a letter from you yet. So strange, I literally hesitated to open it which is something I never would normally do. I was so distressed. I just don't know what to say. Perhaps by now Barbara has had the MRI and other tests and they have ruled MS out. Perhaps they have concluded that it is MS. Perhaps it is still unclear.[147] I write you within hours of getting your letter, so I

147. Barbara has suffered from undiagnosed or misdiagnosed pain and other symptoms for years. No test or doctor has ever been able to give them

don't know. But even this much anxiety and suffering is terrible. And it sounds as if Barb has really had a hard time physically, and I know how hard it must be for you as well. I just feel that you both don't deserve this. I also wish that I were with you, able to make you laugh and give massages and just go through it with you.

You have been a very important friend to me. Your books had spoken to me from a distance for many years. But, our first get-together, when we shared the experience of the struggle to come home and what it took and what it was like, I truly felt that we connected around a very profound personal and political process, and it meant a lot to me. Your ability to be so open personally through your writing and poetry is something I envy—I don't think I can do that. Sometimes I think it's situational and sometimes I think it's temperament and a personal decision. Perhaps it is some of both. I consider our friendship one of the deepest and most important that I have. And I truly appreciate the fact that you have consistently kept in touch with me. I know you are busy and have lots of commitments and people with whom you connect so I feel very happy. Now that you move through this crisis, I would like to be there for you and Barbara.

One question that I have is should I put you on my phone list. I would pay for the calls so that money would not be an issue for you. I can have a limited number of people on my list, so it would make sense to do it if you feel that you would like me to call somewhat regularly. Or do you have too many friends and you don't need at this point more people to be involved in the day to day or week by week process?

---

a name or determine their origin. It is clear that childhood trauma is at the root. Today she treats the symptoms and continues to live a productive life.

I think being ill is hard for both people, very hard in different ways. For the person who is struggling with their health, it is obviously hard in many ways—physically, emotionally, practically. And for the partner, the person who is not sick, it brings in so many other issues—of helplessness, of exhaustion, of redefining their own life. I hope that you, Margaret, can find the sources of support that you need in order to take care of yourself as well as Barbara. I was glad and not surprised to read that your relationship has been very sustaining for both of you.

I have both your letters side by side. Reading your letter of March, with your questions and concerns about me, and your anticipation of all your plans for work and travel, and then your letter of today with the update and description of your travels as they were influenced by and influenced Barb's health. The beauty, the incredible beauty of the photos means to me that you live in a way that takes in so much positive energy, and all that must give you strength to face hardships.

Your own struggle with the physical realm, with your weight, your ability to be active physically, to exercise, and then to take on major physical activities that require courage, has been an amazing journey. In my long struggle with my weight in my late teens and early to late twenties, it interfered with my childhood love for physical activity. Now, with my weight no longer a problem, sports are a very important part of what keeps me relaxed, even though I may go for long periods not doing them because I can't figure out a routine that works. But I have never liked activities that pose a physical threat. I have no doubt I would be too anxious to take the kind of river trip that you took. It sounds extraordinary. On the other hand, as a result of having a friend who is into sports at the same level as I, I've devoted my summer evenings to being in a stuffy gym and playing paddle ball which I never played before coming to prison and which I really enjoy. I love the intensity of it and the challenge to improve. Unfortunately, my friend will be going to another prison probably this week and I'm not sure what will happen to my intense involvement since it makes a big difference to have a partner with whom plans to play can be made and there is a kind of energy that comes. I have also really enjoyed watching the women's professional basketball league this summer. If I were 35 or 40 years younger, I would perhaps be involved in one sport or another. I don't think it would be basketball because I am too small.

I have had a wonderful several months in relation to Chesa. He visited in May after no visit since January—that was very hard, too long, I think possibly unnecessarily, but he has had a lot of traveling this year because he has been involved in a model UN program which took him to the University of Michigan one weekend, the University of California Berkeley for five days, and Toronto—combined with visiting his father in March and June for two days, three actually, plus his regular life—it just wasn't possible. But my May visit was great. He brought a friend with him from his class, not his best friend but one of the guys in his group of friends. And that was exciting for him, to share me and the prison experience with his friend. I then just saw him for three days, two of which were shared with his middle brother, Malik, who is a year ahead of him. Malik came from Chicago with him also to spend time with me. And I had one day alone with Chesa during which we had some very deep discussions. At the end of August, we will have a two-day overnight visit. Last year's was the first one ever. It was complicated. I think this one will be easier for us and I think we will have a lot of good talks. He is an amazing person, and just exploding with issues: from relationships to politics to exploring his own personality and what it derives from. He will be a junior in high school and hopes to finish six months early and take time to live in a Spanish-speaking country and learn Spanish. He worked for six weeks in a factory in Chicago this summer. His best friend Mwanikik with whom he spends his summers flew out to Chicago for the six weeks and they had the factory experience together. They made about $6.50 an hour. The work force was 40% Hispanic and 60% Black, so for Chesa it was his first experience being a minority. And since Mwanikik is Black and so was the other boy from Chesa's class who worked, it was a pretty deep experience for him. He was making display cases, cutting metal, screwing sides together, etc. I had been worried when he was moving toward thirteen or fourteen that adolescence would take him from me, but it just hasn't happened. I have felt very very connected and involved. He is always willing to talk on the phone. I think that my role as mother involves a lot of being a friend for him, and in spite of the loss of not being able to be a normal mother, I have been able to get certain positive things from this role, namely a kind of closeness around certain types of issues and talking that I might not have otherwise. He remains the major source of energy on a personal level for me.

The AIDS book is somewhere in the printing process, so hopefully this fall. My self-reflective pulling back and writing plans have not succeeded to the degree I hoped this summer. However, I have put a lot of effort into trying to imagine the possibilities for a short book on mother-child relationships when the mother is incarcerated. And with the help of two friends with whom I have been in dialogue, I have been able to focus some reading, journal writing, and ideas. My next step is to send a letter with a proposal to an editor along with the materials I have already written. One of the issues I have been struggling with is that my own deepest day to day involvement is with the mothers, their struggles, their world. I could do a kind of ethnographic oral history type of book (your strength). Even though that is a possibility, I feel the political reality requires that if I am trying to portray the importance of supporting the possibility of mothering from prison, then I have to involve children's experiences and voices. And I have to think about how to do that in a way that feels okay, not exploitative. I am grappling with how much of myself to put in it. When I get an outline, proposal done, I will send it to you. But I am slowly making progress. So, although it isn't as much as I hoped, it is enough to give me encouragement. And when this book is done, I have a clear plan for the next one. So, we'll see.

You ask if I am depressed. You comment in your last letter that depression must be built into the prison experience in a certain sense, and the struggle against it a large part of life. I have never thought of myself as someone who gets depressed. I haven't really known what the word means. My personal problems in the past just had a different form. But I have to say that I think recently I am looking at it in myself on some level. I think the combination of regrets, losses of family members with no easy ability to create a strong set of intimate friends inside, the experience of getting older and the fear of dying in prison, along with anxiety about the kind of public struggle that I will have to go through to simply try to get out—the political period, the victim's rights movement and how that particularly impacts on my situation in terms of the kind of opposition that exists around my getting out: all of this has been hard for me. Maybe that's why I stay so busy with projects and projects and find it hard to settle down and find some peace.

Last weekend I was reading a book called *Death Without Weeping: The Violence of Everyday Life in Brazil,* by anthropologist Nancy Scheper-Hughes. It really captured a lot of emotions of people grappling with things over which they had no control. I found it very moving, and it also resonated emotionally for me.

Anyway, enough on that. Yes, I would love to both read the 80-page interview—it sounds incredible—and have a copy of your new book of poems.

Let me know what is the best way that I can be of support to you and Barbara. I love each of you, Kathy.

I have wanted to re-create the long and rich conversation that Kathy and I had throughout her years in prison and since her release. Unfortunately, the archive doesn't contain more than a couple of my letters to her. I must not have made copies, and the following letter is the exception because, once I'd entered the era of digital communication, archiving my letters became easier.

Albuquerque, New Mexico—August 23, 1997

Dearest Kathy:

Your letters are wonderful. They fill us both with such a feeling of support and caring. I started to cry when I read what you say about my friendship meaning so much to you. Yours also means a tremendous amount to me. When I think of the people I am lucky enough to have in my life, you are always way up on the list. I am blessed with so many deep friendships. I do feel your support, through those horrible walls, and always have the sense—in any situation—that when the chance arises to visit, we will pick up where we left off the last time around. There are few people, even among those I truly love, with whom I have that certainty.

I don't know what to say about your phone list. I would love to be on it, love to have the possibility of talking with you on a regular basis, especially now that my times on the east coast are so few and far between. But I am wondering if the list is full, if there is room for us, and who might be sacrificed if we were included. So, I guess I leave it up to you. I know that you need a number of slots for family, Chesa's important people, etc. Please don't feel that because of Barbara's illness you must include us. If you do, we would just want it to be so that we could have a more regular connection.

There are so many things in your letter that I want to respond to. I will talk about Barbara first. Coincidentally, we found your letter on our return from the doctor this afternoon. This was our visit following the MRI, which was a week ago. The wheels move fairly slowly in an HMO, but as such situations go, this seems to be a pretty good one. (I constantly find myself comparing the sort of health plan Barbara has with the situation of the very rich, who go to specialists immediately, rather than, as I should, with the vast majority of people who don't have medical attention of any kind. A class problem, as we would have said in the old days!)

Anyway, we already knew, because the nurse called and told us (even though she wasn't supposed to) that the MRI had come out fine. "An unremarkable brain" were the exact words on the report. Apparently, all this means is that there are no scars on Barbara's brain from the exacerbation of whatever it is she has been suffering from for the past eleven years. She may still have MS (which could show up on a different kind of MRI—with contrast dye—or in a spinal tap). But there is a good chance that she doesn't have that disease. The next step is for her to see a neurologist. Her primary care doctor will refer her on Monday, and we'll see when that appointment will be.

As the doctor said today, she has something but it's beyond him what it is. Our thoughts exactly. Meanwhile, the way she feels goes up and down. I'd say that in general she is feeling slightly better than a few weeks back. One morning she even woke up feeling fine, absolutely fine, as if the whole problem had shut off like a light. But that only lasted a couple of days. Just enough to set us up so we could fall hard. Then it was back to the symptoms again: pain in different parts of her body, different sorts of numbness, difficulty walking, and extreme exhaustion.

The only thing that has seemed to help at all is acupuncture, which she has begun doing once a week, with a very good doctor of oriental medicine. We know that the effects of acupuncture are cumulative, so have some degree of hope that this may be helpful in the long run. Right now, it just seems to help with the symptoms on and off.

So, our life at the moment is one in which Barbara does very little but go to work, do her best in the classroom, come home, and rest. Occasionally we see friends. Occasionally we go to a movie. And very occasionally she will feel like riding her bike. We were able to go for a bike ride this morning, a short one. We're hoping to go again tomorrow morning but won't know until she wakes up if she can do it or not. Additionally, I had something of a hard time this morning, because I broke one of my toes a week ago, one of those stupid little nothing accidents that are more trouble than they should be.

There has been some good news at Barbara's school, though. I'm sure she'll write you about it. Yesterday, in what appeared to be a very sudden turn of events, her principal quit. It seems to have been a firing that was allowed to look like she "resigned for personal reasons." After an almost two-year struggle through the union, through the school administration, and even through the board of education, it was all somehow anti-climactic. Plus of course this woman succeeded in almost destroying the school. Twenty-two of the best teachers left. Lots of parents have removed their kids. Whole programs have fallen apart. It's going to take some work to try to get things back to where they were. And it may turn out to be impossible. A lot depends, I suppose, on who is hired to take this woman's place. Here's hoping it will be someone who knows how to work collectively.

What an enormous number of personal losses you are sustaining just now. Reminds me of several years back when first one and then the other of your parents died, and Ruthie left and the distancing from David began, and more. It must be so hard to deal with these losses in the kind of isolation prison imposes. Because your choices of "replacements" are so limited. I'm glad that your work is going better and that you have sports as well as other projects in mind. Talking on the phone with Ruth the other day, she mentioned that she and Debbie had been down to see you and that you seemed really good. In fact, she ordered some of my note cards for you and I sent them direct—I hope you get them in good time and shape. I didn't know what images you would like best, so made a selection from the Canyon and elsewhere.

What you say about Chesa makes me joyous. I'm so glad that you have been able to spend such quality time together and can look forward to more. When I think about him, which I do often, with both parents in prison, and what that implies in terms of decisions to visit, etc., I imagine his immense growing. What strengths he has had to develop, far beyond others of his age. The factory experience Chesa had this past summer reminded me so much of an experience my son, Gregory, had in Cuba for several summers in a row. He and some high school friends, most of them Latin American and some Cuban, founded a brigade back in the seventies that went to different parts of the island to do hard summer work—first at a nickel plant in Moa, then other projects, some of which I've forgotten. I know they went four or five years. They would work for two months, earning regular laborer's pay, and then donate the money collectively to some internationalist organization or project. It was an incredible experience. And Gregory, there, was also in the minority. He was the only "Anglo" kid from the US (though he speaks no English and is clearly not US in culture or temperament). In more recent years he and I have sometimes talked about those summers and what they meant to him.

Your project to write about mother-child relationships when the mother is incarcerated sounds very important and exciting. And I can't wait to see your AIDS book when it appears. By the way, under separate cover but on Monday as well, I will send you a copy of my new collection of poems (the food poems)[148] and the initial interview with the two women about whom I am now trying to write this book.[149] About the interview, please just disregard the first nine pages. They are a sort of introduction I wrote when I thought I might submit this

148. The book is *Hunger's Table: Women, Food, and Politics* (Watsonville, CA: Papier-Maché Press, 1997). This is a poetry collection in which each poem is also a recipe.

149. I am referring here to an interview I did with María Suárez and Nora Miselem, two women who reconnected fourteen years after they had been thrown together in a prison cell and tortured. They survived thanks to the courage of one of them. They reconnected in Managua, when we were all part of a women's delegation to monitor that country's 1996 election. I first did this long interview and later traveled to Costa Rica and Honduras, where these women live, to do further research and interviews. This fieldwork did finally result in a book, *When I Look into the Mirror and See You: Women, Terror, and Resistance* (New Brunswick, NJ: Rutgers University Press, 2002).

initial interview to some journal or other publication. A way of introducing the subject. But then I realized I wanted to do a book, there is so much material there, and that the initial interview is really only the tip of the iceberg, so to speak. Now I think I will use some pieces of the introduction throughout the book in other ways. I should talk to you some about this project, though, because I am having a lot of trouble with it.

Kathy, writing has always come so easily to me. I mean the act of writing, working on a particular project. I have never thought of myself as someone with writing blocks though—increasingly, it seems—I find that I need to write and then rewrite and rewrite to get things the way I want them. But this book is giving me a lot of trouble. I don't really think it's the book itself. I continue to feel immensely committed to the project. I think it's this moment in my life, the fact of Barbara's illness, the unsettled nature of things right now. Some days I work okay, some very badly, some not at all. Some days I procrastinate and bake bread. I finally finished the transcription and translation of the tapes I made with both women when I was in Honduras and Costa Rica in April. I had gotten to think of that as the "grunt work," pages I labored through day after day but finally finished. And I somehow thought that once the thinking and organizing and writing had begun, I would move faster and be in better spirits about it.

But I'm not. I can't seem to get a handle on it. I think that some of this may come from the fact that I have absolutely no support for this project. No editor interested. A literary agent who doesn't really specialize in this sort of book. And no prospect of foundation grants or other forms of support. Which basically means that I struggle day after day without any funding and therefore feel that I must accept any and every little gig that comes along, which in turn of course takes me away from continuity with the book. I guess I need a breakthrough of some sort. Hopefully, it will come.

The up and down nature of Barbara's condition tends to immobilize me somewhat. I don't know if I'm prone to depression. Certainly, I've never thought of myself as a person who is. I've known sadness, rage, irritation, etc., but not what I think of as depression. But lately I've felt myself literally immobilized in my work. And this seems to me to be a depressive state. Then, when I think maybe I should call my old therapist and see her once or twice, it doesn't seem that bad and I don't.

One other thing I will stick in the envelope with the interview and my book of poetry is something I wrote about our river trip this past summer. That is, something I wrote about the women who row the dories. Again, I wrote this to submit to magazines and I have sent it out, but it has been rejected so far. I think it may be one of those things that falls between categories—it is neither a story nor an article really, nor does it focus on some breathtakingly dangerous act (which seems to be what the sports magazines want). It's about women's strength and courage, which may not be a very popular subject. But I want to share it with you.

Being on that river is so special to me. Both times I have been fortunate enough to do that trip, it has changed me in very deep ways. Who knows if I will ever be able to do it again. Barbara has said in no uncertain terms that she doesn't want to. Unless she heals a great deal, it's just too hard on her. But I do not give up hope that I may once again be able to experience that place. "Secretly," I have been putting money aside, hidden in an envelope in a file cabinet—a twenty-dollar bill one week, a ten the next—in the hope that I can save enough to repeat that trip!

As usually happens in the fall, after a dry summer, I've got a few gigs over the next few months. One of them may be in Storrs, Connecticut, on November 5th. If that one materializes, I'm wondering about the possibility of coming to visit on the 6th. Let me know if that would work for you.

Well, enough for now. Kathy, we loved your letters. Each read her own, then traded. We both feel very close to you. Thanks for being the friend you are. Be in touch when you can.

Much love, Margaret.

September 27, 1997

Dear Margaret,

By now there is probably new information from all the tests that have been done on Barbara. I haven't done anything around my phone numbers because the bureaucratic process of changing numbers just pushes towards doing nothing. But for the moment I feel good about our frequency of writing, so I want to continue that. I have been so happy to be in touch as much with both you and Barbara during these months. It's strange how out of bad things can evolve good things.

I appreciate your sensitivity to my own ups and downs.

I wonder if by the time you receive this letter you will have made some sort of breakthrough with your writing. I read the interview with a lot of different feelings. One of the first feelings that I had was a flash memory of the time that you and I first met and exchanged stories and feelings about our period in "exile"—and the struggle to come back "home." Two women, having shared a very different yet similar experience, meeting years later and looking back at it. Of course, it was different qualitatively from the torture that they underwent, but there was enough in common that it made me think about it.

Another feeling that I had all the way through was what a good movie it would make. Maybe that was partly because I had just had a visit with Chesa's brother, Zayd, who is hoping to write screenplays and movies and that was on my mind. But I think it was more because I felt that a movie would be able to go back and forth between the present and the past, as they are talking and remembering. That is beside the point, since I know that you are not writing a screenplay for a movie. But perhaps it relates to something which I felt. Somehow, the writing did not create the emotional reality which clearly the women had experienced when they were undergoing the experiences which they describe. Or maybe then the question is how to capture for the reader the horror of it even though their own description of it may not have the same effect. Perhaps it was understanding that necessary split that made me think of a movie because you could do both at the same time. Parts stand out, the ocean, the whole theme of menstruation, the connection to memories that so many women have been part of as they try to work on the childhood horrors that they experienced, the relationship between the physical/body feelings and the emotional.

I like the exploration that you do about what it is like for them to go through the process of reconnecting. I am looking at page 75 where Nora talks about the need to make things abstract in order to live through them, the experiences, and then when someone provokes you to start associating, you enter this place but sometimes you get lost.

I also felt as I was reading it a sense of connection to them. I wonder if you are still having trouble writing, if you would find it helpful to write down on a separate journal area what is going on with you during the struggle to write. Those themes might be ones that relate to the material you are writing about in some unknown way, and they may enrich the writing of the piece itself.

I have been keeping a journal of all the reasons that come into my head about why I am so reluctant, afraid, ambivalent etc. about writing. I find that the things that I write about are actually raising issues about my writing, I mean the content of it. I think that there is a lot in the piece and that you are clearly in the process of sculpting. I imagine that by now you are taking, I mean have taken, it further and I would be eager to see it as it goes through stages if you think I can be helpful. But definitely stay with it. I think that it is very very important.

It's interesting that you speak about the issue of depression. I, too, have never thought of myself as a person who gets depressed. My feelings come out in many ways, but being depressed just hasn't been one of them.

From what people say, depression in the most precise sense is a much deeper state of inability to function. But there is no question that these last years for me have left me feeling more often than I remember in the past with a feeling of just not being able to mobilize myself to do what I want, much of the time. I can mobilize myself to do things that interact with others but when it comes to the writing, to the going inside myself, I have found it very hard. In fact, my ability to write poetry has almost completely disappeared. And yet, occasionally I will have an experience that lets me know just how many emotions are bottled up in me. For example, this week a woman I connected with, a woman who was a good friend of my parents—her name is Letty Pogrebin. I had never met her before my parents had their 50th anniversary party at her and her husband's house in New York. We spoke a lot about my parents and tears just flowed freely from my eyes in a way that I haven't experienced for months (and from hers). We had never met and it kind of blew my mind. I know that there are emotions that we have inside us that we don't explore, and they are enormous. And without ways of connecting (through close friendships, love, writing, whatever it is that works) they just stay bottled up. I know that all that you have experienced, and Barbara, in this period in terms of anxieties, uncertainties, losses, changes, are very dramatic and it doesn't surprise me if it is affecting your writing.

The river story was wonderful. I don't know about the issues of getting it published. I understand what you are saying about neither story nor article. Maybe you have to reshape it for size and orientation. But I loved reading it and it helped me to feel closer to that experience that was so important to you. I personally would not have participated on such a trip. I have no desire to experience physical challenges that involve risks. But the beauty of it draws me, the power of nature, and the physical intensity of it all. I think if I could play paddleball for eight hours a day in the beauty of such a place like the Grand Canyon, that would give me the experience of being in the magic of nature and the physical activity and intensity that I love. (That is just meant to be a funny image.) But I loved meeting the women on your trip, understanding something about your experience, and of course Barbara's experience. I can certainly imagine how much stress it might have added to her already stressed-out body.

Thinking back to your own feelings, my sense is that when two people love each other and one of them gets sick, the impact of that changes so much in both lives. And the stress is incredible. I wonder if depression or immobilization relates to not connecting to the whole range of natural feelings: guilt, anger, rage, irritation. It is so hard when everything mainly reflects no one's fault—but is still natural.

I envy you that writing has always come so easily, the act of writing. I am completely a person for whom it is so hard.

Anyway, right now, as soon as I finish this letter I am going to try and write for one hour on my mother-child relationship project. I have been in dialogue with different friends who write. I have lots of ideas, and I always feel so energized from a conversation and then I sit down to write, and I freeze.

One question that is concrete and perhaps reflects my slowly moving into grappling with the actual writing instead of with my various fronts/blocks is my uncertainty about how to bring the real material of women's and children's lives into the book. I have kept a journal from my parenting programs over the past several years, but I don't have people's voices since it is my notes of what people talked about. I can interview a lot of people if I want, including some of the people who are still here if I want them to talk about a situation which I refer to in my notes. I don't have anything from kids themselves and that is much harder for me to get, raises issues of exploitation, etc. I am also looking for a dynamic process, a story, something that moves, the way the groups move, so as to show some process of development. And there is the issue of whether to create composite characters.

As I have thought about writing recently, sometimes it has struck me that an oral history process would be easier, but that isn't actually what I have set out to do. There is so much of a stigma against mothers in prison that I am struggling with how to frame it in a manner that it is clear that working with the mothers is beneficial to their children who most of them will rejoin, and even if they don't, having a solid relationship even from prison makes a difference.

I haven't dealt with the situation you are facing around not getting support for your project, no funding, etc. I know that makes a difference. Somehow, I assumed something would come through for me around that. For the moment I am struggling with conception and lack thereof, and how to start when I don't have a clear sense of organization yet knowing that that may only emerge after I start.

I woke up this morning to see that a tooth that the dentist here has been working on (root canal, etc.) for a year seems to have split in half. I am so depressed about losing my teeth that I am finding it hard to concentrate.

I am going to end now and send you my love and I look forward to our next exchange. Oh yes, your poetry book. I loved reading it. First of all, I love food, and I love cooking, and as I wrote to you about these poems from when you sent me some of them, many do a wonderful job of combining family and personal dynamics with the particular food and recipe.

Much much love, Kathy.

In Kathy's letters to me, she often referred to our first meeting, when she remembered our talking about our respective "returns from exile." And she repeated her use of the word *exile* throughout her correspondence. I don't remember if I ever questioned this description of my time in Latin America or of hers underground. I think the term may be more valid when used in conjunction with her life than with mine. I certainly never thought of myself "in exile" during my many years outside the United States. I had left of my own free will and, despite the complications arising from my having taken Mexican citizenship and the U.S. government's decision to order me deported when I did come home, I was never forced to live outside the country. I knew many Latin American revolutionaries who suffered real exile.

The following letter, written on the sixteenth anniversary of the crime that landed her in prison, was not written only to me. Perhaps Kathy meant it for the victims of the action she had participated in so many years before, the action that resulted in her incarceration. Perhaps it was like a personal journal, and she was speaking mainly to herself. In any case, I received a copy. And I don't know if she mailed this letter to the families of the Nyack police who died in the action in which she took part; doing so would have required a discussion with her lawyers as to how it might affect her possibility of parole. This draft is disjointed in many ways, a stream-of-consciousness record of her emotions around the crime for which she was in prison. In places it reads as if her exploration of the trauma propelled the writing, more like a series of notes to herself than a letter intended for others. There are sentences that begin an idea and then trail off, as if she herself can't yet make sense of what she is feeling. With all this, it is a valuable document, self-critical and heartfelt, that reflects her struggle to come to terms with the pain she caused the families of the men who died.

Middle of the night, October 19, 1997

Dear . . .

On October 20 that year I could not sleep. I saw your faces and kept wondering what you had gone through, what was going through, your minds that night. It is 16 years later. What has happened to your lives, to the lives of your children.

I lay there with a sense of anxiety and sadness at the losses you had to deal with. I tried to imagine what that next day was like for you, your breakfast, saying goodbye, whether you usually ate breakfast together as a family or whether you spoke during the day. And then what was it like for you when you heard the news? Was it on the radio? Was it from a phone call? Was it someone coming to tell you at the door? Today, 16 years later, slowly over the years I have come to a point of being able to see you and your experience of incredible tragedy that day as a very separate part of that day, as something I was not able to foresee.

When the day occurred, my own life was so destroyed, and that of my family, my son. I could barely survive it, and my focus was to try to pull something out of the rubble, to rebuild.

I didn't go into it with any sense of the potential destruction it could cause. My own role was so distant in my mind, and not involved in or responsible for any relationship to possible hurt, hurt, hurt, that I went into it just not assuming that anything could happen, that anyone would be hurt, that everything would be fine, and that I personally, not being there, not being able to hurt anyone, had no relationship to any of that.

Now, years later, I know at the time, from the moment it all happened I realized that there was something terribly wrong, I knew that my own reason for being there was not just about trying to do something, however misguided, about society but also was tied to my own needs to work out things about myself in a very destructive and self-destructive way.

I think I realized there was something really wrong with our whole approach, in which in the name of valuing human life lives were lost. And yet, in response, there was a constant willingness to mourn those who were known, to acknowledge their deaths, yet the loss of your husbands somehow didn't get mentioned. When I spoke at my conviction/plea, I felt that it was very important to say how much I felt terrible about the loss of the men in your lives. I think at the time I knew that innocent lives had been lost, and for what? For something that had been wrong. Yet it was hard for me to imagine your experience. I was so wrapped up in my own experience, the horror of it.

I had been at a point in my own life of trying to get out of a situation that was terrible for me. But it was hard to make the change—so I thought somehow this peripheral role would give me the confidence to be able to leave, within the framework in which I saw the world.

Sometimes, I guess, the horror of an experience is hard to take in, to fully grasp, even if it happens to oneself or one's family. For me, with you, there are many things that have happened that have led me to begin to approach trying to understand what this meant, to understand your feelings. Without knowing you, hearing from you, knowing what happened to your lives, it is impossible for me to have a full picture.

Developments:

a) Going over the newspaper file
b) *Dead Man Walking*
c) The picketing that took place
d) Parenting from a distance, the kids' loss
e) Listening to story after story of women talking about loss in their lives, about violence, and seeing you in their stories

I don't remember what came first, but I do remember at some point beginning to be able to face in human terms the damage for human lives I had to take responsibility for. I needed to know who you were, who had been your family at that time, who was affected by the loss of a husband, father, son, brother, friend. I needed to know, had you been able to repair your life? Were you remarried? Resettled? Had your life moved on? Was there any healing? How did you manage to recover? The newspapers articles told me a little. Maybe I wasn't ready to receive more at that time. They just gave me the beginnings of connecting to you.

I think the fact that I wasn't there, wasn't in a position to hurt anyone, didn't want to be in a position to hurt anyone, felt myself in danger, afraid, running, panicked, had no relationship to it, meant that I was very disassociated from feeling responsible or even connected, yet just being even a peripheral part of something means having to grasp and take a level of responsibility.

At my plea when I said I will never personally participate in a situation of violence for political change, there was for me the beginnings of understanding that I personally could not in any way be associated with an approach to trying to better the world and people's lives that could end up in a tragic loss of life such as this one.

I want again to look at the papers, to see now what it is like.

Then there was the clemency process and the picketing outside, the demonstration, the dogs against me. Here I was, a person whose life since childhood has been on picket lines against injustice of one kind of another, and now I was the object of protest. I remember when I was a substitute schoolteacher and the kids began disrupting the class, maybe even throwing spitballs, perhaps at me, I was about 24 and part of me identified with the kids, remembering seven or eight years earlier in my teen years when I, too, gave the substitute teacher a hard time. A sense of power I guess in a usually powerless situation. I was split, half of me was embarrassed and insulted and knew I had to regain composure in the classroom, and the other half of me was laughing with the kids, remembering, identifying with their glee in their moment of empowerment at the expense of a poor substitute.

And on that day, in my solitude in the prison, in my sense of despair and my horror at the fact that I was an object of your hate or of your blame—there was no one else for you to blame, to focus your hate on—it brought me back to the irony of how being so totally peripheral, out of there, not in on the planning or anything, the newspapers focused on me, and here again so many years later, I had a sense that it was still my name that is for you the symbol of responsibility and therefore the focus of all your hate.

I too was traumatized that same day, yet I put myself into the situation, unable to allow myself to imagine the danger that it might involve, seeing it as completely safe, blinded by my own needs to prove myself.

Suddenly violence, death, an elderly woman pushed out of a car, a car stolen, near or possible death, and then a changed life, fear, what were your feelings? I think it is time to go back into another round of that.

I had heard about the movie. I wanted to watch it. As it turned out, I watched it alone, in the corner where I work, disappearing into it in my own drama, my heartbeat, my breathing, my imagination with no one else around.

Dead Man Walking

As I think about it, I remember their outrage at her being sympathetic to the man on death row, as if he were the victim of the crime, the crime being that of the death row penalty. When they were the ones who had suffered the loss, the loss of their two children. They were furious, aghast, how could it be that the nun was so sympathetic to the person who had committed the crime?

It made me think a lot about Katherine Power and the way in which she became the sympathetic figure at first, until it turned against her. And how do I or someone in my position, struggling to get out, try to explain what might have led to the act, yet always also keep in perspective the damage that was suffered by those who were hurt?

But probably most important of all was the way in which the movie took me into the hearts and souls of those parents who had lost their children to a horrendous crime and how they were so bereft, they had lost their children, the horrible needless loss, and I could feel the loss of your family, what it must have been like to lose a husband, a son, a father, a brother, regardless of knowing that his life's work always carried with it the possibility of injury or death. Still, that is really irrelevant. The total bereavement resulting from a crime and then the anger against the criminal and the desire to hurt back, to kill back, the desire for revenge. I could understand it. I could understand what you felt towards me, how much you believed that somehow I should pay for what happened, the need for someone to pay, it just doesn't . . . I don't know what I was going to say here, but I came to accept in some sense your feelings of hatred and anger and desire to hurt, desire for revenge against me. I cannot say that I felt happy or resigned to it or like exactly I deserved it, but more that I felt compassion for you and understood why you felt that way. And, in a sense, in really being able to see me though your feelings and understand the loss and how it felt, I reached a kind of inner peace or acceptance of the whole situation.

Parenting:

When I began my deep work with women, and with myself, around trying to understand how we had come to leave our children, for me the process began with trying to understand myself. But, as I worked month after month, listening to the stories of mothers who had been left as children and mothers who had left their own children, the stories of loss, the experience of loss and of hurt, of abandonment . . . I was aghast that this had happened, in a way knowing that I did not deserve what you were feeling and at the same time knowing that somehow history had created this craziness, in some way even I had created it, so wanting to be known as a person who was committed, willing to go to the end, and so craving that self-definition, I ended up getting into a tragic situation in which there was no greatness associated with it, only tragedy and hatred. I could imagine myself in your place, imagine myself on a picket line protesting someone being let out of jail, imagine myself, as if you were using the tactic that symbolized my life, and it all felt so ironic. And somewhat then, despite my own sense of despair, I think I was able to imagine that your feelings were ones I could understand. But I just wished that you could believe in forgiveness. I don't know, that day was one on which I really struggled alone.

Within days after that, I had the beginning of what would be a long friendship, my first real experience in listening face to face to the story of someone who had experienced that day.[150] I don't think it could all be said at one time, or all be absorbed, to describe what a traumatic, scary, terrifying event it is, and to begin to see it through the eyes of a person who lived through it and to know that you were involved, even if peripherally, to the occurrence, but it changes it. It is in the details of the actual experience. I was doing this that day, feeling like this. Suddenly, unexpectedly, I found myself in a . . . this happened, this happened, and then there were the next three years of my life.

150. This indicates that one of the victims of Kathy's crime met with her in prison and that they established an ongoing friendship. She never spoke of this to me, and I was moved to learn of it in this letter.

It is in all these details of life that one is able to really understand the impact of what one does. My imagination did not have to create understandings. A person, face to face, told me what happened to her that day and what it meant to her life.

It is time to listen again, to go over it again perhaps.

When I saw the movie, it took everything down an even deeper road.

(December 21, continued)

In hearing about her life, one day shopping for her daughter, in an area where she worked, looking for a skirt I think, or a dress, then caught behind a kind of roadblock, in a car that stopped, getting out to see what is the holdup, why do they have to stop, suddenly the back of a van opens, men jump out shooting, her car is suddenly occupied, her mother is pushed out and the car is driven away. And then for three and a half years she is involved, her house is under protection, her life is changed. I try to put myself in her place, it takes time to do this, not just minutes or months but years, to be able to take down the fences that protect me from having to feel too much of the pain that I am in some way partly, at least on a moral level, responsible for. It is so much easier to feel another's pain and suffering when you are not the person or a person who played some role in it happening. To watch a movie, to read a book, lives unfolding, each so separate yet brought together by an event, an event in which one person played some role and the other was involved by coincidence. When you step back and can look at it like a movie, maybe that is the best way to get closest to it, to view it from a distance and then allow it to fully unfold in front of you. And then to jump into it, open the door.

How often have I read about trauma and thought about the victims of trauma, worked with people on retrieving memories and reliving them and healing from them. And that connects to this, the knowledge that I am in some way related to a trauma that someone experienced and trying to imagine what your children experienced when they were told that their father had died. I have studied families wrecked by drugs, by incarceration, by battering and violence, immersed myself in the wreckage trying to help women understand what the loss can do to their children and helping them heal from their own losses. And so, it brought me closer into the pain and horror that your children went through on that day when the event occurred. I could never again be involved in the idea of making society better in a process that put human life at risk.

January 1, 1998

Dear Margaret:

It is hard to believe that after I got the basically good news about Barbara's health, I not only did not keep up the level of correspondence between us that was really needed but I'm not sure that I ever even wrote to say how relieved I was. It is as if I was immobilized from active writing by potentially a tragic health situation instead of good news. I am just shaking my head as I think about it. Well, I want you to know, or I hope that this last experience will be clear proof of the fact, that I will definitely be completely there when bad things happen—if anything should happen. Now I have to get myself back together around being in touch during the normal ups and downs of life.

Wow, I realize that you were going to come and visit me a week or so after the birth of Ana's baby, which was predicted for December 22. What happened? Did I blow a visit by not responding quickly to your letter? Oh god, I hope not.

In your letter of October 5, you wrote about your recurring dream, the dream about feeling useless, used up, with people who were going to be eliminated, your interpretation of it relating to your feelings of being directionless, uncertain about your work. You write about feelings of being "nowhere, really, with regard to my life."

I wonder how you are feeling now, several months later. In your December letter (Dear Family and Friends) you refer to the prolonged crisis around writing. So, I guess you are still in some way in it. I agree that probably it will be valuable in the long term but that doesn't make it easy to figure out or live with. The feelings that you express about your life are pretty low: "My own work in that effort for social change came to nothing. The revolution my generation hoped to make was a failure. My books have mostly fallen between the cracks." Your questions about your life raise the deepest questions about the meaning of life, the value of social activity, objective and subjective views. There can be no argument, just the thoughts and feelings that your own words evoke.

Recently I have been struggling deeply to grapple with the idea of "what if I never get out of prison because parole just never lets me go" or "if I get out when I am truly in old age, unable to enjoy some years of real active life outside." You may wonder why I have those thoughts. They exist because although I was sentenced to 20–life and the judge said he felt 20 years was adequate, he does not have the real decision-making power, and currently in New York State there is a policy of simply not letting anyone with a violent crime out of prison, they go to parole and are told to come back in two years. The present governor will be reelected and will be governor when I go to the parole board in three and a half years, so there is a basis for my fears even though obviously there are many years between me and old age and history is always unfolding. Nevertheless, I have been very absorbed with it. I have had to look at my life and try to figure out what I think. Some people do not want to live with regrets. In here they say: "It must have happened for a reason." I wish that I believed that. I don't. I have deep regrets. And after I was arrested, I faced another type of crossroad. Here I was going to spend so much of my life in prison for an approach to social change that had done a lot of damage. It wasn't even heroic, brave. It was not only a wrong path but was clearly psychologically driven by deep personal issues leading to my participation. I know that I survived by trying to express the different parts of it, by feeling the horror of it all, the grief, the loss. And by also feeling good about being part of a long tradition of people who had been involved century after century as long as human history has existed in trying to devote their lives to bettering society, to accepting the limitations of what is possible in terms of change yet feeling good about being part of the process. I struggled for a way to feel and define life that would allow me to survive, literally survive, under the conditions of terrible repression and loss which I myself had caused (to make things even worse). And now I feel that I am once again struggling to make sense of things.

I think of my many friends with AIDS, so many of whom have died. I take from them a lot of questions about the meaning and essence of life. For me, this expresses itself in continually figuring out ways, however small, to improve life for whomever I can touch, be it an individual with a problem concerning visiting her children, or a group that has a need and this sparks an idea for a program, to finding good friends with whom I can share closeness, to feeling a sense of family and commitment to my son and other family members, to enjoying a good movie, a good book, and a beautiful day, and to write a good poem and get exercise. It involves both expressing my values in small ways and in the day-to-day relationships. If I were to die now, I would feel wonderful about my relationship to my son and wonderful about my work here. I would feel unbelievable regrets and sadness about the path my life took.

So, how does this connect to you and not become a letter just about me when I started out with you? I wonder whether your sense of the futility of it all is coming from your writer's crisis, since I think the depression about the failure to make revolution in our generation is something that we have been living with for a while now. And when you are feeling good about your own ability to act, to write, then it is possible not to have it be so controlled by certain larger issues which truly are beyond our control.

I guess, as I read this the next day, it doesn't sound very coherent. I am trying to get at two things: there is no question that our generation's dreams were not fulfilled. We were wrong about what was possible, but it's not that we failed. Is it depressing? Well, when I think about what we lived through, then I try to imagine what it was like to have been witness to the Holocaust. My god, what human beings are capable of is enough to take away any sense of faith. Yet somehow, within the worst of the worst situations, each person must find a way that works for her/him. I have seen people in here who are sentenced to 25 to life when they should have gotten 5–10, a big, big difference in time. And in some cases, a woman will be bitter, in others very depressed, and in others a woman will retain a sense of humor and, while fighting to get out somehow maintain a philosophic acceptance knowing that injustice has been done. I think my own inability to accept the fact that there was not going to be a revolution, that change could not come on the scope that we had believed, played some role in my ending up here. But there is also the personal involvement in it. Maybe each of us has to reduce our sense of what we as individuals can do, as well as the broader movement. To me, your books have made a major contribution.

Before college, Chesa wants to live for a while in a Latin American country. Venezuela is one possibility, Mexico is another. I thought that perhaps you might have some thoughts on it.[151] He will be eighteen by then. He doesn't want to just go and live with a family. He wants to be sure that he could do hard work because he is someone who has to be doing something. I know that this experience for him will be very profound as it has been for every person I know who has lived in another country, especially Latin America/Caribbean.

In addition to my deeply thinking about issues of getting out of prison/not getting out, on a broad level I have been beginning to talk with friends and lawyers about what makes sense to do during these next three and a half years. No big ideas yet, but taking it seriously really is different and changes my dreams, my ability to sleep, my focus.

My greatest frustration is around writing. I have within me the desire to write two books. First, the experience of mother-child relationships across this prison separation. I have simply not been able to really start, even though since July I have been working on it in terms of possible outlines, etc. How much is it the voices of mothers that I want to allow to become the centerpiece? What about children and how do I involve them in this project which is such a vulnerable issue without in any way undercutting the legitimacy of my ongoing work? How much do I take on issues of public policy in a situation in

---

151. Over the next few months, I gave some thought to places where Chesa might live, work, and learn Spanish between high school and college. Mexico was a possibility, and my daughter Ximena and her then husband, Fito, offered to receive him at their home in Mexico City. Chesa ended up choosing an option in Guatemala.

which I don't have access to what would prove some of the things I am trying to capture as positive? How much is it about myself and what does that mean for Chesa and/or relate to issues about me and my public definition? I don't want to do an oral history type of book. I am looking for a way to capture the dynamic of the process in here, of a community in which parenting is supported and learned. I have been very moved by a number of ethnographic type books, *Number Our Days,* about a small Jewish community in Venice, California; *Death without Weeping* about a community in northeast Brazil, *Amazing Grace* about the South Bronx, in which people become alive and there is a dynamic in the book which captures the flow of their lives in day-to-day reality. But I don't have the kind of data those writers collected over years, tape recordings (which I can't do). I have my own life experience living here and the ability to interview people as they talk and I type, the ability to live here and observe. I lack the confidence in my writing. I have done so much thinking, some level of outlining, no writing.

I also want very much to write poetry. It is a way for me to connect to an inner river, but I lose myself in the day-to-day projects and seem unable to stop. So, these are my struggles.

I send you so much love and I look forward to hearing from you and I promise to pick up on our wonderfully engaged correspondence of the early fall. Much love, Kathy.

January 1998 [this letter is dated January 24th, which is inconsistent with its content]

Dear Margaret,

It is well into the beginning of the year. And winter really hit. Because my life is so full of so many different projects that work with people, when I have several days in a row off from being able to do my normal work, it is usually a real relief. But sometimes all I do is try to do things and don't accomplish them. Yesterday and today, I had only one goal: to connect with my friends, such as you and Barbara. And I am happily writing to both of you. We have been better at writing in these last couple of months—although in general this past year was pretty good.

I am going to catch up by looking at your last two letters.

First, Chesa. I know that you spoke finally with Bernardine. I hope that you had a good conversation. I am very grateful for your energy spent on helping develop a place for Chesa. It meant a lot to me that you engaged it seriously, came up with ideas, and also were part of the process with me. In a sense, what is important to me is not the possibility of Ximena and Fito's house working out or not working out, but that I felt you were really going through it with me. I very very much appreciate it. Naturally, for me to be able to take initiative with friends of mine to try and find something for him was, in itself, a pleasure. Since I have so little actual responsibility for helping him concretely. As you probably know from Bernardine and, I think, my last letter, he is going to San Andrés in the Petén region in Guatemala, to the Eco-Escuela. The person who suggested it had been there last year and she had a wonderful time. Chesa met with her, saw pictures, and learned what was true in the brochures and what wasn't. It gave him a sense of certainty about a place that had enough going for it in terms of his goals. So, he picked it.

Personally, knowing him, I am not sure it is the best situation. But it was his choice based on the options that we had. And it clearly made a big difference to him to know someone who had been there. He leaves next Thursday January 7. And returns March 16. I am very excited. It brings back many memories of my own journeys to other countries and cultures. At precisely his age and at this time—end December, early January—I went to Cuba age 17, my senior year of high school. It was 1960–61. I think it changed me as much as any other experience in my life. I have a journal that I kept, and I gave it to Chesa to read. He was pretty amazed by it. I am of course a little anxious for him. But he is very mature and steady, and this was very much his idea, his decision, where to go. And he is ready, as he has said, to take a step on his own out there. I can't wait to see him when he comes back. I am already taking a leap forward.

Your description of the impact of the global economy plus natural forces such as hurricanes on that area of the world is quite devastating. The situations with your children and with Nicaragua and Honduras are rough. I know when Chesa's best friend, Mwanikik, went to Kenya this summer (his father was born in Kenya) he did some volunteer work with a Christian children's association. He described watching children eating garbage in the street. He couldn't take it, he said. It was beyond anything he could imagine. I remember at age 19 traveling on a bus along the Albanian border in Yugoslavia and seeing little kids begging, all bone, begging. I was shocked at that. So, Chesa is going into a world that I am sure will shock him. How it will affect him, who knows. But it will change him.

He just had the experience of applying to Harvard "early decision"—meaning they could accept him, but he didn't have to decide until spring. They deferred him. He didn't seem too upset, mainly irritated. But his school was upset. And the Harvard admissions department called him and asked him to come to Harvard for an interview. He had already been interviewed by an alumnus in Chicago. But they said that a number of people want to interview him, that they would arrange their schedules to suit his, including coming in Christmas week. To make a long story short, it became clear that they were embarrassed that they had not accepted him because he does present a lot of outstanding qualities and yet they were anxious about who is this kid with two parents in prison, two well-known 60s radicals raising him, going to Guatemala, etc. They did everything they could to convince him to come to Harvard for an additional interview. They clearly don't want to accept him without the big shots grasping who he is. After some discussion about what it means that he has openly put himself forward as embracing all of his parents, brings with it power but vulnerability, the possibility of impacting people yet also making them anxious, he is going to Harvard on Monday for an interview, then leaving for Guatemala on Thursday. He is on a journey, my son, that is his and of his making.

I would very much like it if you would extend my thanks, my gratitude, to Ximena and Fito for their willingness to open their house to Chesa. Even if at this point it would not have worked out for them, they went through a process of decision-making and that means a lot to me. I don't know whether he will get to Mexico on this trip. He doesn't know. All he knows is where he is beginning. If you think it would be nice for me to write directly to them or send a note to you, I will be happy to. But I very much want them to know that I appreciate their good will and support.

Needless to say, I am very relieved that there were no lasting effects from the summer. It is strange how I was living with such a different reality. I assumed, not hearing from you, that everything had deteriorated, and I was very anxious and lived with that anxiety for August, September, and October, until I wrote to you and heard back. A little bit of light, the story of light years transformed into sharing lives through the mail.

Above left: The author with Kathy Boudin on a visit to her at the Bedford Hills Correctional Facility, 1980s. Photo by prison photographer. Below and right: Kathy in 2013, after her release from prison. Photos by Margaret Randall.

As for the *Breaking the Walls of Silence* book. Wow. What a frustrating experience. So far, no one has reviewed it other than *Kirkus*, outside of a couple of AIDS type journals. I have worked so hard to get copies sent to people, sent out cover letters with a perspective on the meaning of the book, asked for help. Almost everyone who has received copies has said that they thought it was very important, many felt that it was compelling to read, etc. etc. All of that makes me feel good. And the people who have said that are very good respected people from all walks of life. But we have had no breakthrough publicly. However, I am not discouraged because a wonderful woman has just been hired to do publicity for it and I believe that something good will happen. By the way, while we are on the subject of reviews, David asked me to tell you that when he was doing monthly reviews for a paper in Albany, you are the person whose books he reviewed the most. He was excited to know that we are friends.

Yesterday I saw *Wag the Dog.* I believe you wrote me about it last year. Quite apropos of the present. Although of course there is a lot about the present that is not in the movie.

I also want to thank you very much for always sending me photos. I love nature and I love your photos. And I can paste the plain photos onto cards and then send them to people. Thank you very much.

As for our benefit to raise money, I cannot describe what a wonderful experience the whole process was. The writing workshop was great. Hearing and seeing talent at the level that we saw read our words, giving them the meaning that was intended but, because of the acting, magnifying and deepening it 100-fold, it was tremendous. And when they did the actual benefit in front of 800 people, apparently they had been energized by doing it for us, meeting us, performing for 200 prisoners, and they really let loose that night and the audience response was tremendous. I am sending you and Barbara the writings that I submitted, some of which were used, so that I can share with you some of my writing and thinking. I am also sending you some of the pictures of our group.

I hope that you have had some wonderful trips, to Grand Canyon and to Peru, and I look forward as always to hearing from you.

Congratulations on your 12th anniversary. All my love, Kathy.

February 7, 1998

Dear Margaret,

I just got your letter, and I decided to write back a quick note. I was glad to hear about the fact that you were able to make a visit here that was solely family. Of course I was disappointed not to see you, but I was happy to get your letter with an explanation and it makes a lot of sense.

It's good news that you are writing again. It's true, we can try to analyze the "why's" of things in retrospect, but sometimes it is hard to really know the truth and it is interesting to me that you have been able to unfreeze through the focus on a "real memoir." And I'm thrilled that with that center to your energy and work you are waking up each day feeling eager and inspired. I have a feeling that something like that will happen with me and my writing of the mother-child book. It is hard to explain. I'll either do it later in this letter or in another.

I want to address the issue that you raise about my description of how I feel about the choices I made. I guess it is part of clarifying things for myself and this is an ongoing process. Someday I will find a synthesis of my feelings and understandings. The best way I can say it is something like this: the night that I was arrested I consciously understood that my presence there that day was driven in part by a political framework (which was flawed in its analysis, yet inspired by certain values and principles which were/are honorable), and at the same time driven by deep personal needs that came out of my personality, life experience, etc., which I didn't clearly understand but which had absolutely nothing to do with politics. And which, if they had not been as much of a force, perhaps I wouldn't have ended up there. I have been struggling to understand the psychological factors and I have reached some understanding of them, enough that I have some sense of peace about it. Although had I another set of circumstances, I would probably still be spending time each week trying to understand things in a structured way. As it is, I explore things on my own. Obviously, any human being who is a political activist, revolutionary, or a doctor, or a writer, can wonder or search to understand why it is that they chose that route. Biography and autobiography often explore the combination of psychological, historical, life experience, political factors which combine to make a person who she is and to act the way she acts. When something goes very wrong, as it did for me during the last years that I was a fugitive—panic attacks, unable to make up my mind to do something I needed to do, a process of self-destruction, and then the ultimate act of two parents leaving a child at a babysitter under an illusion that there really is no risk, and two parents involved when there was absolutely no historical pressure or tactical necessity—you have to really deeply question what is going on. And that is what I have been doing.

It was far and away not solely a mistake in terms of specific ideas about what was right. It was so driven by my own personal needs that it not only blinded me to risk and forfeited responsibility to a child, but to what I wanted for myself yet could not tolerate or do. I think I survived the aftermath by, on the one hand feeling that my life as a whole was part of a long tradition of people trying to make a better world, one that included Jesus, the abolitionists, people throughout the world and throughout history that I did not have to take my identity from that act. And, on the other hand, I survived by knowing that one day I would begin to figure out why I had ended up there. The psychological elements are intertwined with the political: race, level of militancy, commitment, gender roles. I have been trying to piece together the ways in which my own personal life experience as a child and young adult led to the path I took, good and bad. I guess when I see you, we will talk more about it all. A lot has come together for me during the past year in terms of understanding.

Some of it involves coming closer and closer to experiencing in myself what that day must have been like for the families of the victims. The kids without fathers, the women without husbands. It's a lot to actually absorb.

The most fluid writing that I myself have done is really recording that journey, trying to piece all this together during the past eight or nine months. Just journal writing, but it has helped a lot.

As I try to move forward on the mother-child book, one of my issues is that I experience myself here as part of a community of mothers. And I know that I cannot approach it as a memoir. Not that someone else couldn't do that, it's just not in me to do that about this experience. I know that my own experience has to be part of it, but at the same time I want to make it not in the form of a memoir but something that expresses through the voices the shared experience of mothers and their children and the staff of the children's center who are inmates and those who are civilians. My wish would be to do some kind of ethnographic book in which there is a story, a dynamic, rather than interviews with people. I don't know if I am capable of writing such a book and I don't want it to take forever. I really want to do it this year. I have been struggling with form and conception a lot. Love, Kathy.

March 15, 1998

Dear Margaret,

I'm going to try and continue for a few minutes picking up on the present energy of our correspondence. This has not been a great period for me. Over these years I have watched different friends struggle emotionally when they are working to get out of prison. They get angry, depressed, thrown off course. And I have always said that I am glad that I haven't focused on trying to get out because it seems to make people crazy. But there comes a point when it is unavoidable, and I feel that I am at that point. And it is amazing how the entire universe inside and around oneself shifts. Up to now, I have picked my choices of work and what I do by that which has worked for me interacting with my environment. There is some interchange between my own growth, development and needs and the immediate environment where I live that has determined those choices and my day-to-day schedule. Suddenly, a whole new factor is thrown in: is there something I should be doing that could make a difference? Perhaps there is nothing, and whatever I think is really an illusion. I am constantly asking myself that question. And, when I more or less continue to just lead my life as I have been, I am filled with anxiety and dissatisfaction. The issues surround some things I feel it would be better to discuss face to face and others that are obvious, and I can write about them. For example, I have had a completely low public profile.

I have written quite a lot, but it is all in academic journals so the sense of knowing that I and my work are acceptable and fairly non-controversial is certain. Shouldn't I be doing something that begins to be more public, so that who I am now begins to chip away at the image of myself as a symbol of "the violent wing of the radical left" or, more specifically, "a symbol of terrorism?" Well, if I should, then what should it be? Should it focus on my work here? Should it focus on my expressions of regret and remorse? If I do the former without the latter, is that problematic? But if I do the latter, what is the level of detail to get into? Should I be spending my time working on a brief or lengthy self-analysis which would include for public consumption (in some later form) how I understand why I made the choices that I did? But this would have to include not just the last event but the period leading up to my becoming a fugitive and the whole history of my political work during those tumultuous years. And then there is the content, how to weave together a life—any life—defined and created by a combination of family dynamics, personal childhood and young adulthood experiences, history, and social forces? How do I do that so that I don't take away from the positive which is part of not only how I see myself but what I am publicly known for, and yet at the same time can explain the wrong things? And then, what about some things that are wrong and yet it is complex? Complexity doesn't work in this situation. I have a lot of journal notes that come from the structured self-examination that I went through during the past four years, and I think I should probably try to come up with some coherent summary for myself. I know that I should be writing poetry. It is a way to anchor myself in myself and, also, poetry is a good way to communicate who I am. But I have not been able to. Instead, I create project after project of interesting work with women here, all of which is useful yet none of which is absolutely urgent. It is as if I fill my life with an enormous amount of work connected either to parenting or health or college, which involve meetings, teaching, organizing, and have no time to do either the deeper intellectual work or the reflecting. And, although I can see it and say it, I have not been able to stop. Maybe I am hoping that by writing it down it will help me to alter things. I am working on a book prospectus about mother-child relationships across the prison separation. I have been working on it for about two months. It has been very difficult for me to get it done. I made some headway last week and I am feeling good about that. When I have a draft, I will send you a copy. I am hoping to have a rough draft this week.

I think I also suffer from loneliness. There are many people in my life, but no central person, other than my son. And that is not the greatest situation because it makes me kind of dependent on someone who needs to be encouraged to be independent and not responsible for me. I guess it's a lot of things.

Someone suggested to me in terms of poetry that maybe it would be helpful if there were someone outside who kind of wanted to work with me in a mentoring relationship. This person has the name of a woman who teaches at Sarah Lawrence College and is a poet who might be interested in working with me. I think I have it in me, but I just am frozen in the poetry workshop that I go to and haven't written anything. I tend to censor myself on anything of importance to me so the whole point is lost.

I am going to end now because I want to mail this off to you. Please give Barbara my love. I will answer her wonderful letter this week. We all seem to be on a similar energy current, which is wonderful. Much love to you, Kathy.

Barbara and I got together in the fall of 1986, and whenever she could join me on the East Coast, she accompanied me to the prison. She, too, became close to Kathy. Even after my immigration case was resolved in my favor, that wasn't to be the end of my political troubles in the United States. Finding a permanent university job was impossible, and Barbara—who was teaching by this time—and I were forced to separate for months at a time when I was hired for a semester far from Albuquerque. In far worse circumstances than mine, Kathy remained an example of someone who was able to make the best of even the most negative situation. I tried to learn from her.

During the next few years, we and all those who loved Kathy were increasingly focused on securing her release. Although in the 1981 Brinks armored car attack for which she had been convicted, she was only in one of the getaway cars and hadn't carried a weapon, New York State law stipulates that anyone involved in a crime in which someone dies is as guilty as the person who pulled the trigger and thus merits the same punishment. During her trial, the judge had sentenced her to twenty years to life, meaning she wouldn't come up for parole until she had served twenty years and could be forced to endure a life sentence. In issuing his sentence, he made it clear that he believed that in her case twenty years was enough.

The end of the decade of the 1990s was marked by coordinated work by Kathy's legal counsel and core support group as well as personal letters from Kathy in which she wrote about the anguish the whole process was causing her. She had gone through a lengthy and intense period of trying to understand the choices she had made and her responsibility in having been part of a process that resulted in the loss of human life in the name of bettering society. She was able to begin to identify with the families of the victims, and this caused her immense grief and regret. She was sincerely remorseful. Now an important theme was how painful it was to move from focusing on the many projects she created and participated in within the prison walls to the attention public scrutiny around campaigning for release would bring. Those close to Kathy were asked to write letters of support and I wrote an enthusiastic one.

At that first hearing on August 22, 2001, which lasted less than an hour, Kathy was denied parole. She was disappointed, of course, but intent on working toward her next board appointment two years later while continuing the several projects she was involved in on the inside as well as the work she was doing to deepen her understanding of her own life and choices.

Two months after the denial, Kathy sent a collective letter of thanks to supporters and friends:

> I am writing to thank you for supporting the effort to win my freedom. Only a short time has passed since my parole hearing . . . yet only two weeks after the hearing, on September 11, terrible and tragic events took place that made the parole board seem so far away, and the future filled with many questions concerning all of humanity. It took me many years working on the issue of my own freedom. Once again, I found it hard to focus on myself. Yet I know that part of living in this period involves moving forward with the lives that we have created and that we care about, so that the life force of hopes and dreams continues to carry us.
>
> I thank many of you for taking the time to write your letters. In the parole file, all of the letters together created a quilt or mosaic that added up to a portrait: who I have become, what I have done, my remorse. I drew strength from them during difficult moments. When I reached the parole hearing, the impact of your letters was evident. The hearing officer put her

hand on top of the parole file and, patting it, said that clearly I had helped many people and made a positive impact on their lives, and that I was remorseful. Your letters made a difference in how I was treated during the hearing. . . .

When the parole board denied my release and told me to come back in two years—the maximum time between boards—I was not surprised since it has been their general policy towards people with violent crimes, but of course I was disappointed. Then the horrendous attacks of September 11 took place. I was horrified by the atrocities, filled with sorrow for all who suffered, and I became engaged with the larger issues facing us, grappling with the changes, the emotions, and the meaning at every level. Yet, amidst these profound changes, I am moving forward in prison with my life's work, my education, being a mother, and actively trying to win my freedom. I send you my energy of hope, my concern for humanity, and my deepest appreciation. Love, Kathy.

At the end of this collective letter, Kathy added a handwritten note to me:

Dear Margaret,

I gulped as I opened this letter to you. I am so remiss in maintaining our friendship and correspondence. I just haven't been able to. But that does not mean that I don't treasure our friendship, or care about you. I just haven't been able to sustain it in this period. This is just a short note of thanks. Thank you for your letter of support. As I reread it, it shines with your reflections on my process and combines your knowledge of a shared history with real dilemmas and conversations between us. Thank you very much for writing it and, more, thank you for always having your hand out in friendship. I hope you are well. Love to you and Barbara, Kathy.

The following two years were full for Kathy. Her son, Chesa, won a Rhodes Scholarship, enabling him to study international law at Oxford. As was to be expected, even the liberal press made a point of contrasting his achievements with his parents' radical histories. In every interview, he stressed his pride in his parents and admiration for their worldviews, which he said he shares. The terrorist attacks of September 11, 2001, necessarily complicated Kathy's efforts to get out of prison but also contextualized them within a larger framework. That event doomed Bill Ayers' book, *Fugitive Days,* which had the misfortune of being released two days after the attack.[152]

Kathy went before the parole board again in August 2003. This time she was successful. I immediately wrote:

Albuquerque, August 23, 2003

Dearest Kathy:

AMAZING! WONDROUS! AND SO VERY DESERVED!!!!! Barbara and I have our arms tight around you, celebrating with you from this physical but totally fictitious distance.

Yesterday, from very early in the morning, I thought of nothing but your parole hearing. I had called Ruth Hubbard a few days before, remembering that it would be around now. She told me Wednesday. I must admit that I had very little hope. Even when Ruth told me that your committee was "cautiously optimistic" I guess I didn't want to set myself up for renewed disappointment. We have had so few victories of late. But how could someone like me be completely without optimism?

152. *Fugitive Days* (Boston: Beacon Press, 2001).

Then, around 3 p.m., Ruth called me with the news. I stared crying from joy and also from a sense of the complexities—Judy, your parents not having lived to experience this day, and also, I must admit, because I had no way to connect with you and tell you myself of my great happiness and relief. I cannot even begin to know what you must be feeling. Through a subsequent round-robin of telephone conversations (with Ruth, Suzanne Kessler, Cory Chertoff and others) I learned that you will remain at the prison perhaps as long as a couple of weeks and then go to live with Charlotte Phillips. I'm glad you will have an opportunity to say important goodbyes. I'm sending this note to you both at Bedford Hills and at Charlotte's, hoping you will receive it at one place or the other.

Kathy, I know that the terms of your parole will keep you in New York for the foreseeable future. But I want you to know that Barbara and I hope you will visit us here when that's possible. This is such a powerfully healing place. Needless to say, our home would be yours for whatever time you wished, and long walks in these foothills might be a great transitional aid.

The other thing I want you to know is that I want to come east to see you and to celebrate. My first comment to Ruth was: "I'm flying east right way," thinking I could be at the prison door to welcome you out. Ruth thought I was being extremely precipitous, and of course she was right. I had no idea when your exit date would be, nor whether you even wanted that moment to extend beyond immediate family. Still, I assume there will be a celebration of some kind, and I want to be at it. I hope someone will let me know in time to buy a plane ticket.

Lately, over the past few days, I have written a poem which I want to share. I began writing it last week, so it didn't start out being for you. But I finished it yesterday, and knew it was.

TO STAY RIGHT HERE

—for Kathy Boudin

Waiting changes. The patience
for it. How time becomes
time alone, unburdened with images
of what may happen next.
Unspoiled by fibers of memory.
Clean.

I listen to the seconds now,
the minutes.
They are not fused one to another
but stand alone: complete.
Each itself, its fullness
embracing the jawbone.

To experience the call of a canyon wren
vying with my own steps
reaching from one lichen-covered boulder
to another,
each vowing movement: erosion or violence
the promise.

Deep into my seventh decade and at peace, finally,
with the balance.
The running to or away
behind me now. The long-drawn-out stillness
not yet upon me,
a tangle of arms.

To stay right here. To breathe.

September 10, 2003

Dearest Margaret, Dearest Barbara,

Your letter is with me. I am thinking about each of you, how you have shared your lives with me over all these years and how dear you are to me. I feel your hugs. The distance is nonexistent. We are celebrating together.

Not too many people were optimistic, but we kept forging ahead and it happened. My son, among others, played such an important role. He was tremendous.

Although there are of course complexities, getting out is a good thing, unqualified. My last two years were so bad that I came to the end of a useful life in here. Not from an objective standpoint. I still did lots of good things. It was something deeper. Judy and David of course weigh heavily on my mind. I will be very involved in working for their release when I get out. It's different from my own experience—we did this in a little over two years only, not a long time, just a tough time—and that gives me hope for the "impossible," meaning nothing is impossible. And I learned a lot, really a lot. I remember, Margaret, when you too won and how I celebrated from here.

I'm still here, so a celebration is not yet happening. But, of course, I will figure that out.

I loved your poem. I feel in such an enormous moment, change, waiting, it's happening.

It hasn't happened yet, but I am calm rather than having the heavy anxiety about the future that I was living with for the past two years. I remember, Margaret, our early discussions about your return from exile, my arrest and coming back. Now I am in another moment of coming back, yet with strong ties with those I leave, wanting them to come, committed to helping, of course missing my parents at this moment, wanting to connect to friends of theirs as a way of connecting to them. Thank you, Margaret, thank you Barbara, for being such wonderful friends. Now when you visit New York I will be there! Much love, Kathy.

Sometime in December 2006, Kathy wrote the last written communication I have in my archive. This was on a card that accompanied the gift she brought to my seventieth birthday celebration, hosted by my daughter Ana at her home in Brooklyn:

Dearest Margaret,

How extraordinary to celebrate your 70th birthday with you. But, even more extraordinary to know you, to have shared your life—first through your books about women in times of revolution, then through trying to contribute to your legal case from the prison law library, then through visits in the prison visiting room with Barbara, then through your wonderful poetry books and photographs, and then seeing you outside the prison.

But these are a partial picture of who you have been in my life. Our early conversations about "coming back" after "leaving," you as a friend who shared the richness of my years inside, you as a person who is a mother, who combines art, poetry, political commitments, love of nature, loving Barbara, caring for your parents. Margaret, you embody in yourself all that brings out the best in me, that inspires me, and that makes me so happy that you entered my life as my friend.

I give you the birthday gift that I chose both to celebrate you and Barbara and to celebrate the beginning of this next decade of your life which I look forward to being part of.

With all my love, Kathy.

Once Kathy was out of prison, our correspondence stopped. Now we were able to see each other outside the prison walls, walk together in the street, be free of the watchful eyes of prison guards. It was a gift I never expected.

Kathy visited us in New Mexico, and I remember a trip to Chaco Canyon, where we reveled in her freedom and in the mysteries of the people who constructed that extraordinary site. Whenever I was on the East Coast, we'd get together. Occasional long phone calls allowed us to catch up, and we remained close. The postprison work she did was rich and leaves an indelible legacy, particularly the center for prison projects she created at Columbia University. It has an endowment but, like all such institutions, must struggle for funding. It hires mostly ex-inmates.

But Kathy was to know freedom for only two decades. She was diagnosed with cancer and waged a seven-year struggle, which she lost on May 1, 2022. She had lived long enough to further her higher education, take some long-dreamed-of trips with her son, Chesa, and see him marry and become a father. Following her release from prison, she and the extraordinary support network that had worked for her release also did so for David Gilbert and Judy Clark. They were both freed, David after more than forty years and Judy for close to that number. Kathy was able to enjoy a few months with David after his release in November 2021 and before her death.

Kathy Boudin, despite—or perhaps because of—her enormous challenges, was truly larger than life. This is a description that has become clichéd by virtue of its frequent use and the broad range of personalities it invokes. Nonetheless, it encompasses a unique quality. Her largeness transcends her death.

Kathy's continued presence in my life was reaffirmed by a strange experience I had while constructing this chapter. I would reread a letter in which she posed some of her probing questions about our generation, the historical periods in which we lived, the choices each of us made, and the many other concerns we shared. I would catch myself thinking I needed to tell her this or that and then be startled by the knowledge that she was gone. This happened at least a dozen times during my reading and selection of the material. Each repetition surprised me, as if it were the first.

INDEX

D

R

S

ACKNOWLEDGMENTS

AFTER CHOOSING WHOM I wanted to include in this book, I had to access the correspondence that would make that possible. Jane Norling provided me with copies of my letters to her and I was able to get copies of hers to me from my archives at the Center for Southwest Research (CSR) at the University of New Mexico. My gratitude to Dr. Margie Montañez, curator of Latin American Collections there, and to graduate assistant Daniela Geovanna Galvis Garzón for copying this material. They also provided me with copies of Kathy Boudin's letters to me. Unfortunately, I was unable to locate my letters to her. Bill Ayers and Chesa Boudin attempted to track them down, unsuccessfully. It's possible that they are deposited at Columbia University Library and may be accessible in the future. Because I wrote this book shortly after Kathy's death, my lack of access may simply have been due to timing.

Arturo Arango kept our correspondence in both directions from 2004 to the present. Mail service between the United States and Cuba has been problematic since the victory of the revolution, so we've communicated almost entirely by email.

Our letters are in Spanish; the English translations are mine. And finally, Robert Schweitzer copied and sent me the few letters from me to him that he's saved over the years. The guardians of my archives at CSR provided me with copies of his to me. Jane, Arturo, and Robert also read drafts of their respective chapters, adding information and correcting my errors. Chesa Boudin read my chapter on his mother, permitting me to correct a few inaccuracies taken from misinformation in the press or online. Discussions with my son, Gregory, helped me think through some of the issues in the chapter about Arturo. He took time from a busy schedule to read the entire book, as did my friend Greg Smith; both made suggestions that greatly improved the text. And as always, my wife, Barbara, supported this project by providing a sounding board for my ideas, putting up with the long hours in which I sequestered myself in my studio, and adding my household duties to her own when I needed to focus on the project. My deep gratitude to you all.

As it was for its predecessor and a number of my other titles in recent years, New Village Press was a perfect home for this book. Lynne Elizabeth, my wonderful editor there, got excited at my initial mention of the project, committed to it sight unseen, and supported it every step of the way. I thank her and the rest of New Village's excellent staff for their vision and skills.

ABOUT MARGARET RANDALL

MARGARET RANDALL (New York, 1936) is a poet, essayist, oral historian, translator, photographer, and social activist. She lived in Latin America for twenty-three years (in Mexico, Cuba, and Nicaragua). From 1962 to 1969, she and Mexican poet Sergio Mondragón coedited *El Corno Emplumado/The Plumed Horn,* a bilingual literary quarterly that published more than eight hundred writers and visual artists from thirty-five countries—some of the best new work of the sixties. When she came home in 1984, the government ordered her deported because it found some of her writing to be "against the good order and happiness of the United States." With the support of many writers and others, she won her case, and her citizenship was restored in 1989.

Randall's most recent poetry collections include *Stormclouds Like Unkept Promises, Vertigo of Risk, Home, and Wild Card* (Casa Urraca Press) and *This Honest Land* (Wings Press). *Che on My Mind* (a feminist poet's reminiscence of Che Guevara, published by Duke University Press), *Thinking About Thinking* (Casa Urraca), *My Life in 100 Objects, Artists in My*

Life, Luck (New Village Press), and *Last Words* (Casa Urraca) are recent titles. In 2020 Duke published her memoir, *I Never Left Home: Poet, Feminist, Revolutionary.* A second volume of selected poems, *Time's Language II: Poems 2019–2023*, from Wings Press, followed *Time's Language: Poems 1959–2018* as compendiums of her best work in that genre.

Many of these titles have appeared in Spanish translation from Siglo XXI, Alforja, Ediciones de Medianoche, and Heredad in Mexico; Casa de las Américas, Ediciones Matanzas, and Vigía in Cuba; Abisinia and Tinta Limón in Argentina, Rumbo in Uruguay, and independent publishers in Nicaragua, Brazil, Ecuador, Peru, Colombia, Venezuela, Spain, Holland, Japan, Turkey, and India.

Margaret also translates from the Spanish. She has produced English-language poetry collections by Roberto Fernández Retamar, Roque Dalton, Otto René Castillo, Carlos María Gutiérrez, Daisy Zamora, Kelly Martínez, Israel Domínguez, Alfredo Zaldívar, Laura Ruiz, Chely Lima, Rita Valdivia, Reynaldo García Blanco, Yanira Marimón, and Gaudencio Rodríguez Santana, among others; novels by Freddy Prestol Castillo, Juan Antonio Hernández, and Tomás Modesto Galán; memoirs by Gregory Randall, Lurgio Gavilán Sánchez, and Stefano Varese; and anthologies of Cuban poetry and short stories, Ecuadorean poetry, U.S. poets for Mexico, and Beat poets in Spanish. She has read her own work and delivered keynote addresses in hundreds of venues throughout the United States, Latin America, and in other countries.

Two of Randall's photographs are in the Capitol Art Collection in Santa Fe. In 1960, Randall was a recipient of a Carnegie Fund for Writers aid grant, and in 1960 a grant from the American Academy of Arts and Letters revolving fund for writers in need. In 1989, she was a cowinner of the Mencken

Award, and in 1990 she received a Lillian Hellman and Dashiell Hammett grant for writers victimized by political repression. The Barbara Deming Money for Women Award was given to her in 1997, and in 2004 she received the PEN New Mexico Dorothy Doyle Lifetime Achievement Award for Writing and Human Rights Activism. Randall received the 2017 *Medalla al Mérito Literario* from *Literatura en el Bravo,* Ciudad Juárez, Mexico. In 2018, she was awarded the Poet of Two Hemispheres prize by Poesía en Paralelo Cero in Quito, Ecuador. In 2019, she earned an honorary doctorate of letters from the University of New Mexico. In 2020, she received the George Garrett Award from the Association of Writers & Writing Programs (AWP) and the Paulo Freire Award from Chapman University. In 2022, she received the City of Albuquerque's Creative Bravo Award. Randall lives in Albuquerque with her partner (now wife) of thirty-nine years, the painter Barbara Byers, and travels extensively to read, lecture, and teach.